English Medieval Settlement

English Medieval Settlement

Edited by P. H. Sawyer

Edward Arnold

© Edward Arnold (Publishers) Ltd 1979

First published 1979 by
Edward Arnold (Publishers) Ltd
41 Bedford Square
London WC1B 3DQ

ISBN 0 7131 6257 0   Paperback

British Library Cataloguing in Publication Data

English medieval settlement.
    1. Anthropo-geography—England—Addresses,
essays, lectures
    I. Sawyer, Peter Hayes
    301.34'0942   GF551

    ISBN 0–7131–6257–0

Printed in Great Britain by
Fletcher & Son Ltd, Norwich

Contents

Preface

With the exception of chapter 1, which has been revised, and the note by John Hurst on recent work at Wharram Percy, the contents of this book were first published in 1976 in *Medieval Settlement: Continuity and Change*, a collection of papers discussed at a colloquium in the University of Leeds in 1974. The purpose of that colloquium, and of the consequent book, was to provide an opportunity for specialists working on different aspects of the subject to explain their aims and methods and to report recent discoveries. The emphasis throughout was on the interdisciplinary character of the subject and, although the main interest was in the British Isles, continental scholars provided stimulating contrasts and analogies on the basis of recent work in Denmark, France, Germany and Poland.

The present book is intended as a complement to *Medieval Settlement*. It will make available to a wider audience, and in more accessible form, studies of English settlement first printed there. The following contributions to the original volume have been omitted: Walter Janssen, 'Some Major Aspects of Frankish and Medieval Settlement in the Rhineland'; Rosalind Hill, 'Some Parish Boundaries in Hampshire'; T. M. Charles-Edwards, 'Boundaries in Irish Law'; Axel Steensberg, 'Store Valby and Borup: Two Case Studies in the History of Danish Settlement'; Charles Thomas, 'Towards the Definition of the Term "Field" in the Light of Prehistory'; Robert Fossier, 'Land, Castle, Money and Family in the Formation of the Seigneuries'; Niels Lund, '*Thorp*-Names'; W. T. W. Potts, 'History and Blood Groups in the British Isles' and E. Sunderland's comment on that paper; Krzysztof Dabrowski, 'Kalisz between the Tenth and Thirteenth Centuries'; and Brian K. Roberts, 'The Anatomy of Settlement'. The introductory comments on the sessions of the colloquium prepared by the chairmen (G. W. S. Barrow, Charles Thomas, P. D. A. Harvey and Robin E. Glasscock) have also been omitted.

P. H. Sawyer

I

Medieval English Settlement: New Interpretations

P. H. Sawyer

In the past decade the combined efforts of archaeologists, geographers, historians and place-name scholars have resulted in major, even fundamental, changes in our understanding of the way English settlement developed between the fifth and fifteenth centuries. The interpretation that was, until recently, generally accepted assumed a more or less continuous process of growth, from small beginnings made by early colonists after the collapse of Roman authority until the fourteenth century when population started to decline and the process of village desertion began. Domesday Book has been cited in support of this theory. It names over 13,000 places in those parts of England controlled by William I in 1086 and therefore appears to be a comprehensive guide to the stage then reached in the colonization of the English landscape. One of the founders of the modern study of Domesday, J. H. Round, was led by its evidence for Sussex and Kent to assert that the Weald 'was still, at the time of the Norman Conquest, a belt some twenty miles in width, of forest, not yet opened up, except in a few scattered spots, for human settlement' (Round 1899, p. 3). It has consequently been assumed that many of the settlements that Domesday Book does not name, and that are first recorded in later sources, were the result of post-Conquest colonization. So, for example, Frank Emery, in his account of the colonization of Oxfordshire, wrote: 'Hardwick did not appear until 1199, and hints of similar expansion in a different environment come from the Cotswolds: Upton was first recorded in 1200 and Signet . . . in 1285' (Emery 1974, pp. 81–2).

A similar argument has been extended to the pre-Conquest period. The fact that very few of the settlements in Domesday Book are named in earlier sources has encouraged the idea that the centuries before the Norman Conquest witnessed a slow process of colonization. Many early charters granted large estates but they rarely hint that these included any subsidiary or minor settlements, and in texts written before 735 only 224 places are named, and not all of these were settlements (Cox 1976). Sir Frank Stenton was led by the tendency of early charters to describe estates in terms of major natural features, such as rivers and forests, to argue that they reflect 'the conditions of a time when river valleys determined settlement and village communities had not yet defined their rights in the woodland which overshadowed them . . . A comparison of this vague language with the definite place-names and exact boundaries of a late Old English charter indicates the nature of the unrecorded changes which had come over English country life between the eighth and the tenth centuries' (Stenton 1971, p. 285). Further support for this theory has been found in place-names, for it has appeared possible to distinguish early names, generally used for the more important settlements, from later ones that usually refer to minor or secondary settlements, often established on less desirable sites, in clearings or on newly colonized land. One group of names that can be dated with some confidence to the ninth century or later are those incorporating Scandinavian elements, most commonly *by* and *thorp*, which occur in large numbers between the rivers Welland and Tees. These have been taken to prove that large areas of eastern and northern England were empty and awaiting colonization when Scandinavian settlers first arrived in the ninth century (Fellows Jensen 1975; see now Fellows Jensen

1978*b*). Many of these place-names incorporate a Scandinavian personal name—Aslackby and Roxby in Lincolnshire, for example, are named after Áslákr and Hrókr respectively—and it has been argued that such names commemorate Scandinavian colonists. Outside the Scandinavian areas it has similarly been argued that the names of estate founders are preserved in such place-names as Woolstone in Berkshire, the *tūn* of Wulfric, or Aughton in Wiltshire, the *tūn* of Æffe (Stenton 1929, pp. 42–4; see now Gelling 1978, pp. 180–90). The fact that some of the people whose names are thus preserved in place-names can be identified in the tenth or eleventh centuries—there are thirty in Domesday Book apparently named after tenants of 1065 (von Feilitzen 1937, pp. 32–3)—has seemed to confirm the theory of slowly expanding settlement.

The inadequacy of this theory has been demonstrated by archaeologists who, by excavation or by the discovery of such surface indications as crop marks, seen from the air, or occupation debris, found in ploughed ground, have identified, and sometimes dated, many settlements that flourished long before they are first named. So, for example, several ninth-century houses have been discovered at Goltho, some ten miles northeast of Lincoln, under Norman structures that show the site was occupied when Domesday Book was compiled, although it was first named in the thirteenth century (*Medieval Archaeology* XIX, 1975, pp. 223–4). Many other examples could be cited. John Hurst shows, in the supplementary note written for this volume (pp. 83–5), how complex the early settlement pattern was on the Yorkshire Wolds, and in another part of Yorkshire Alan King has excavated a ninth-century house, with other structures, at 1,100 feet in the Pennines, at Ribblehead, an area that is almost completely blank on the Domesday map (King 1978). William Ford has drawn attention to even earlier examples in Warwickshire (below, p. 156) and Christopher Taylor has recently noted others in different parts of the country (Taylor 1977). The list of excavated settlements prepared by Philip Rahtz in 1974 (but not published until 1976) already needs substantial revision, as the annual survey of pre-Conquest archaeology in *Medieval Archaeology* clearly shows.

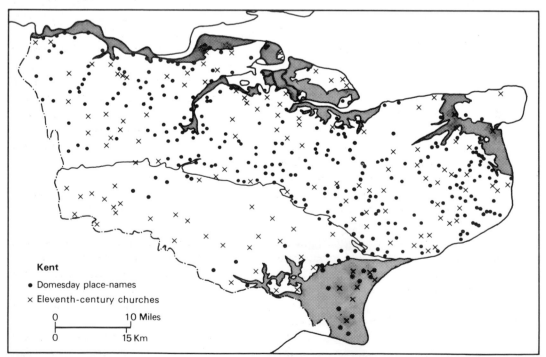

Figure 1.1   Domesday settlements and eleventh-century churches in Kent (*from Darby and Campbell 1962, pp. 496–7*).

Such discoveries have encouraged historians and geographers to re-examine Domesday Book. Its deficiencies as a record of eleventh-century settlements have been well described by H. C. Darby in the concluding volume of his great enterprise, the *Domesday Geography of England* (Darby 1977, pp. 15–26). One of the most striking demonstrations of its inadequacy is illustrated in figure 1.1. This shows the 347 places named in the Kentish Domesday as well as 139 of the 159 places that had churches at that time, but which are nevertheless omitted from Domesday Book (Darby and Campbell 1962, pp. 494–501, from which the figure is taken. Twenty of the churches cannot be identified and are therefore not shown on the map). Omissions on this scale are not surprising, for Domesday Book was not intended as a list of settlements. The reasons for its compilation, more fully discussed by S. P. J. Harvey in chapter 8, were clearly stated in the contemporary Anglo-Saxon Chronicle as follows: to record the possible yield of estates to their lords so that when they fell into the king's hands, by confiscation or death, the king's government could quickly determine how much could be demanded from a new tenant, and secondly to record what dues, including taxation, should be paid to the king. The compilers were therefore interested only in places through which such payments of rent or tax were made: hamlets, farms or villages which paid tax or rendered dues to their lord through some other estate might well not be named in Domesday Book. So, for example, the great archiepiscopal estate of Sherburn-in-Elmet in Yorkshire is described as having berewicks, but these are neither named nor numbered, although contemporary sources show that there were at least twenty. The places in the Weald that were omitted from, or unnamed, in the Domesday description of Kent, Sussex and Surrey, were dependencies of estates that lay elsewhere and there was, therefore, no need to describe them separately. Round, whose comment on the settlement of the Weald at the time of the Conquest has been quoted above, misread the evidence of Domesday because he misunderstood its purpose. The idea that the Weald was an area of very late colonization is, however, deeply rooted (Darby and Campbell 1962, pp. 579–82) and has influenced Peter Brandon's recent discussion of the Sussex landscape. He draws attention to some estates in the north of Hastings Rape that 'had been detached from their former manors in the Eastbourne and Lewes district and were separately distinguished in the Sussex Domesday. These appear to have been isolated farms, thinly scattered over the bleak forest ridges. Some had not been previously assessed for taxation, and were probably recent clearings. The presence of new farms so early in this relatively unfavourable environment has never been fully explained' (Brandon 1974, pp. 79–81). He rejects the suggestion that 'at some uncertain date claims in the Hastings backwoods were allotted to such lords of the Pevensey triangle as would take them up and that this forest district was deliberately colonized' (Salzman 1931, p. 23), because it 'does not explain why the Pevensey manors chose to settle their colonists in such distant wastes when most, if not all, had extensive and more favourably situated forest lands nearer at hand'; instead he favours a geological explanation. The Kentish evidence, however, shows that the Weald was not uncolonized forest and the explanation for this group of Sussex estates is simply that they had been detached from their parent estates and therefore needed separate treatment. The reason they had not been assessed for taxation was not that they were recent clearings but that they had formerly been treated as parts of larger estates.

It would, of course, be quite wrong to assume that all medieval settlements existed in the eleventh century. The chronology of settlement can only be determined by detailed local studies and these may well show that in some areas there was a significant extension of settlement in the centuries after the Norman Conquest; but in all such studies it should be recognized that the silence of Domesday Book is not necessarily significant and that the onus of proof rests on those who wish to claim that settlements were created after the Domesday enquiry.

Our main documentary evidence for settlement before Domesday Book consists of the 1,500 charters that have survived, the earliest being from the seventh century (listed in Sawyer 1968). Unfortunately they are very unevenly distributed throughout the country and large areas have few or none. Even in areas like Kent, Hampshire and Worcestershire, which are well provided with charters, there is the difficulty that, as guides to settlement, these documents tend to suffer from the same weakness as Domesday Book; they often deal with estate centres and do not attempt to name the contributory settlements. Many charters clearly granted large tracts of land which were exploited from many settlements, most of which are unnamed. This is shown very clearly in a late seventh-century grant by Cædwalla, king of Wessex, 'of land whose name is Farnham', in Surrey, for the construction of a monastery. After giving the assessment of the estate, sixty hides, it continues: 'of which ten are in Binton, two in Churt, and the rest are assigned to their own places and names, that is *Cusanweoh*; with everything belonging to them, fields, woods, meadows, pastures, fisheries, rivers, springs' (Sawyer 1968, no. 235; Whitelock 1955, no. 58). It is possible that the copyist left out some names after *Cusanweoh*, a word meaning 'sanctuary of Cusa', but the plural forms of 'places and names' are as clear as the conclusion that there were other places in this estate and that they had their own names. The estate was very large, for Binton lies some four miles east of Farnham and Churt five miles to the south. This seventh-century grant may be compared with the Domesday description of the same estate, then held by the bishop of Winchester, and still assessed at sixty hides. As Maitland remarked, 'we certainly must not draw the inference that there was but one vill in this tract. If the bishop is tenant in chief of the whole hundred and has become responsible for all that is levied there-from, there is no great reason why the surveyors should trouble themselves about the vills. Thus the simple *Episcopus tenet Ferneham* may dispose of some 25,000 acres of land' (Maitland 1897, pp. 13–14). Many early charters similarly grant large estates and it is significant that these are sometimes described not by the names of places but of districts, like the eighth-century *Timbinctun* with bounds that extended over six Gloucestershire parishes (Sawyer 1968, no. 141). There is also an important group of early names incorporating the element *hām* which was sometimes used for districts rather than for individual settlements, a meaning that led the Old English translator of Bede to use it to render *civitas* while *villa* is translated *tūn* (Smith 1956 I, p. 227; Sawyer 1978, pp. 159–60).

The problems posed by the documentary evidence have led historians of settlement to put great weight on the evidence of place-names. Their interpretation has, naturally, been influenced by the ideas generally held about the evolution of settlement, and the recent changes in those ideas have had a significant effect on the study of place-names. As Margaret Gelling remarked in 1974, 'work on the historical interpretation of place-name evidence has not kept pace with the etymological aspect of the study. . . . The chronology and historical significance of English place-names should be regarded for the moment as an open field', to which she added the caution that it would be regrettable if any new ideas or methods 'were to harden prematurely into dogma' (Gelling 1974b, p. 93). Apart from such obvious problems as how to date names that may not be recorded until centuries after they were first given, there are two particular difficulties. First, as already observed, names serve different functions. Some describe particular farms or villages, or even subdivisions of settlements, while others refer to large estates that included many settlements. Thus the common word *tūn* has a range of meanings from a small enclosure such as an orchard, *æppel-tūn*, or church-yard, *cyric-tūn*, to such a large estate as *Timbinctun*, already mentioned. The word *hām* has, in addition to the sense of estate or district, a more limited meaning; it is the source of modern English 'home'. The second difficulty is that names need not be permanent. Some have doubtless disappeared with the settlements to which they referred, but there are also some examples of changing names. One is Wilmington in Kent, a name that origin-ally meant *Wighelm's tūn*, and was certainly used for the place in the ninth century. In the seventh century the same place was named after someone else, Pleghelm (Sawyer 1978, pp. 152–3; Ekwall 1962). Margaret Gelling has drawn attention to the frequent occurrence of personal names in the boundary clauses of charters and she has reasonably concluded that a boundary mark such as *ælfheages gemære* is shorthand for 'the boundary of the estate now or recently in the possession of Ælfheah' (Gelling 1976, p. 828). While many of these names in boundary marks have been completely forgotten, others have survived in modern place-names. The probable explanation for most, if not all, examples of such permanent associations of individuals with places is that these people were the first to acquire full rights of ownership. In and before the seventh century individuals appear not to have owned land in the sense that they could alienate it. It belonged rather to a lord, or to a family whose members had rights that could not be disregarded. An individual only had a life interest in inherited land and could not make grants that would, in effect, disinherit his heirs. Similarly a retainer might expect to receive from his lord an estate appropriate to his rank and service but the land was lent, not given, and lords, even kings, were themselves subject to the same restraints on alienation as anyone else (see chapter 7). In such circumstances places were more likely to be named after kinship groups than individuals (Charles-Edwards 1972, p. 30). These early attitudes to land ownership were already changing in the seventh century, largely as a result of the need to endow churches with land, a need met by royal grants, made with the full support of the leading nobles. In time, similar grants were made to laymen and when, thanks to such a grant, an individual was seen to own land that was at his disposal, it might well be remembered as his, especially if he chose to make that place his permanent home. Such names therefore reflect not the foundation of settlements but a significant change in their status (Gelling 1978, pp. 180–85; Sawyer 1978, pp. 154–6). The Scandinavian conquests in England resulted in the creation of many such private estates, often on land that had formerly belonged to religious communities and churches. This explains why a very high proportion of places in the Danelaw are named after Scandinavians. This was not a habit imported by the Danes from their homeland, where place-names in *by* rarely have a personal name as the first element (Hjorth Pedersen 1960; Fellows Jensen 1978a, pp. 276–86).

Some names appear to define the relationship of one place to another. Thus the name *throp*, and its Scandinavian equivalent *thorp*, is generally interpreted as a secondary or dependent settlement, and it has sometimes been assumed that such places were founded after the parent settlements. The argument, clearly stated by Margaret Gelling in this volume (chapter 9), is that relatively marginal land was settled some time after the preferred sites on which the primary settlements were established. It is indeed likely that the best land was occupied first, although it is important to note that climatic change can alter the relative value of sites. It is, however, most improbable that many of these secondary settlements were first established in the post-Roman period; it is more likely to have happened in the Iron Age, or even earlier when the main clearances took place (below, pp. 135–40). The description of a place as secondary implies that it was subordinate to its parent estate rather than that it was founded later. As Dorothy Owen explains below (chapter 3), the relations between settlements are sometimes reflected in the status of their churches (see also Owen 1978 for Bedfordshire), but here too we may well be observing a functional hierarchy of settlements rather than a process of colonization.

The Scandinavians must have disrupted the links between many old estate centres and their subsidiary or tributary settlements. The *thorps* of the Yorkshire Wolds, for example, are most unlikely to have been new settlements established in the tenth century; and the recent discoveries near Wharram Percy (below, pp. 83–5) have reinforced the suspicion that this rich area is unlikely to have been left unoccupied by the English (Fellows Jensen 1972, pp. 222–4; Sawyer 1978, pp. 161–3). It seems more reasonable to suggest that the *thorps* of the Yorkshire Wolds were long-established settlements that, before the Viking conquests, were regarded as component parts of large estates based on the very good settlement sites around the Wolds. The disruption of these estates by the Scandinavian invaders in the ninth and tenth centuries may be compared to the separation of Wealden properties from their coastal centres after the Norman Conquest of Sussex (above p. 3).

The fragmentation of old estates, and the creation of private rights over their component parts, helps explain the changing character of charter boundaries. In the early days bounds did not need to be described in detail because they were well known; indeed some very early charters give no bounds at all or say simply that they are well known or 'ancient and known by the natives'. Desmond Bonney and

William Ford offer good reasons for thinking that some of these estate boundaries were very old indeed (below, chapters 4 and 12). The more detailed boundaries of tenth-century charters are not an indication that the landscape was then more intensively occupied; they were needed because when old estates were broken up the old bounds no longer served, and the new rights had to be carefully defined.

The argument that the settlement and exploitation of the English landscape was already extensive in the seventh, and earlier centuries, is supported by the palaeobotanical evidence discussed below by David Bartley (chapter 11; see also Bartley *et al.* 1976). Only rarely is there any indication of a significant change in the balance between woodland, grass and arable in the post-Roman period. The main clearances occurred in the Iron Age, or earlier, not after the English conquest. A similar conclusion is suggested by the assessments of estates given in early charters. These assessments, expressed in terms of hides, households or ploughlands (Charles-Edwards 1972), were the basis on which various dues were levied, including military service and food renders to the king and his agents, and the burden could be very heavy. In the early eighth-century laws of Ine the food-rent from an estate of ten hides is given as ten vats of honey, three hundred loaves, twelve ambers of Welsh ale, thirty of clear ale, two full-grown cows or ten wethers, ten geese, twenty hens, ten cheeses, an amber full of butter, five salmon, one hundred eels, and a quantity of fodder (Whitelock 1955, p. 371). This may be compared with the details given in a charter concerning the tribute payable in the eighth century from the sixty-hide estate of Westbury in Gloucestershire, which was to be 'released from all compulsion of kings and ealdormen and their subordinates except these taxes; that is of the tribute at Westbury two tuns full of pure ale and a coomb full of Welsh ale, and seven oxen and six wethers and 40 cheeses and six long *theru* [a word of unknown meaning] and 30 ambers of unground corn and four ambers of meal, to the royal estate' (Sawyer 1968, no. 146; Whitelock 1955, no. 78). These texts imply that the estates were fully exploited and that there was very little room for unworked resources. When, in 681, an abbess was given twenty hides by the river Cherwell for her monastery (Sawyer 1968, no. 1167; Whitelock 1955, no. 57), she was not being given empty land in need of clearance; the assessment meant that the estate was due to render a substantial tribute to the king, or anyone he wished to favour, in addition to the produce it was expected to yield to its owner. The appurtenances listed in early charters reinforce the impression that the estates being described were well developed. These clauses were not routine formulae for they seem to have been chosen with the actual resources of the estates in mind (Sawyer 1974, p. 112) and imply that the exploitation was thorough and that the organization of the estates was well developed.

Recent archaeological discoveries have drawn attention to the scattered nature of many early English settlements; the term 'polyfocal' has been used to describe them (Taylor 1977). It has indeed been argued, in this volume and elsewhere, that medieval settlement developed by a process of concentration from scattered settlements, and that nucleated settlements tend to be relatively late. It is however possible that some nucleated settlements were very early. If the numerous buildings found at Chalton in Hampshire or at Catholm on the Trent were occupied simultaneously these places would certainly be examples of early nucleations, but they may, on the other hand, represent a succession of rebuildings (Addyman and Leigh 1973; *Medieval Archaeology* XXI, 1977, pp. 212–13). The fact that the English were familiar with nucleated settlements in their homeland encourages belief that they did introduce something similar to Britain (Parker 1965; van Es 1967; Hvass 1975). It is also possible that the English found nucleated settlements when they arrived in Britain; some villas must have been hard to distinguish from nucleated villages. It is, however, clear that alongside any early English nucleated settlements there were numerous scattered, single farms. Continuity of occupation can never be proved archaeologically and we may therefore look forward to a continuing debate about the fate of the British population and their settlements after the English conquest. That conquest must have caused much disruption and destruction, and it seems likely that the plague of the mid-sixth century left a lot of land vacant for reoccupation by the English; but the survival of many single farms after the English conquest (Foard 1978; Taylor 1977; and below, p. 84) does suggest either that many Britons survived, or that the English quickly adapted themselves to the patterns of settlement that they found in Britain.

Too little is known about the development of fields and field systems for much usefully to be said here about them. Many studies have been based on recent surface indications that are a poor guide to early arrangements. It is possible, as suggested below (pp. 84–5), that large open fields of the kind familiar in post-Conquest England were not an original feature of the English landscape and that they were formed relatively late in the pre-Conquest period. It would however be wrong to assume that communal cultivation was similarly late. Ine's laws (c. 42) show that in late seventh-century Wessex both arable and meadow could be shared or held in common, and contemporary Irish laws show kinsmen and neighbours cooperating in exploiting the land (Hughes 1972, pp. 51–3, 61–4).

Early settlements, whether nucleated or single farms, were not self-contained units of exploitation, isolated from their neighbours. Many were in fact grouped together in larger units variously called federal, discrete or multiple estates by modern scholars. These large estates contained the varied resources needed to sustain life: arable, pasture, woodland, and probably fisheries as well. In the post-Roman period there may have been many markets in which surplus produce could be bought and sold, some associated with former Roman towns, others in the open countryside, but they are unlikely to have played a major part in distributing food, raw materials and equipment. Lords and their dependants had, therefore, normally to rely on what they, or their neighbours, produced. It is significant that for the one essential commodity that was not universally available, salt, elaborate arrangements were made at a very early date to distribute it widely from the inland brine springs of Worcestershire and Cheshire (Sawyer 1978, pp. 225–6).

Some of these estates survived and can be recognized in Domesday Book or later, but there are no grounds for assuming that they had done so without alteration from the earliest English period, for they could be reorganized, amalgamated, divided, and probably even created. The extraordinary similarities between such estates in different parts of Britain does however strongly suggest that they had a common basis (below, chapter 2; Barrow 1973; Barrow 1975; Phythian-Adams 1978). They were, of course, not uniquely Celtic; organizations of this kind must have been a normal feature of many primitive societies with limited means of exchange. If, as seems likely, the English were familiar with such lordships before they came to Britain, their conquests in the island would have been facilitated, and it would certainly have been in their interest to re-establish, or to preserve, such units of lordship as quickly as possible, so that they would have the same tribute and services as their British predecessors.

These large estates appear originally to have been royal. In time many passed into the hands of nobles, some of whom claimed royal descent, and after the conversion to Christianity others, or parts of them, were used to endow churches. Later, either by grant or usurpation, many laymen acquired fuller rights of ownership over parts of such estates. It is possible that this fragmentation of 'royal' estates was associated in some way with the development of nucleated settlements observed by archaeologists. It is also possible, even probable, that the enhanced rights of lordship resulting from the break up of these old estates led in their turn to the more rigorous exaction of servile obligations from tenants who were unable to resist the encroachment of seigneurial authority. Twelfth-century surveys make it possible, for the first time, to study manorial lordship in some detail, and they reveal great variations in the status and obligations of peasants (Lennard 1959); but it would be wrong to conclude that this form of manorial lordship was only developed late in the Old English period. The earliest English law-codes, of the seventh century, show that there was then an elaborate hierarchy of unfree and semi-free men and women, and that freemen, of all ranks, had dependants, servants and slaves. As T. H. Aston has shown, the essential features of later manorial organization are well evidenced in the seventh and eighth centuries (Aston 1958). It was the labour and renders of their subordinate peasants that made it possible for lords to pay the food-rent owed to the king, or whoever else held the 'royal' estate. When these lords were freed from all, or part, of their obligation to pay this food-rent and to render other services, their own resources were obviously increased, and it would not have been surprising if many of them attempted to reorganize their servile tenants to their own advantage.

Whether or not the number of unfree peasants was growing before the Norman Conquest, a large number successfully preserved their independence. Domesday Book records many freemen in eastern England and there are grounds for suspecting that its compilers were not consistent in their treatment of this class. In Derbyshire and Staffordshire early twelfth-century surveys of Burton Abbey estates show that Domesday omitted large numbers of *censarii*, rent-payers (Walmsley 1968). Some of these may have been villeins whose labour services had been commuted to a money payment, but others clearly had a higher status than their fellows, having the obligation to go on errands for the abbot of Burton, and to attend the courts of shire or wapentake. They also owed some small ploughing service, and additional duties at harvest time. These obligations are very much like those owed elsewhere by drengs, thegns, *radmen*, rad-knights, gavel-kinders and sokemen, the varied names given in Domesday Book and other sources to men who in Old English appear to have been called *geneats*, 'companions' or 'retainers' (Barrow 1973, pp. 13–19, 27–8).

It was in the remoter parts of Britain, in Cornwall, Wales, Northumbria, Cumbria and Scotland, that such men, and the estates to which they belonged, tended to survive rather better than in the south and east. In the Danelaw it was the Scandinavians who hastened the break up of estates, while in southern England new forms of royal government, including markets under royal control, had a similar effect. In all parts of Britain, however, some traces survived, often in the form of obligations or renders of obscure significance preserved by the conservative tendencies of rural society.

The period between the English and Norman conquests was therefore not marked by a great movement of colonization. Conquests, natural disasters, climatic change and partible inheritance all led to changes in the pattern of settlement as new ones were formed and old ones abandoned, but from the earliest period after the English conquest the resources of the landscape were fully exploited in most parts of England. The pattern of settlement was, however, being changed in a more significant way by the progressive abandonment of single farms and the formation of larger nucleations. That change was only a symptom of a more fundamental change in social organization. New ideas about kingship, and the rights of landlords, effected great changes in the way settlements were organized. Domesday Book may be an unsatisfactory guide to the settlements in which the English lived in the eleventh century, but by revealing the contrast between the archaic society of Northumbria and the more developed south (Sawyer 1978, pp. 201–3), it casts a flood of light on the changes that were, in the centuries before the Norman Conquest, transforming men's ideas about their rights over the land, and their relations with each other.

2

Multiple Estates and Early Settlement

G. R. J. Jones

Some sixty years ago, towards the end of an inconclusive debate about early settlement history, Sir Paul Vinogradoff asserted that 'the history of Great Britain rises on a rock-bed of Celtic institutions' (Vinogradoff and Morgan 1914, p. v). Yet, until recent decades, no serious attempts were made to test the validity of this assertion. Archaeologists, geographers, historians, and place-name scholars held, and usually still hold, with tenacity to the ethnic interpretation of settlement history (Meitzen 1895, I, pp. 199–201; II, pp. 119–22). The Celts were dismissed rather pejoratively as footloose tribesmen who roamed at will with their herds and when in due course they settled, did so in scattered homesteads or, at best, hamlets; for the latter, by some elusive train of thought, were considered to be as appropriate as scattered homesteads for the allegedly almost exclusively pastoral tradition of the Celts. In accordance with this interpretation it was claimed that, on the departure of the Roman legions, the Celts were fairly readily displaced from the lowland areas of eastern Britain; and here, therefore, so it was argued, a new beginning was made by cooperative communities of Anglo-Saxon freemen housed in large nucleated villages. The purpose of this paper is to demonstrate how models of territorial organization which were presented by Welsh lawyers in medieval lawbooks but, nevertheless, had been derived from ancient exemplars, can be used to provide a more satisfactory basis for the interpretation of early settlement history.

The most comprehensive of these models is that provided for north Wales in a group of related law-texts of the thirteenth century known as the Book of Iorwerth (Jenkins 1963, p. 39; Wiliam 1960, pp. 59–65). Reduced to tabular form and its major components this model is as follows:

4 acres	= 1 homestead		
4 homesteads	= 1 shareland	=	16 acres
4 sharelands	= 1 holding	=	64 acres
4 holdings	= 1 vill	=	256 acres
4 vills	= 1 multiple estate	=	1,024 acres
12 multiple estates + 2 vills (i.e. 50 vills)	= 1 commote	=	12,800 acres
2 commotes (i.e. 100 vills)	= 1 hundred	=	25,600 acres

Within each commote the two vills or townships distinguished from the twelve multiple estates were said to be for the use of the king. One was to be land of the reeve's vill or settlement (*maerdref*), the mensal land cultivated under the guidance of the lesser reeve for the sustenance of the royal court. The second was to be the king's waste and summer pasture. Of the twelve multiple estates which were to be in every commote, four multiple estates, that is sixteen vills, were assigned to the king's bondmen. The chancellor, an important royal officer was assigned one multiple estate of four vills, and a second important royal officer, the greater reeve, was assigned a similar estate. There therefore remained six multiple estates which were assigned to free notables.

The affectation of numerical precision in the model reveals clearly that Welsh medieval lawyers fully appreciated the importance of landed resources and indeed recognized that land was the ultimate source of all wealth. The subtle nature of this preoccupation with resources in the model is implied by the linking of the two vills for the use of the king. This linkage reflects the essentially mixed nature of the agrarian economy and also points to the integration of lowland resources with those in the uplands. The king's court was normally in the lowlands and in its vicinity therefore was located the mensal land, arable demesne cultivated in order to satisfy some of the demands of the royal table. On the other hand, much of the king's waste and certainly his summer pasture would usually be located in the uplands. The main exceptions in north Wales would be low-lying areas like Anglesey, where lowland marshes were used for pasture in the drier months of the year. Even today on the moist coastlands of northwest Wales where climatic conditions are favourable for the growth of grass the appearance of 'the first bite' in spring is still a matter of concern to the farmer. In the medieval period, before the advent of scientific aids to farming, these considerations were of even more crucial significance. Hence the traditional practice of seasonal transhumance which applied even to the herds of the king. Thus the king's summer pasture was singled out for mention. It was the grazing of the upland pastures of mainland commotes during the summer months from May onwards which permitted the conservation of lowland pastures for the winter months and, above all, the lean days of Lent.

Associated with the Iorwerth model were statements about royal income in the form of services and rents. The latter in their uncommuted form consisted of cereals, meat, butter and, not least, drink, preferably mead, but if that were not available bragget or, seemingly as a last resort, ale. The four multiple estates assigned to the king's bondmen were stated to be for the support of 'dogs and horses and for progress and quarters'. This is an allusion to the ancient custom whereby the king and his court, including the household troop and groups of youths under military training, made periodic circuits or progresses around the kingdom, and were quartered for a certain number of nights on a particular district. Among those with this right to make a circuit, so as to be fed and housed *en route*, were the grooms with the royal horses in their care. This kind of ambulatory feeding was adopted also for the falconers with the hunting birds, and the huntsmen with the dogs. The appearance of the dogs in the Iorwerth model is a salutary reminder that although hunting made but a relatively small contribution to the economy, it nevertheless remained a highly prized index of social standing. Nor were the other wild products of the woods, wastes and waters neglected. Thus the Book of Iorwerth records that since the bondmen of the king were not to support him or his household 'they are not to retain their honey, nor their fish, but are to send them to the king's court; and he may, if he will, make weirs upon their waters, and take their hives'.

In conveying some impression of the disposition of resources the Book of Iorwerth helps to illuminate the functioning of the economy. It also casts some light on the nature of the social structure. This was essentially hierarchical, with the king at the apex followed in descending order by his royal officers, then the free notables and, still lower down the social scale, the bondmen. The Iorwerth model has the added advantage that it gives some hint of the relative proportions of freemen and bondmen (Jones 1961a; 1964). Contrary to the beliefs of earlier investigators there must have been a majority of bondmen. In Wales at least these were *adscripti glebae*, tied to the soil. Besides the occupants of the four bond multiple estates in the commote, and the bondmen of the two royal vills there were, as other sections of the lawbooks make clear, many bond under-tenants. Such bond under-tenants provided the necessary support not only for the chancellor and the greater reeve but also for the free notables. In addition the lawbooks refer to slaves. Some of these were owned by bondmen, hence the Welsh proverb which indicates that unfortunate indeed was the lot of the bondman's slave (Evans 1885, p. 546).

As the post-Conquest extents of north Wales show, these social differences were to some degree reflected in differences of tenure (Jones 1972, pp. 320–49). By the time the Book of Iorwerth was compiled, royal officials, free notables, and even many bondmen, held land by a hereditary tenure. According to this, equal shares were normally inherited by brothers on their father's death, save that provision was made for a re-partition among members of the same agnatic lineage as far as second cousins. Under-tenants held land by what appears to have been a smaller scale variant of this tenure best described as nucleal land. A minority of bondmen, however, held geldable land which was not shared 'according to brothers'. Instead, it was 'right for reeve and chancellor to share it and give to everyone in the township as good as to each other'. On that account it was called reckoned land and the township was known as the reckoned township or vill. In the same way the land of the reeve's vill, other than the mensal land, was to be shared out among the bond tenants by the lesser reeve. No matter what the tenure, however, land was generally cultivated on the infield–outfield system (Baker and Butlin 1973, pp. 430–79). The well-manured infield, normally located in the immediate vicinity of the settlement, was cultivated year in year out for the spring cereals, oats and barley. After harvest the stubble was grazed in common, save where favourable physical conditions, coupled with a flexible use of fencing, permitted the cultivation of a winter cereal, usually wheat. The outfield was normally used as a common pasture but periodically portions of this would be dunged and then cultivated for as long as they would bear a worthwhile crop, before being allowed to revert. Such land was often known as mountain land (*terra montana*) or mountain ground, though it was sometimes located at low altitudes (Eyre and Jones 1966, pp. 199–230).

Implicit in the Iorwerth model is a hierarchy of estates, whose existence is independently confirmed by the post-Conquest extents of north Wales. The most important estate was clearly that of the king. Within the royal estate there was an admixture of agrarian and political lordship. In the agrarian sense this lordship extended from the lowland arable demesne of the court to the waste, which was always the king's waste (*desertum regis*) and on to the upland summer pastures. In the political sense all the king's free tenants owed military service and, in addition, suit to the court of the commote or hundred. The latter had probably been the original unit of political organization in Wales, for there is evidence to show that many a Welsh hundred (*cantref*) was co-extensive with a petty kingdom (*tud*) until the absorption of a number of these units into larger kingdoms, a process already well advanced by the sixth century (Charles-Edwards 1971; Jones 1972, pp. 287–8; Williams 1899, pp. 77–88). The estates of the chancellor and greater reeve, like those of the free notables were presumably more circumscribed, consisting, according to the model, of only four vills each. Even these smaller estates, however, would have contained more than one significant centre of settlement and would thus merit the designation 'multiple estate'. The Book of Iorwerth indicates that at least by the thirteenth century some rights of jurisdiction attached to these estates. Thus notables could exercise rights of lordship over aliens (*alltudion*), literally men from outside the kingdom (*tud*), after the forbears of these aliens had occupied the same land under them for four generations and, as a result, had become tied to the soil in bondage.

The lawbooks of south Wales present a much more sketchy outline of territorial organization. The commote was certainly a unit of royal administration for its boundaries were said to belong to the king, but neither its components nor those of the hundred were defined. The only multiple estates described contained either thirteen or seven vills (Emanuel 1967, pp. 135–6, 226, 239; Williams and Powell 1961, p. 71). Thus the Book of Cyfnerth, a lawbook of the early thirteenth century, records that 'there should be thirteen vills in every multiple estate, and the thirteenth of these will be the supernumary vill' (Wade-Evans 1909, pp. 54–5, 204–5). Such supernumary vills were usually located in the uplands. A gloss in a fourteenth-century manuscript of a law-text adds the explanation that 'a supernumary vill is a vill of notables, without an officer over it, without an officer from it' (Owen 1841, II, pp. 768–9). Nevertheless the remaining twelve vills of these multiple estates supported the royal officers mentioned in the Iorwerth model, namely the chancellor and the greater reeve. Despite the alienation of these larger estates to notables some regalian rights were reserved to the king;

but although some south Welsh texts refer to the estate of thirteen vills as the 'complete multiple estate', rents and services to the king seem to have been contributed by only twelve of the constituent vills.

The Book of Cyfnerth also records that there were to be seven vills in the multiple estate of bond vills. Correspondingly, other south Welsh texts specifically used the plural, rather than the singular, when referring to those bond vills adjacent to the court which were subject to the authority of the lesser reeve (Emanuel 1967, pp. 120, 349; Richards 1954, p. 75). In the Iorwerth model the king's single vill in the lowlands was matched by one containing summer pasture in the uplands. A similar matching is not unlikely to have been adopted in any model that the lawyers might have devised for south Wales. Since the lesser reeve who controlled the vills of the king's court in south Wales was also responsible for the king's cattle, there could well have been as many as seven vills in the uplands to provide summer pasture. One would expect the complete multiple estate of the king to have been larger than that of the most well-endowed notable. In this event we can envisage that, ideally, in the model commote of south Wales there would have been a multiple estate of fourteen vills belonging to the king with seven inhabited by his bondmen in winter and the remainder grazed by their herds and especially those of the king in summer. If to these fourteen vills are added three multiple estates each containing twelve vills from which the notables provided rents and services, then the commote of south Wales would have contained fifty vills or townships, exactly the same number as in the model commote of north Wales.

In hierarchical terms the highest rank would have been accorded to the multiple estate of the king. The *caput* of this estate would have most merited the appellation *maenor*, the original Welsh term for what has been described hitherto in this paper as a multiple estate. The term *maenol* used of the multiple estate in north Wales was a later dialectical variant of *maenor*, a south Welsh word. The first element in *maenor* has been taken to be *maen*, meaning stone (Lloyd 1890, pp. 32–4, 57–8). Thus *maenor* is deemed to have meant originally the stone-girt residence of the king, which was readily distinguished from the less substantial dwellings of lesser men. By extension this same term appears to have been applied to the territorial unit from which rents and services were contributed to the stone-girt residence.

Like all models those presented by medieval Welsh lawyers were simplified structurings of reality presenting supposedly significant features in a generalized form. Nevertheless, as the post-Conquest extents of north Wales show, these models despite their obvious schematism were not totally divorced from actuality. That this accordance should occur, it could be argued, is only to be expected, for the presentation of models might well have distorted subsequent portrayals, in the same way that the very act of prediction in human affairs can affect subsequent human actions. But such considerations do not explain all the parallels between the lawyers' models and the extents, for some elements of the former existed in various parts of Wales long before the oldest extant text of a Welsh lawbook was written *c.* 1175 (Emanuel 1967, pp. 9–12, 97).

For Gwent in south Wales, Domesday Book records the existence in 1086 of multiple estates containing thirteen or fourteen vills each subject to the authority of a reeve. Here there was also one group of seven demesne vills. In addition there was one group of fourteen vills which had been fissioned into smaller groups, consisting of three or two vills and even single ones. In mid-Wales a memorandum attributed to *c.* 850, and inscribed in a gospel-book, records the donation of one bond vill to the church. Given by a territorially well-endowed agnatic lineage, this township had clearly been carved out of a natural topographic unit corresponding with the upper reaches of the river Cothi and its tributaries (Jones 1972, pp. 304–6, 311–20). For this area which appears to have been roughly coterminous with at least the northern portions of the medieval commote of Caeo there are pointers, even in the Roman period, to an organized integration of upland and lowland resources. Thus, in order to exploit the lowland gold deposits at Dolau Cothi by hydraulic techniques Roman engineers constructed long aqueducts to convey vast quantities of water to the mines (Lewis and Jones 1969; Jones and Lewis 1972). As would be expected these were obtained from the headwaters of the Cothi and one of its tributaries. But the particular points chosen for tapping these water supplies lay just within the limits of the later commote, a disposition which suggests that this boundary, probably a zone rather than a line, had already been delimited. The oldest known reference to a *maenor* occurs in a marginal entry in the same gospel-book, and has been attributed to *c.* 800. Appropriately the unit thus recorded contained seven townships in later centuries (Jones 1972, pp. 308–11).

For north Wales, a good example of the organization of both natural and human resources within the framework of the hundred and its subdivisions, the commote and the smaller multiple estate, is provided by the hundred (*cantref*) of Aberffraw in Anglesey (figure 2.1). Although Anglesey is low-lying this was a fairly well-defined natural unit. On the southwest it was bounded by an ancient arm of the sea which merged inland into the most extensive tract of marsh on the island, Cors-ddeugae. Likewise on its northwestern and northern margins the boundary of the hundred passed through the large marsh known as Cors-y-bol (figure 2.2). Elsewhere on the landward margins of the hundred the boundary for the most part followed the courses of rivers. Only about half of the hundred consisted of readily drained soils suitable for cultivation, but the nuclei of the most important settlements were sited on the margins of these well-drained soils. They were therefore well placed to make use of arable resources for both infield and outfield cultivation while, at the same time, they had ready access to adjoining permanent pastures usually located on less well-drained soils.

This unit was still called a hundred (*cantref*) for purposes of secular administration as late as the fourteenth century. It comprised the two commotes of Llifon and Malltraeth but, of the two, it was the latter which contained the larger expanse of well-drained soils (Roberts 1958). Significantly the *caput* for the whole hundred was located here at Aberffraw, a royal court, regarded as the traditional capital of the whole kingdom of Gwynedd during the latter part of the dark ages. Despite its royal associations the hundred of Aberffraw did not contain the one hundred vills or townships envisaged in the lawyers' model. An extent of 1352 records only sixteen secular vills in Llifon and eighteen in Malltraeth (Ellis 1838, pp. 44–55). In addition nineteen lesser units known as hamlets were recorded for the former and seventeen for the latter. Some of these were described as free and some as bond. But there were still others said to be inhabited both by freemen and by bondmen; these for convenience have been designated as mixed. In the Iorwerth model, as distinct from other sections of this lawbook, no mention was made of church land. Yet, in Llifon, six vills had been alienated to the church, and in Malltraeth the same was true of no less than nine vills and six hamlets. The majority of these had been alienated to the bishops of Bangor, but there were a few vills alienated to monastic communities (Ellis 1838, pp. 104–6, 234–8). Among these was the vill of Eglwys Ail which, according to the extent of 1352, was said to be free and held 'of Saint Cadwaladr the king [*de sancto Cadwaladr rege*]', save that certain dues were reserved to the crown. The church of this vill was, and still is, known as Llangadwaladr. Since it contains an inscribed stone commemorating Cadfan, a member of the ruling dynasty of Gwynedd who died *c.* 625, the vill was probably donated to the church by his grandson, Cadwaladr ap Cadwallon, the celebrated warrior, and later monk, who died during the latter half of the seventh century (Nash-Williams 1950, pp. 55–7). The church whose existence is indicated by the name *Eglwys* Ail, was no doubt re-named Llangadwaladr during this period as a tribute to the memory of its pious royal benefactor. A church had probably existed on this site long before, for Cadfan was the great-great-grandson of Maelgwn Gwynedd, allegedly a more sinful benefactor of the church, who died in the mid-sixth century (Alcock 1971, pp. 244–5). Maelgwn's designation of 'island dragon' in the writings of his contemporary Gildas implies his secure possession of Anglesey, and thus of the court at Aberffraw (Williams 1899, pp. 76–88). As the probable burial-place of Cadfan, and the holy retreat of Cadwaladr some two miles distant from Aberffraw, Eglwys

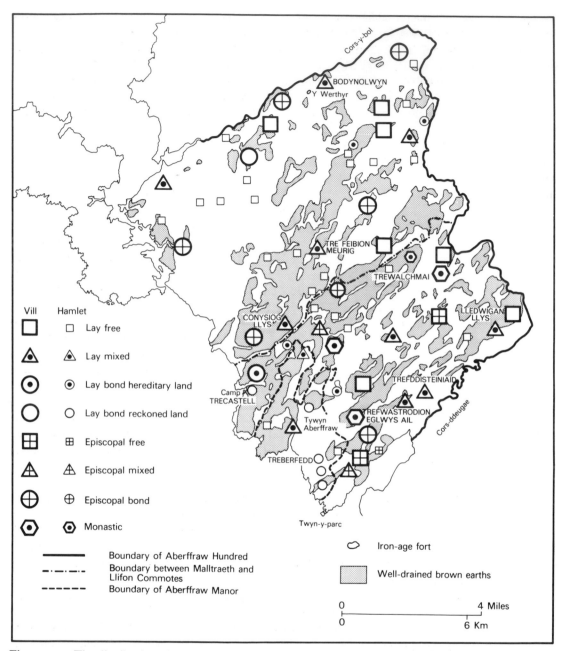

Figure 2.1   The distribution of medieval vills and hamlets in the hundred of Aberffraw.

Ail was almost certainly old-established. Although quite distinct from the court chapel, it clearly served the palace of Aberffraw.

In keeping with the Iorwerth model many components of the hundred of Aberffraw had been alienated to royal officials (figure 2.1). Among these was the hamlet of Trewalchmai which was named after the noted court poet who flourished at the close of the twelfth century. Members of lineages descended from Gwalchmai also held land in the vill of Lledwigan Llys near the southeastern border of Malltraeth, and nearer to Aberffraw at the meaningfully named Trefddisteiniaid (The Vill of the Stewards) and Trefwastrodion (The Vill of the Grooms).[1]

Despite this alienation of estates to laymen, regalian rights were preserved. This is most apparent in relation to the royal court of Aberffraw, a group of separate buildings dominated by the king's timber hall, and surrounded by a wall. According to medieval surveys the various structures of this court complex were built and maintained by the labour services of both freemen and bondmen residing in various parts of the hundred of Aberffraw. Thus the two members of the free Lineage of the Gatekeepers, who apparently resided at Aberffraw itself, among their other rents and services made and repaired one length of the wall of the lord's manor there on either side of the gate. On the other hand the four bond lineages holding hereditary bond land in Tre Feibion Meurig (The Vill of the Sons of Meurig), in the neighbouring commote of Llifon, were also said to 'make the walls around the lord's manor of Aberffraw', presumably the parts not built by the Gatekeepers. These bondmen of Tre Feibion Meurig, who included occupants of land on Moelfaenol (The Hill of the Multiple Estate), also made part of the roof of the hall and of the chamber at the manor of Aberffraw. Besides, as the extent of 1352 put it, 'they make and clean the lord's privy [*latrinam*] there'. In addition they made good against the rain the roof of the chamber of the bailiff, and they were to pay for every circuit. A few years later in 1356 it was also found that 'each bondman having pigs should give 2d. for each pig as long as the lord should please; however, each one having several pigs used to render one pig worth 20d. to the lord'. Yet, perhaps the most noteworthy of their obligations was that recorded in 1352 whereby they were 'to carry the lord's victuals and fuel from his vill'. The destination is not specified but it is perhaps significant that Tre Feibion Meurig is roughly midway between Aberffraw proper and the small hill-fort of Y Werthyr near the northern border of Llifon (figure 2.2). This hill-fort has been ascribed to the iron age but a post-Roman or even an early medieval date cannot be ruled out (Lynch 1970, pp. 231–3). It was located within the almost exclusively bond vill of Bodynolwyn, whose tenants were the only ones said in 1352 to owe pig dues, these matching those of Tre Feibion Meurig in 1356. Within Bodynolwyn, moreover, there were four bovates of free land held in return for various obligations including the usual suit of the hundred court. Although the tenant of this land lived some ten miles distant from Aberffraw proper, he was obliged to make part of the lord's hall and chamber there and, in addition, paid for the circuit of the king's warhorse.

Nearer to Aberffraw proper constructional duties loomed larger, especially among the bondmen. Thus, whereas the freemen of Trefwastrodion with others of the commote of Malltraeth made part of the lord prince's chamber, the tenants of bond hereditary land in this same vill made part of each house (*domus*) of the lord prince's manor of Aberffraw. That they should also owe the circuit of the king's warhorse is only to be expected in The Vill of the Grooms but, in addition, they paid the circuit of the falconers, that of the otter hounds, and that of the bailiff. In Conysiog Llys, the nearest secular vill to Aberffraw in Llifon, the members of one free lineage paid their share towards the works of the manor of Aberffraw, and each time they brewed ale they paid to the bailiff for the time being six gallons of ale or 6d. The members of a second free lineage here, who also held land in Treriffri, among their various obligations, maintained 'the roof of the lord prince's hall and chamber at Aberffraw against the rain'.

Within the framework for extensive lordship provided by the hundred of Aberffraw a smaller multiple estate called the manor of Aberffraw had emerged, certainly by the late thirteenth century, and probably long before. Within this manor the chief settlement was at Aberffraw proper where the court was located. The major royal officers had a lodging either in the court itself or in the adjoining vill. Here too in 1352 lived minor royal servants, including the four occupants of the Holding of the

[1] Trefddisteiniaid is originally likely to have borne a different name, for *distain*, its middle element, is a Welsh borrowing of the Anglo-Saxon, *discþegn* (Binchy 1970, p. 23).

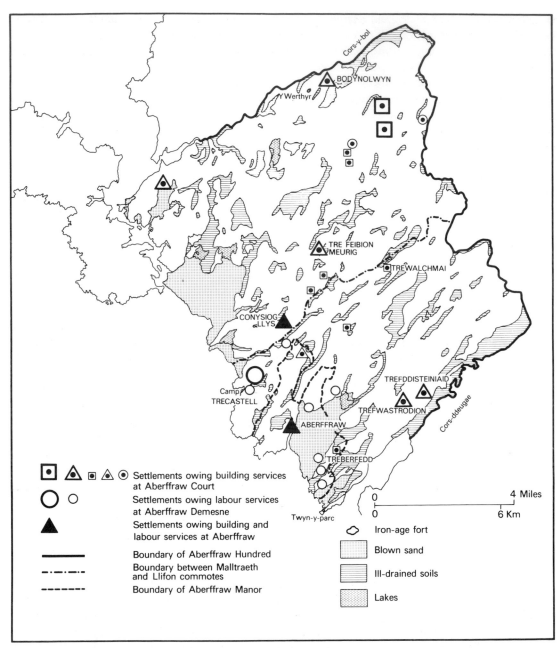

Figure 2.2   The distribution of medieval settlements owing building and labour services at the manor of Aberffraw.

Carpenter, the two members of the Lineage of the Gatekeepers, and probably some members of three other free lineages. Within Aberffraw proper there were also two other sub-units which for administrative purposes were accorded a separate identity. One was the hamlet called *Maerdref* (Reeve's Settlement) inhabited by reckoned-land bondmen, and the other was the hamlet called *Garthau* (Gardens), with its fourteen gardens of *terra nativa* each containing one acre. In 1294

Maerdref was occupied by at least one group of nine bondmen and Garthau by another nine bond-men. This settlement, the largest in the manor, was flanked on the west by four carucates of arable demesne land, each of sixty acres, which lay intermingled in open-field with the lands of free and bond tenants (Public Record Office, SC 11/768; 769).

In addition to this main settlement the multiple estate known as the manor of Aberffraw contained seven, or possibly eight, other dependent hamlets. Of these, five were exclusively bond, one was mixed, and two were free, though there is some doubt about the inclusion of one of the free hamlets. One of these dependent bond hamlets was located beyond the boundary of the manor. Named Trecastell (The Settlement or Vill of the Castle), it adjoined a small promontory fort called Camp, and, significantly, contained one carucate of arable demesne. But, that this outlying hamlet formed an integral part of the manor is clearly revealed by later records which state that rights of intercommoning were exercised on the sandy waste (*vasta arenosa*) named Tywyn Aberffraw by the lord and his tenants of Aberffraw, Garthau, Trecastell and the other exclusively bond hamlets of the smaller multiple estate of Aberffraw. In 1352 moreover, the bondmen of all the dependent hamlets of this manor of Aberffraw with 'all the lord prince's bondmen of Aberffraw' were said to pay 2s. each year for 'work on the animal house of the said manor'.

Typical of these dependent hamlets was Treberfedd whose name indicates that it was literally 'The Middle Vill'; although a hamlet, it was said in 1352 to be 'of the nature of reckoned vill'. At that date the relatively onerous obligations of its bond tenants included suit at the lord's mill of Aberffraw, for which they also made the ditch, watercourse and roof. To this same mill they carried timber and millstones; in addition they performed carriage for the lord with a man and horse hired at 2d. daily. In 1294 this same hamlet of Treberfedd was held by nine *villani*, a total which is in exact accord with the number of houses envisaged by the lawyers as the ideal for the bond hamlet. These bondmen, besides paying an old-established cash rent, made newer payments (Jones Pierce 1941). These were in lieu of barley flour, butter, sheep, lambs, hens, eggs, and instead of labour services on 161 days.

As would be expected the most burdensome obligations were those of the bondmen of Aberffraw proper. Hence by 1294 particularly heavy cash rents were contributed by these *villani* in lieu of labour services. Before their commutation into substantial cash rents these had included harrowing, reaping and other autumn works, as well as the duty, stipulated in the Book of Iorwerth, of providing fire and straw for the lord's court. Some labour services for the cultivation of the court demesnes had also been provided by the *villani forinseci*, the bondmen of outlying settlements, of the hundred of Aberffraw; but in 1294 the value of these services was less than a quarter of those provided by the bondmen of the manor of Aberffraw. Clearly, therefore, the agrarian duties imposed on this manor, the smaller multiple estate at the *caput*, were more intensive than those characteristic of the remainder of the hundred.

The focus for this activity was undoubtedly Aberffraw proper where recent excavations in the present village have revealed traces of what appears to have been a Roman fort. This was probably refurbished once in the Roman period, and later, arguably in the post-Roman period (White 1974). The ditch of this fort was re-cut once in the Roman period. It was also lightly re-cut on a different profile in the fifth or sixth century when a new rampart, crudely built of clay and rubble, was provided on its inner edge with a revetment wall of stone. This refurbishing of the fort has been ascribed by the excavator to the reign of Maelgwn Gwynedd, or possibly to that of his great-grandfather, Cunedda, who expelled the Irish from Anglesey in the early fifth century. The tentative placing of the fort suggested by the excavator on the basis of various finds made within the village is such that the later court chapel named Eglwys y Beili (The Church of the Enclosure) would have been sited within the defences of the fort (Eyre and Jones 1966, pp. 211–14). Accordingly Aberffraw proper may well have been the site of the court from at least the late Roman period onwards. Eglwys Ail, as we have seen, certainly existed by the seventh century, if not long before, and earlier could have been a pagan cult centre. A division of functions between the component settlements was very characteristic of multiple estates whether large or small. Such a division of functions could have applied at an early date not only to the hundred of Aberffraw but also to a sub-unit slightly larger than the medieval manor of Aberffraw. If, for the hundred, the court at Aberffraw was the secular focus, and Eglwys Ail the church focus, then the large iron-age fort on the promontory at Twyn-y-parc was probably the main retreat of the inhabitants in times of strife. Behind the massive ramparts, which almost completely cut off the cliff-bounded promontory from the mainland, fragments of a Roman *mortarium* have been found (Lynch 1970, pp. 231–3). It may be suggested, therefore, that this coastal retreat could have remained in use during the period when the Roman fort at Aberffraw was occupied. It is possible, moreover, that a sub-unit embracing Aberffraw proper, Eglwys Ail and Twyn-y-parc fort was even then in being. The name Treberfedd (The Middle Vill), applied to a settlement which is roughly equidistant from all three components, would have been entirely appropriate for such a sub-unit but, given its eccentric position, entirely inappropriate in relation to the hundred as a whole.

The multiple estates of Wales, whether large or small, were matched in Northumbria by similar groups of vills or townships. In Northumbria the group of vills administered from the lord's court was usually known as a *shire*, but the parallels with Wales are very striking (Jones 1955, p. 55; 1961a, pp. 194–6). As in Wales the occupants of the shire vills were responsible for the entertainment of the lord and his retinue, as well as the maintenance of his huntsmen and dogs at certain seasonal progresses. Again the building and repair of the lord's court were duties apportioned among various vills of the shire. In the case of Auchlandshire, according to a survey of 1183, the list of buildings erected for the lord, the bishop of Durham, is virtually identical with the list of buildings constructed for the typical Welsh king. The only significant difference is that in Wales the buildings were permanent structures in the lowland court, whereas the survey of Auchlandshire dealt in detail with the building of the bishop's hunting lodges in the forest of Weardale, and only incidentally with the lowland court (Greenwell 1852, pp. 23–30). Moreover, near identities of usage are matched by identities of terminology. Thus, for example, some townships in Auchlandshire rendered to the bishop one cow in milk known as the *vacca de metreth*. The qualification of this particular render had, as its main element, the Brittonic word which later became the Welsh for *treth*, meaning tribute (Rees 1963, p. 161). That similar obligations should be characteristic of multiple estates in Wales and of shires in Northumbria seems to be too great a set of coincidences to be explained away by parallel growth, especially given the usage in both areas of words like *treth*. There are so many parallels between Wales and Northumbria that we are justified in postulating a common origin for multiple-estate organization in both areas; and this common origin must date from the period before the seventh century when the Anglo-Saxons finally severed the overland links between Wales and the north.

Some of these parallels were recognized by Seebohm as early as 1890 and they were developed further in 1926 by Jolliffe in a classic paper (Jolliffe 1926; Seebohm 1890, pp. 68–72). As Jolliffe observed, 'Northumbria shows so many parallels to Celtic custom that one is forced to suppose a historical continuity.' When he wrote of this continuity Jolliffe was clearly thinking of the early Celts as mobile pastoralists rather than permanently settled practitioners of mixed farming. Like Seebohm and Maitland before him, he was profoundly influenced by the ethnic interpretation of settlement history. He thus regarded Northumbrian institutions as an amalgam of two cultures, the one pastoral and the other agricultural. Celtic community, by which he meant solidarity of kinship, united with Anglian lordship to form a distinctive Northumbrian society. To Jolliffe, direct exploitation of the soil in both Northumbria and Wales followed a political lordship relatively recently introduced. Thus he regarded cultivation of the demesne land as even more of an innovation in medieval Wales than in Northumbria. But in Wales, as earlier sections of this paper show, permanent settlement associated with mixed farming, and territorialized arrangements closely resembling shire organization, date back to a much more remote period.

Even Maitland had conceded an earlier beginning when dealing with 'the scattered steads and isolated hamlets' of southwestern England. There, he considered, when Germanic conquerors had spared or failed to subdue the Britons, they 'adapted their own arrangements to the exterior framework that was provided by Celtic or Roman agriculture'. Thus, 'Very often in the west and southwest of Britain, German kings took to themselves integral estates, the boundaries and agrarian arrangements whereof had been drawn by Romans, or rather by Celts.' The conquerors fitted themselves into 'an agrarian scheme drawn for them by the Britons,' and 'in the small scattered hamlets which existed in these tracts there was all along a great deal of slavery'. Maitland cited as an example the gigantic manor of Leominster whose members at Domesday were scattered about over a wide tract of Herefordshire. In this manor of eighty hides he discerned 'strong traces of a neat symmetrical arrangement—witness the 16 members, 8 reeves, 8 radknights, 16 beadles; very probably it has a Welsh basis'. But since it was a single unit for fiscal purposes it was the kind of manor to which he applied the epithet 'discrete'. He also recognized that the manor of the eastern counties at Domesday was 'a discrete, a dissipated thing [*sic*]'. To Maitland, in the north as in the east, the manor was the centre of an extensive but very discrete territory known as its soke. Given this existence of discrete estates in east and west, in south and north, it need occasion no surprise that he was prepared to concede some survival of Britons in England but 'against the hypothesis that this was the general case the English language and the names of our English villages are the unanswered protest' (Maitland 1897, pp. 112, 115, 220, 321, 351).

In his later work Jolliffe drew attention to the similarities between the commote of Wales, the shire of Northumbria, the rape of Sussex and the lathe of Kent. The latter he regarded as the exact synonym of soke. Thus, beside the then current phrase of the 'discrete manor' for the scattered lordships of eastern England, he placed that of the 'federative manor'; moreover he argued that soke arose from a federation of folk-land and folk-right under private or royal lordship. To Jolliffe the persistence of immemorial ties between a *villa regis* and the upland hamlets pointed to the era of the folk in English history when the only dependence of the people was that of the common man upon the king. Thus the lathe and the rape imported by the Jutes to southeastern England showed how life in the fifth or sixth centuries could be 'lived without servitude, without debasing inequality, and yet preserve a fabric of order, adequately protected justice, and continuity' (Jolliffe 1933, p. 119). There is much to be said for Jolliffe's views that Welsh and English met on grounds of common government and found that their differences needed little adjustment (Jolliffe 1934). Recently other historians (Binchy 1970, pp. 1–14; Charles-Edwards 1972, pp. 3–33) have cogently demonstrated that the institutions of the Celtic west and the Teutonic east stem from common Indo-European roots. But for eastern England, Jolliffe, like Maitland and most other historians, seriously underestimated the survival of Britons. Since much of this survival appears to have been in an involuntary capacity, within the framework provided by pre-existing units of territorial organization, Jolliffe's phrase 'federative manor' with its implications of consent, seems singularly inappropriate. Similarly Maitland's use of the epithet 'discrete' for a unit consisting of scattered fragments, which he described as 'a dissipated thing', betrays an atypical inconsistency on his part. It is for these reasons that the more neutral phrase 'multiple estate' is used here to describe the system of territorial organization with which Maitland, Jolliffe, and many other historians have been concerned. It is also contended in this, as in earlier papers (Jones 1960; 1961b; 1961c; 1961d) that, although these territorial units were certainly not solely of Celtic origin, they continued during the making of England in the sub-Roman and post-Roman periods to be occupied by Britons who were confined in the main, but not exclusively, to the lower social levels. In earlier papers this contention was based largely on the analysis of English institutions in the light of the conditions prevailing in medieval Wales. It is particularly significant that G. W. S. Barrow, working quite independently from different premises, and largely from a Scottish base, has come to virtually identical conclusions. Thus in a recent paper he envisaged for the area extending from the northern shores of the Firth of Tay to southern England a system whereby goods and services were 'due from outlying dependencies to a royal centre' (Barrow 1973). This, he argued, 'must have implied, at a more or less remote period of time, some domestic or domanial slavery, or at least pretty thorough-going servitude.' But, he averred, 'it must also have necessitated a ministerial or serviential horse-owning aristocracy or gentry, among whom, given customs of partible inheritance, a wide variety might easily develop not only in the amount of land held by any one individual but also in the status of the individual within society.' The discerning reader will recognize that this evocative statement would serve equally well as a verbal description of the Iorwerth model presented in the opening sections of this paper.

The parallels between the multiple estate of Wales and that of southern England are well illustrated by the estate of Malling in Sussex, part of the territory of the kingdom of the South Saxons (figure 2.3). According to Domesday Book the archbishop of Canterbury held, in the hundred of Malling (*Mellinges*), the manor of Malling, or South Malling. The hundred of Malling later became the hundred of Loxfield (Anderson 1936, pp. 97–100; Mawer and Stenton 1929–30, pp. 353–57), with which the manor of Malling was almost co-extensive. As Domesday Book records, 'in the time of King Edward it was assessed for 80 hides, but now the archbishop has only 75 hides, because the Count of Mortain has 5 hides outside the hundred [*extra hundredum*]' (DB I, fos 16a, 16b).[2] These five hides, carved out of the archbishop's holding of Malling, were possibly in Framelle hundred, which was co-extensive with Little Horsted, itself a detached portion of the later hundred of Rushmonden (*Victoria County History, Sussex*, I, pp. 388, 415). Nevertheless that part of the manor still held by the archbishop was said in 1086 to be sufficient for fifty ploughs, and the whole comprised a huge estate. Thus, 'On the demesne are 5 ploughs; and 219 villeins with 35 bordars have 73 ploughs and 43 crofts. There are 5 mills yielding 4 pounds and 10 shillings and 2,000 eels. There are 195 acres of meadow and woodland yielding 300 swine from the pannage. From the pasturage come 38 shillings and 6 pence and 355 swine for pasturage.' It extended up and over the chalk of the South Downs, across the Weald clay vale to the north, and on to the well-wooded sandstones of the High Weald. The meeting-place of the hundred of Loxfield was at Hundred House, approximately half-way between the southern and northern extremities of this estate which was so well endowed with varied resources. Parts of this large unit were held by mesne tenants. Among these were the canons of St Michael's, the collegiate church of South Malling, who held four hides. Moreover, as Domesday Book records, 'the archbishop himself has in Lewes 21 haws [*hagae*] . . . and they are appurtenant to *Mellinges* [Malling] manor' and, as a result, part of Lewes remained in South Malling until recently. Most of the places which, in this sense, were contributory to Lewes were located further west, beyond the Ouse (Darby and Campbell 1962, pp. 466–9). This suggests that Lewes, which by 1086 had developed into an important commercial and military centre, was the *caput* of an older provincial unit, the primitive rape of Lewes. It was from this larger unit that the hundred of Malling, and probably the neighbouring hundred of Rotherfield, had been carved.

The Malling estate, with the probable exception of the urban haws or closes at Lewes, appears to have belonged to the archbishops of Canterbury from the early ninth century. An agreement of 838 records that it was granted to them some years earlier by King Baldred of Kent. Then it was restored to Christ Church, Canterbury, by the agreement made in 838 between Archbishop Ceolnoth and King Æthelwulf, with the consent of his father Egbert, king of the West Saxons (Birch 1885–93, no. 421; Sawyer 1968, no. 1438). A hint that the archbishop's estate extended as far north as Wad-

[2] L. F. Salzman and J. H. Round in their analysis of Domesday Sussex (*Victoria County History, Sussex* 1905, I, p. 360) argued that this was one of many 80-hide units in that county, and suggested that these resulted from a beneficial hidation of 20 per cent applied to original 100-hide units. The Welsh 'acre' in the Iorwerth model was small so that the vill of 256 'acres' contained by statute measure only 76 acres or thereabouts. The vill of the Iorwerth model would therefore bear comparison with the small hide of the extra-Wealden areas of Sussex (Wilson 1959, p. 108).

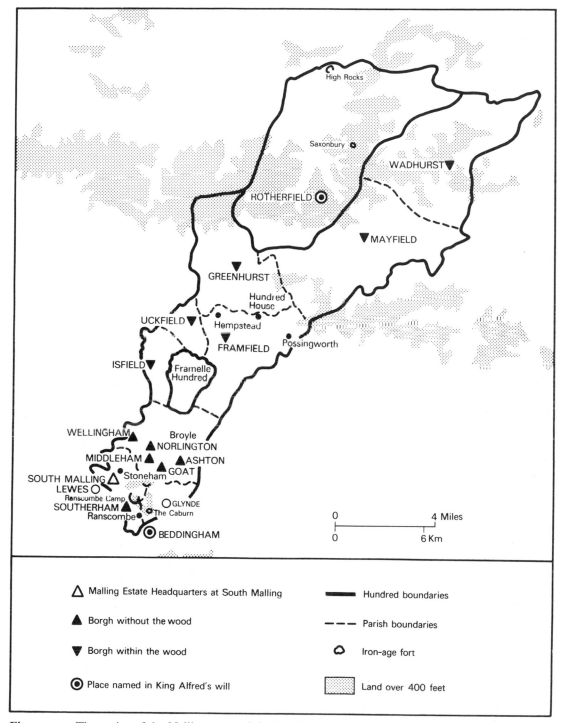

Figure 2.3   The setting of the Malling estate of the Archbishop of Canterbury.

hurst is provided by a charter of 1018 recording the grant by King Cnut to Archbishop Ælfstan of a 'copse called *Haeselersc* in the well-known forest of the Weald'; for its northwestern limit ran down along 'the broad stream by the archbishop's boundary', which has been identified as the Hook river which marks part of the northeastern border of Wadhurst (Sawyer 1968, no. 950; Ward 1936, pp. 126–7). Further confirmation is provided by the propinquity of two royal estates recorded in the will of King Alfred, a document ascribed to the period 873–88 (Sawyer 1968, no. 1507). One of these royal estates was Beddingham just beyond the southern boundary of the Malling estate; this was still in royal hands in 1066 when it was assessed for $52\frac{1}{2}$ hides, and also rendered 'one night's farm [*firma unius noctis*]'. The second was Rotherfield near the northern limits of the Malling estate and named as a royal residence in King Alfred's will. There was certainly a royal estate here *c*. 1015 when, according to his will, Athelstan granted land at Rotherfield to the nun's minster at Winchester (Whitelock 1930, pp. 167–8). In 1066 the royal estate at Rotherfield was held by the powerful Earl Godwin, but although this then passed into the fee of the bishop of Bayeux, by 1086 it was held in demesne by his brother King William. Even though this *caput* of the hundred of Rotherfield was said to contain land for 26 ploughs it was assessed at only three hides. In the words of the Domesday survey, 'On the demesne are 4 ploughs, and 14 villeins with 6 bordars have 14 ploughs. There are 4 slaves [*servi*] and woodland yielding 80 swine from the pannage. There is a park' (DB fo. 16a). Despite its low hidation this estate was of considerable extent. During the thirteenth century the forest of Rotherfield alone was twelve leagues or more in circuit (Public Record Office C 132/27). Appropriately this embraced the park, and on its northern fringes, the iron-age hill-fort misleadingly named Saxonbury, the local retreat for Rotherfield, as distinct from the more distant retreat at the larger hill-fort known as High Rocks (Money 1941; Winbolt 1930). If these dispositions for Rotherfield recall some attributes of the Iorwerth model, notably those concerned with the royal waste, there are other features recorded in the Domesday survey for Sussex which resemble elements of both the Cyfnerth and the Iorwerth models. The primitive rape, before its reorganization after 1066, was 'an organic fiscal and jurisdictional entity, a body politic having its meaning in the past of law, taxation, and government, and in no way reflecting contemporary reality' (Jolliffe 1933, p. 84). The rape was in a sense an abstraction, not the land as a whole but only the hidated area. As such the rape was at least as old as the hidation. Although new land was inevitably brought into cultivation with the growth and redistribution of population, the rape remained as a fiscal and legal network, gripping one acre but avoiding another. By Domesday, however, these newer lands had to be taken into account, and this was done, but in the process they were deemed to be 'outside the rape [*foris rapum*]'. Thus for example in Framelle hundred there was one virgate outside the rape but, in the words of Domesday Book, 'it never paid geld'. The restriction of the ancient hidation to the rape recalls the way in which cash assessments were restricted to arable lands in the Iorwerth model (Jones 1972, p. 327). At the same time the recognition of land 'outside the rape' bears a resemblance to the supernumary vill of the complete multiple estate in the Cyfnerth model.

A custumal produced *c*. 1273 (Redwood and Wilson 1958, pp. 30–120) reveals that the characteristic major subdivision of the Malling estate was the *borgh*, a territorial tithing. Within the estate there were two groups of *borghs*: Wadhurst, Mayfield, Greenhurst, Framfield, Uckfield and Isfield were said to be 'within the wood'; on the other hand, Wellingham, Goat and Middleham, Norlington, Ashton and Southerham were 'without the wood'. The *borghs* within the wood were further subdivided into hamlets. Thus there were fourteen hamlets in Wadhurst, twelve in Mayfield, nine in Greenhurst, no less than seventeen in Framfield and eleven in Uckfield. No subdivisions were recorded for Isfield, because it was said to be held of its lord for one knight's fee by free service of arms; hence the lack of detail about settlement. In the remaining *borghs* so numerous were the recorded hamlets that figure 2.3 shows only the hamlets after which the *borghs* were named, and a few additional hamlets, or other places specifically named in the text.

The customary land of each of these hamlets was normally assessed at one virgate; this was a unit of convenience, rather than a precise area, for some virgates contained 75 acres and others were larger, often exceeding 100 acres. In each hamlet the virgate appears to have been the original core of land; accordingly fractions of the virgate were generally held by a number of tenants. For the *borghs* without the wood there was no subdivision into hamlets but simply into virgates of thirty acres, or as few as ten acres. These smaller virgates, were characteristically subdivided into holdings of a half or quarter virgate. Nevertheless these were components of fairly large common fields. The obligations of the *borghs* within the wood, whether performed by bondmen (neifs, *nativi*), or by freemen, show the unity of the whole estate. Although they included services to the lord archbishop and his attendants when they passed through, or stayed in, the wood, the main predial services were performed without the wood, notably at the court of South Malling or Stoneham.

This is clearly indicated in the borgh of Wadhurst which can be regarded as being broadly representative of the *borghs* within the wood. Here there were some virgates of neif land, and others of free land. Of the 15¾ virgates of neif land in the borgh of Wadhurst it was recorded that 'every virgate [*sic*] shall hedge 1 perch of fencing about the court of Malling' and in addition, four virgates in four specified hamlets had to 'make the gate of the court of Malling and mend it when necessary'. Every virgate, 'with all the other virgates in the wood' had to 'roof the grange of Stoneham with poles . . . from the lord's wood'. From the same source each virgate found beams, boards and laths for repairing the barley grange at Stoneham; each made one hurdle for delivery to Stoneham on the eve of Ascension Day; and each hide containing four virgates made one cook and one trough. On the other hand, with all the other virgates in the wood they had to 'roof the stable at South Malling with the requisite covering to be found by them whenever necessary'. All these virgates, 'with all the other virgates of Mayfield must find 1 sheaf of rushes at Michaelmas. And if the Lord Archbishop lie within the wood in winter they must supply 1 truss from each virgate to feed his horses, namely, half of hay and the other half straw . . . And each virgater who has 3 pigs shall give his third best pig and this is called gavelswine [*gavelswen*], or shall give for the aforesaid pig 6*d*. if the bailiff so please. And each virgate must reap, bind and make ready to carry corn, 2 acres of wheat . . . 2 acres of barley . . . and 2 acres of oats. . . . And must, with all the other virgates in the wood, prepare the privy chamber [*secretum thalamum*] of South Malling when necessary.' Gavelswine was paid for the right of pasture throughout the year, but, as is revealed by the Domesday account of Malling, pannage for swine was also a source of revenue to the lord. Thus according to the custumal, 'each virgate must fence with hedge in mast-time 10 perches . . .' Within the wood, as would be expected, hunting services on behalf of the lord were important. Accordingly, 'each virgate must hunt with 1 man as the lord requires without bow and arrows for 12 days, worth ½*d*. a day, namely for 6 days in winter and 6 days in summer. And the virgates must, with the others in the wood, keep a sparrow-hawk's nest if it be found, and shown to them, and this is called *hundredesnest*. And if it is stolen in their custody, they shall give to the Lord Archbishop 40*s*.' Again, 'he who finds bees or honey must take them to the court and shall have half'. Each virgate had to carry 'to the court of Malling 3 cartloads of wood in their own carts where the bailiff directs them'. Moreover, each virgater owed carrying service inside and outside the estate, including the carriage of the lord's corn whenever, for specified periods, they went to the lord's mill at South Malling. In addition each one had to 'pay suit at the court of the Lord Archbishop every 3 weeks'.

In the borgh of Wadhurst one prominent free tenant owed nothing except 'suit at the hundred of Loxfield every 3 weeks'; but the majority, besides suit of court, also owed cash rents which, by 1273, were paid in lieu of all services. A few in addition owed gavelswine if they had three pigs, and performed hunting services 'at the lord's hunt with bow and arrows for 12 days'. Two of these tenants, instead of hunting, had to 'lodge the bailiffs of Malling and the steward of the Lord Archbishop' when they wished to lie at these tenants' houses; and, besides, they had to 'lead the Lord Archbishop and his men through the midst of the Weald up to Cranbrook', which was beyond the northern limits of the Malling estate.

Within the same *borgh* three tenants of Droflond, known as Drofmen, were responsible, as their name implies, for driving animals within the estate. They also gathered the hen rents, levied for common in the forest, which were paid by large numbers of cottars, free, neif, or serf, in the borgh of Wadhurst, and took these hens to South Malling. Besides these activities the Drofmen, when summoned to do so, had to 'clean all the houses within the court of Mayfield, against any coming there of the lord if necessary'; for, just as there was a court at South Malling without the wood, so there was a palace within the wood at Mayfield (Cooper 1869; Du Boulay 1966, pp. 138, 184).

Without the wood, as for example in the borgh of Wellingham, there were again virgaters holding neif land. Some of their rents and services were of the kinds already cited for Wadhurst. Thus they owed gavelswine, and each holder of '1 virgate, $\frac{1}{2}$ virgate or 1 ferling' had to construct one perch of fence 'about the court of South Malling or Stoneham or elsewhere', as assigned. They cut and transported cartloads of wood to South Malling or Stoneham. To judge from a rental of 1305, they also owed for brewing service (Redwood and Wilson 1958, pp. 122–38). Moreover, their works of ploughing, threshing cereals and making hay were more onerous than those of the neif virgaters of Wadhurst. From Stoneham they also drew out dung, for part of this activity working in conjunction with all the virgaters from without the wood, save those of Southerham. Some integration of the services from within the wood with those from without is implied by the obligation whereby these tenants 'between them, with the others outside the wood except Southerham' were to 'bring in all the corn which the men of the wood, and all the others outside the wood have reaped'. Similarly 'they with all the aforesaid virgates must cut all the aforesaid corn which remained after the reaping of the men of the wood'.

The free tenants of the borgh of Wellingham held their land by more varied services. One holder of a virgate had to be at the lord's hunt with bow and arrows for six days; in addition he had to go with the beadle to Glynde, where the archbishop had created three knights' fees, to distrain on the lord of Glynde when necessary. Another, who held nearly two virgates and a mill, besides such services as these, drew out dung from Stoneham, mowed meadows and made hay in conjunction with all the other virgaters owing works outside the wood; he made palings in the lord's wood and carried them to the court; he thatched the barley grange with straw he had gathered; in addition he ground a quarter of the corn which the archbishop used at South Malling, and also a quarter of the corn used at a manorial feast known, perhaps not inappropriately, as *Gutfelling*. Significantly too he had to 'fence 1 perch of hedging around the Court of South Malling which is called Burghyard'. The latter was an obligation which must have been imposed on a large number of other tenants for, according to an inquisition of 1398, 'the site of the manor', probably near Malling House, contained four acres 'within the close' (Public Record Office C 145/269).

Yet another free tenant, with all the neifs outside the wood, had to find hay in winter, with which to supply the horses of the archbishop when he came to South Malling for fifteen days in winter. As at Wadhurst, the tenants of Droflond contributed to the economic integration of the whole estate. Thus, for example, among other obligations they had to drive the lord's pigs to Framfield, and also as far as a hospital (*hospitalem*) in Lewes.

Most of the remaining tenants of the borgh of Wellingham were cottars. Some were the cottars of neifs and others the cottars of freemen. Any one of these using common pasture in the wood of the Broyle with his animals had to give the lord archbishop one hen in the year when this common was used. There were also five other cottars said to owe works; these were otherwise known as 'the 5 cotmen of *Walecote*' although, according to the custumal, two in fact were widows. Each of these cottars held a cot of $1\frac{1}{2}$ acres. Of their tiny holdings, it was said that one was a 'cot, not built-on', and three were 'built-on'. Each cottar paid a small cash rent and had to do one work each week throughout the year, save during the four holy weeks.

The borgh of Wellingham can be regarded as being broadly representative of the *borghs* without the wood, save that in South Malling the presence of the court made for some variations in the incidence of obligations. Thus, besides their normal obligations the free tenants at South Malling, if they attended the lord's pasture with cows and oxen, had to attend the lord's fold with these animals from Ascension Day to All Saints' Day. Again, a neif here, holding $2\frac{1}{4}$ acres of land, besides paying a cash rent had to go and get yeast as required for 'brewing at the court of Malling against the coming there of the Lord Archbishop'. On the day of the archbishop's arrival the foresters were accustomed to have their food in the court of South Malling and were also provided with provender for their horses. At South Malling there were some tenants known as *bermanni*, each of whom held a messuage and a curtilage usually of less than half an acre. These had to drive whatever animals were handed over to them 'to the Weald as far as Uckfield and Framfield and to the west as far as Lewes bridge'. They carried supplies for the lord archbishop 'from Lewes market to the court for 15 days in winter and 15 days in summer', as well as transporting lead from the court for use in repairs. In addition they had to guard thieves taken with the goods of the archbishop. At South Malling, as at *Walecote*, there were cotmen most of whom held built-on cots. Here, however, they were twelve in number and their holdings were usually of two acres or a little more. The cots of the sacrist of the church of South Malling and of one other tenant were held in return for cash rents. The remainder, whether held by freemen like the carpenter and the tinker, or by neifs, were held in return for both cash and works of reaping and threshing. But whereas at *Walecote* only one work a week was demanded, save for the holy weeks, at South Malling two works a week were required for forty-eight weeks in the year. Here, moreover, other services such as carrying, or duties at the court, could be performed in lieu of agricultural works.

According to the custumal, in times past, there were in South Malling ten oxherds (*bovarii*) each of whom held five acres which he tilled with the lord's plough. In return the oxherds worked with the lord's plough all the year and did other works at the will of the bailiff. One of their number could act as fold-keeper from Ascension Day to All Saints' Day. They also had to hang thieves who had stolen the lord's goods and were condemned. The 'tenements of 6 of these oxherds lay in the middle of the demesne'. This was at Stoneham where the custumal records that '61 virgates $\frac{1}{2}$ ferling' in Framfield and Mayfield had to reap 122 acres 1 rood of wheat, plus identical areas of barley and oats. It was here too that '$27\frac{1}{2}$ virgates 1 ferling' in Wellingham, Goat and Middleham, Norlington, and Ashton had to plough, sow and harrow for *Gauelerthe*, a cultivation service, $55\frac{1}{2}$ acres of wheat, plus $55\frac{1}{2}$ acres of oats and, afterwards, were to fallow 27 acres 3 roods for barley. The inquisition of 1398 confirms that Stoneham was the major centre of demesne cultivation in the Malling estate; and another of 1366 reveals that it was sometimes called the manor of Stoneham (Public Record Office C 145/190). It was recorded in 1398 that the archbishop had a 'halymot of Stonehamme' and a court baron at Uckfield, as well as hundred courts at Loxfield and at Ringmer near Middleham. Since Stoneham was almost invariably coupled with South Malling in statements about obligations given in the custumal, it was probably the original *caput* of the estate. Certainly the land in the vicinity of Stoneham was, and still is, of a far higher inherent quality than that near South Malling.

Within recent years the Agricultural Development and Advisory Service of the Ministry of Agriculture has graded agricultural land according to the degree to which its physical characteristics impose long-term limitations on agricultural use, affecting the range of crops grown, the level of yield, the consistency of yield and the cost of obtaining it (Ministry of Agriculture, Fisheries and Food 1968). Land in grade I is subject to no physical limitations to agricultural use or, at worst, only very minor ones. Land in grade II is subject to some minor limitations sufficient to exclude it from grade I. The best land today within the limits of the Malling estate is classified as grade II, and of this there are only some 550 acres. Nevertheless, Stoneham as well as Goat and Middleham are all sited on this land, on the gentle slopes at the scarp foot of the South Downs.

South Malling proper, on the other hand, occupies a much more constricted site on a spur over-looking the river Ouse where the latter cuts through the South Downs in a narrow gorge. The ancient collegiate church was sited here, originally at Old Malling, and later at South Malling. It was endowed with some territory in this vicinity but most of its landed possessions were in various outlying settle-ments including, within the Malling estate, Wellingham, *Walecote*, Middleham, Glynde and Ringmer. The custumal of 1273 reveals that the four canons of South Malling also had common in the wood of Broyle 'with their animals and piggeries'; moreover each of them claimed to have one log in the Broyle 'for their hearths' and also '6 pigs in the same wood quit of pannage'. According to the in-quisition of 1366 the log in each case was to be an oak 'tall and fit for fuel'. The same source reveals that the dean and three canons [*sic*] of the collegiate church of South Malling, 'by right and custom' had the great tithes of the parishes of Ringmer and Malling; the tithe of pannage in all the woods of the archbishop in Ringmer, Framfield, Bucksted, Uckfield, Mayfield and Wadhurst; but 'all the tithes of the manor of Stonhamme both great and small'.

The archbishop's court without the wood was perhaps moved from Stoneham to South Malling in order to be nearer to the collegiate church. But the court remained at some distance from the church and was also separated from the vill of South Malling by 'half a link' containing one acre of land. Given such dispositions there would have been no room for more than a small portion of the arch-bishop's demesne at South Malling. It is significant therefore that, according to the custumal, the tenants on two tenements of the oxherds served at the court; yet, these tenements were said to lie away from the demesne. Moreover, of the ten oxherds ascribed in times past to South Malling, two were said to care for animals, one keeping cattle, and the other wethers in Southerham.

The borgh of Southerham is of especial interest for within its bounds was located the large iron-age hill-fort known as Ranscombe Camp (figure 2.3). That there were close connections between this *borgh* and the court of South Malling is clearly indicated by the obligations of the tenants. Thus, among the free tenants of Southerham in 1273 were three sisters who held one sheepwalk. In return, among their varied services they were obliged to 'keep 120 ewes on the lord's pasture if the lord will', and the lord archbishop was to have all the wool of these sheep. These and all other sheep in milk which grazed on the lord's pasture had to go to the lord's fold from Lady Day until St Thomas's Day. The sisters contributed a substantial render of cheese and a smaller render of butter or cash in lieu of this pastoral produce. Their agricultural services were for the cultivation of oats, and were light, but they had to 'keep 1 dog of whatsoever breed'. In conjunction with three other shepherds they had to 'do 4 shares in making the baking-oven of Malling' and also repairing it. They had to cleanse the lord's stable within the court. They were responsible for repairing and thatching the lord's sheep-fold. In return for this service, and for keeping sheep, they held one acre of the lord's demesne. Among other rights they were also to 'have 6 pigs in the Broyl quit of pannage; and . . . 1 man in the court at the meal called *Gutfulling* [*sic*]'.

At Southerham in 1273 there were three cottars, tenants of the lord archbishop who owed rents and light agricultural services. There were also seven other cottars, both free and serfs (*servi*) who, in return for rents and services, had 'common in the Broyle', as well as piggeries if they wished.

The virgaters in Southerham who owed works were, in the main, neifs. Within the *borgh* they ploughed 13¾ acres for *Gutfelling*. Here too for *Gauelerth* they ploughed, sowed and harrowed, 26½ acres of wheat, 26½ acres of oats, 13¼ acres of barley and they also fallowed 13¼ acres. In addition they ploughed 11¾ acres in return for pasture rights. They harvested cereals, and also peas, vetches or beans. They sheared sheep, and they mowed meadows, including two near Stoneham. They had to grind malt and carry it to the court. In their own wains they also had to carry 'out of Broyl parks without the Wood, 4 cartloads of wood to the court of South Malling or Stoneham'. Once in winter and once in summer, on the departure of the lord archbishop, they performed carrying service westwards outside the estate, and 'toward the Wood to Framfield'. Every year each of these tenants found one hurdle for the lord's fold, and if he wished to avoid suit of fold, had to make a heavy payment to the lord archbishop. In conjunction with his fellows he had to roof the barley grange at Ranscombe; for this purpose he gathered thatching and also sought rods at Stoneham. In addition he had to draw out the dung of Ranscombe. It is of considerable significance that the majority of these particular tenants of Southerham supplemented their fractions of virgates by means of small plots of *terra montana* on the downs. The total area involved was only $41\frac{1}{4}$ acres, but this outfield cultivation, like their sheep farming activities, would have taken the twenty-two tenants involved into the general area, known as Saxon Down, where Ranscombe Camp is located. This hill-fort was probably constructed in the iron age but, as is indicated by the pottery found during its excavation, occupation continued into the second and third centuries AD. In relation to the medieval outfield cultivation practised on the *terra montana* of Saxon Down, it is perhaps significant that there was a small group of Romano-British lynchets and roughly rectangular fields within the camp (Burstow and Holleyman). Less than half a mile distant and some 350 feet below Ranscombe Camp was the settlement at Ranscombe proper which, as the custumal suggests, was second only to Stoneham as a centre of demesne farming in the whole of the Malling estate. This suggestion is confirmed by the inquisition of 1398 which reveals that the archbishop then had seventy acres of arable land at Ranscombe, as compared with four hundred acres at Stoneham, and only thirty-two acres at South Malling proper.

Overlooking Ranscombe proper from the south was the smaller but more strongly defended multivallate hill-fort known as the Caburn, which though constructed in the iron age was later in origin than Ranscombe Camp. Crowning a summit at 490 feet, the site of the Caburn was better for defensive purposes than that of Ranscombe Camp. Moreover, the Caburn appears to have been permanently occupied, but this occupation came to an abrupt end during the early phases of the Roman occupation. After a break sufficiently lengthy for the outer rampart to fall into decay there was at least a partial rebuilding of the outer defences in the late Roman period. Finally in the mid-twelfth century the site was fortified again as an adulterine castle. The Caburn was sited within the limits of the medieval lordship of Glynde but this, as we have seen, was a component of the Malling estate within which the archbishop had created knights' fees. There are therefore good reasons for suggesting that, just as Ranscombe Camp was an earlier retreat of the ancient precursor of the Malling estate, so the Caburn served this purpose during a later period. The original church focus of this estate was probably at Old Malling and, later, South Malling proper. The secular focus, on the other hand, was almost certainly at Stoneham until such time as the archbishop's court was transferred to South Malling. The division of the archbishop's demesne arable lands in unequal portions between Stoneham, Southerham and South Malling preserved clear traces of these arrangements down to the late thirteenth century.

In the South Malling estate the territory within the wood continued to be much less intensively used than that without the wood (Brandon 1969). Nevertheless, even within the wood there were certainly some old-established settlements in the vicinity of long-cultivated sharelands. In the area of the Malling estate there is only one place-name deemed to contain the Old English *hām*, an element meaning a homestead, a village or an estate, and reckoned to belong to an early stratum of English place-names (Dodgson 1973, p. 34). This is Hempstead, a place-name derived from the Old English *hām-stede* and meaning literally, settlement site. In the custumal of 1273 Hempstead was one of the hamlets of Framfield, located within the wood less than two miles from the hundred meeting-place at Hundred House. Place-names containing the Old English *ingas* and *-inga-* are the names of communities, whether of kinsmen, associates or dependants, extended to the territories in which they lived or had some interest; these are taken to denote a slightly later, though still early, phase of Anglo-Saxon settlement (Dodgson 1967a). Within the wood of the Malling estate there are only four examples, but all are within three miles of Hundred House, among them Possingworth, the enclosure of Posa's folk, the name in 1273 of yet another hamlet in the borgh of Framfield.

By the thirteenth century, the *borghs* without the wood, with their mature open-field systems for crops, their common pastures for cows in milk on the brooklands, and their common pastures for sheep on the downlands, were the most intensively exploited components of the Malling estate. Although the element *ham* appears in a number of place-names without the wood, it is deemed in all cases save possibly one to have been derived from the Old English *hamm*, which had a variety of meanings including land in a river bend, a meadow or an enclosure (Gelling 1960; Smith 1956a, I, pp. 226–33). This element, however, in its early range may well be contemporary with *hām* (Dodgson 1973). In any case, in the area without the wood there are two names in *-inga-*, namely Wellingham, and Chalkham near Stoneham, while South Malling itself is a place-name in *ingas* meaning Mealla's folk. Moreover, a still earlier Anglo-Saxon occupation is represented in this district by pagan Anglo-Saxon burials on the chalk uplands near Goat, at Saxon Down, and notably at Malling Hill; for the cemetery at the latter site, overlooking both Stoneham and South Malling, has been ascribed to the second half of the fifth century (Meaney 1964, pp. 246–66; Welch 1971).

Already in Old English times, to judge from the names of some of the *borghs* without the wood, a subdivision within the framework of the wider Malling estate appears to have embraced Norlington, the *tūn* towards the north, Southerham, the most southerly *hamm*, and between them, but nearer the former than the latter, Middleham, the *hamm* towards the middle. In relation to these *borghs*, whose relative positions are specified, the dispositions of the remaining settlements without the wood, including South Malling and Stoneham, are such as justify the suggestion that they also belonged to the same subdivision which can therefore be regarded as a lesser multiple estate.

The place-name Stoneham, which contains the Old English elements *stān*, meaning stone or stones, and *hamm*, can be interpreted in various ways (Dodgson 1973, p. 28; Ekwall 1960, *s.n.*). One suggestion is that Stoneham is sited opposite a loop in the Ouse but, given the significance of the river as a barrier, this explanation is unsatisfactory. Again the suggestion that *hamm* is a water meadow is contradicted by its combination with *stān*. The interpretation that Stoneham acquired its name because of stony soil would appear to be ruled out by the siting of the settlement on arable land of high quality; although there remains the possibility that the stoniness could have resulted from the presence of ruins. By far the most likely explanation, however, would appear to be that Stoneham was named after an enclosure made of stone; for the name could be a literal equivalent of the word *maenor* in the sense of the stone-girt residence of a lord. This could have served as the *caput* of at least the lesser multiple estate, and probably of the whole Malling estate. The medieval role of Stoneham as the principal centre for demesne cultivation in the Malling estate strengthens this suggestion. The precursor of the English estate of Mealla could well have been a British estate with its headquarters at Stoneham, and its retreat for the *borghs* without the wood at the Caburn. A pre-existing settlement at the site later known as South Malling could have been renamed when it was taken over by the associates or English dependants of Mealla. Chalkham, about half a mile northwest of Stoneham, also provides a pointer to early Anglo-Saxon settlement near the *caput* of the estate, for this name can be interpreted as meaning either the *hamm* of the warrior's folk or, possibly, the *hām* of Scealc's folk (Dodgson 1967a, p. 23; Mawer and Stenton 1929–30, p. 354). But that some of the pre-existing British occupants of the estate were retained *in situ* is suggested by the English place-name *Walecote*. The medial 'e' in this place-name reveals that it was used to designate the cot of the Welsh, or the cot of the serfs. But these two meanings of *Walecote* are not mutually exclusive for, as the Iorwerth model shows, a majority of Welshmen were bond. The precise site of this settlement is not known, but it was certainly located within the borgh of Wellingham and there are hints in the rental of the archbishop's estate for 1305 that it stood near the southern boundary of this tithing. *Walecote*, though separate from Stoneham, was therefore well placed for its occupants, like the five lowly cotmen of 1273, to labour on the demesne. It survived long enough during the Anglo-Saxon colonization for the distinctiveness of its occupants, as well as their lowly status, to be recognized by the newcomers and designated by means of an English place-name. This very survival would have helped to perpetuate a knowledge of pre-existing estate circumscriptions and an awareness of ancient obligations.

As the foregoing account makes clear, there are many striking parallels between the customary obligations of north Wales as illustrated for the hundred of Aberffraw and those of the Malling estate, otherwise known as the hundred of Loxfield. The argument in support of these parallels is not undermined by the existence of apparently quite different inheritance customs in the two areas by the late thirteenth century; for 'the usage of the manor' of Malling whereby the last born normally succeeded his father could well have been a late surviving vestige of the inheritance custom in north Wales, according to which the youngest son normally inherited his father's homestead, alike on hereditary land as on reckoned land. Later custumals reveal that if any tenant were first admitted tenant of any of the assart lands and died seized of assart or bond lands, then the eldest son should be the heir; if however the tenant were first a tenant of bond or yard lands then the younger son should be the heir of the bond lands and assart lands (British Museum Add. MS. 5701; Redwood and Wilson 1958, p. 141). Such parallels as these could, on the other hand, have stemmed from the common Indo-European origins of the Celts and the Anglo-Saxons and, by themselves, do not constitute proof of continuity. Nevertheless, the existence of English place-names like *Walecote* and Stoneham, in appropriate contexts, ecological, spatial and institutional, is best explained in terms of continuity. Especially is this true when, as in the case of the Malling estate, such diagnostic place-names occur in an institutional framework so closely resembling that envisaged in the lawyers' model for north Wales and actually recorded for the hundred of Aberffraw.

The place-name evidence for continuity in the Malling estate though meaningful is admittedly slight, probably because the earliest English onslaught in this part of southern England took place in the late fifth century (Myres 1969, pp. 111–12). For this reason it is appropriate to buttress the argument for Malling by reference to another example on the northern fringe of the Celtic principality of Elmet in Yorkshire which was conquered only in the early seventh century. This is the multiple estate known as Burghshire, the *Borgescire Wapentac* (Burghshire Wapentake) of Domesday Book (figures 2.4 and 2.5). Some of the features of this multiple estate have been considered elsewhere, and therefore only those which bear most directly on the present argument need be considered here (Jones 1971). The limits of this shire can be reconstructed from the evidence of Domesday Book and that of a precursor, erroneously called the Summary (Harvey 1971, pp. 761–3). *Borgescire* was named after the Domesday *Burg*, now known as Aldborough (Beresford 1967, pp. 383, 523–4). This stands on the site of *Isurium Brigantum*, the fortified Roman cantonal capital of the Brigantes. The very name Burg, which bears comparison with the Burghyard of South Malling, is derived from the Old English *burh* meaning fortified place, and is clearly a reference to the Roman fortifications. Isurium was also recorded by the geographer Ptolemy, *c.* AD 150, as a *polis*, a *caput* with its dependent district, one of the nine *poleis* which he attributed to this important British tribe (Rivet 1958, p. 142). When the limits of Burghshire as reconstructed for the eleventh century are viewed against the known, or possible, locations of the *capita* of the neighbouring *poleis*, this *shire* can be seen to fit in a convincing fashion into the outline framework thus provided (figure 2.4). Neatly bisected by the upper reaches of the Nidd valley, the shire extends from a crest line in the Pennines down to the riverine barriers provided by the lower courses of the Ure, the Nidd and the Wharfe. Within this area there was a great variety of resources ranging from rough pastures and woodlands, especially at the higher altitudes, to large expanses of good arable lands in the lowlands.

In 1086 there were 135 vills within the shire (DB fos 299b–374, 380). Of these no less than sixty were partially or wholly royal vills (figure 2.5). Two royal multiple estates were especially prominent, the one with its *caput* at Aldborough and the other with its *caput* at Knaresborough. The latter in later centuries was the headquarters of the royal hunting forest of the same name (Agerskow 1958, pp. 4–26; Jennings 1970, pp. 31–57). Although a distinction must be drawn between a legal forest and woodland, there need be little doubt that the forest of Knaresborough was in many respects the equivalent of the land designated as being within the wood at the Malling estate. Both the Aldborough

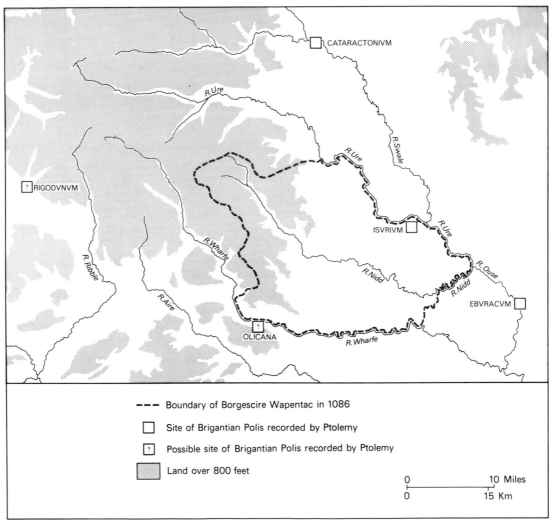

Figure 2.4 The setting of Burghshire.

and the Knaresborough estates included numerous components, some of which were berewicks, outlying portions of demesne, and others sokelands, subject to the jurisdiction of the *caput*. Components of both the main royal estates were intermixed alike in the area extending from Aldborough to the northern border of the forest, and within the forest near its southwestern boundary. This intermixture suggests that both estates had originally formed part of the one unit. Further support for this interpretation is provided by the fact that South Stainley in 1086 was in part sokeland of Aldborough assessed at two carucates and in part a berewick of Knaresborough assessed at two

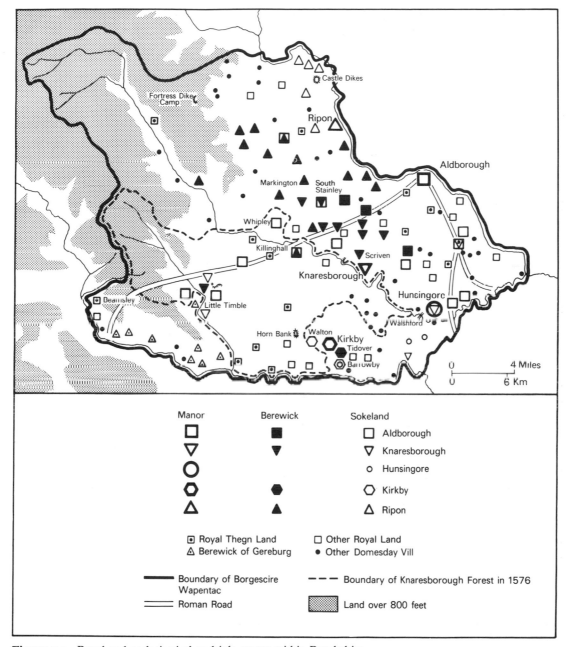

Figure 2.5 Royal and ecclesiastical multiple estates within Burghshire.

carucates. At South Stainley and the neighbouring vill of Markington one carucate was land of St Peter's of York, free from the king's geld. But the greater part of Markington, assessed at 4½ carucates, was part of the Ripon estate of the archbishop of York. Earlier, according to a description of the archbishop's estates dated *c*. 1030, a still larger area of Markington and of South Stainley assessed in hides had formed part of a substantial multiple estate of Ripon (Farrer 1914, pp. 21–3). This in 1030 included many of the berewicks and sokelands recorded for the Ripon estate in 1086 when it was assessed at about sixty-five carucates for geld. Some of these possessions in the eighteen outliers of Ripon in 1086 must have been part of the forty hides of land given by King Alhfrith of Northumbria to Bishop Wilfrid in the second half of the seventh century, along with the recently founded Celtic monastery of Ripon (Colgrave and Mynors 1969, pp. 296–9). Others were no doubt part of the additional endowments which King Athelstan is reputed to have made in the tenth century (Small 1965, pp. 77–9). But whatever the date of their donation, these components of the Ripon estate were in many cases intermixed with the components of the royal estates of Aldborough and Knaresborough. Thus, for example, in 1086 part of Killinghall, assessed at one carucate, was sokeland of Aldborough and the remainder, assessed at one carucate, was a berewick of Ripon. Again Little Timble, a berewick of the archbishop's estate of Otley in 1086, and likewise part of the archbishop's estate of Otley in 1030, was sited midway between two royal sokelands, one belonging to Aldborough and the other to Knaresborough. There are good grounds therefore for suggesting that Burghshire had once been a single royal unit, but was later partially fissioned by the alienation of its components. Royal land was often permanently alienated to the church, but when the recipients were royal thegns the alienation was generally less durable. Lands were also alienated to laymen. Thus, for example, Hunsingore near Walshford, the ford of the Welshman or serf, consisted in part of two independent manors; yet a small part of Hunsingore held by Erneis de Burun, the tenant-in-chief of one of these manors, was in the soke of Knaresborough. The manor of Hunsingore held by Erneis was in turn the *caput* of a lesser multiple estate with three sokelands, one of which was Barrowby. This particular sokeland at Barrowby was assessed at three carucates but a fourth carucate in the same vill was sokeland of William de Percy's manor of Kirkby (figure 3.5). Such dispositions as these are best explained in terms of the fission of a larger unit. Fission, however, was not the only means of transformation. On the contrary there is evidence to show that many a severed component could be fused anew into a different combination. Especially was this true in the period between 1066 and 1086, but that it was also the case at an earlier date is suggested by a charter of 972 which records how Ripon lost and regained two properties known to have lain within the limits of Burghshire (Robertson 1956, pp. 112–13, 359).

In general, however, fission appears to have prevailed over fusion. Nevertheless, a strong impression of a functional integration between the components of the larger royal and ecclesiastical multiple estates of Burghshire is given by their make-up in 1086. A pointer to a similar integration is provided by that part of the secular estate of Erneis de Burun which in 1086 contained Beamsley and Whipley. Thus, although these two settlements were no less than twelve miles apart, they were assessed together at one carucate in 1086; and the same was true in 1066 when they formed part of the estate of Gospatric. Some four centuries earlier the existence of a territorial unit in which uplands and lowlands were integrated is suggested by the analysis of pollen contained in stratified deposits at Fortress Dike Camp, a Romano-British enclosure, which occupies a site at about 900 feet in the northwestern part of Burghshire. A radio-carbon date for a sealed organic layer at this site suggests that *c.* AD 630 agricultural activity including cereal cultivation formerly practised here appears to have ceased or, at least, was markedly reduced (Tinsley 1972, pp. 169–72; Tinsley and Smith 1974). This change appears to have coincided with the military campaigns between the English and Welsh, known to have taken place in the lowlands during this period.[3] Such military activity, by reducing the size of the lowland

---

[3] The radio-carbon date for the organic layer at Fortress Dike Camp is AD 630 $\pm$ 90. The Anglians could have penetrated as far as the Ripon area by the middle or end of the sixth century. At the battle of Hatfield in 633 the forces of Cadwallon, father of Cadwaladr of Gwynedd, and of his ally Penda of Mercia slew Edwin of Northumbria and destroyed his army. The following summer witnessed the destruction of the army of Osric of Northumbria who had rashly besieged Cadwallon 'in a fortified town [*in oppido municipio*]' which the latter had occupied. Bede, who recounts these events, did not name the town but in this area there were only three fortified towns. Bede names two of these, namely York and Catterick (Colgrave and Mynors 1969, pp. 212–13). It is likely, therefore, that the un-named town was Burgh, the later Aldborough.

population, could well have removed the need to use a marginal upland, like that in the vicinity of Fortress Dike Camp, for agricultural purposes.

Be that as it may, Roman occupation of the lowlands is well attested not only at *Isurium* but also at the villa of Castle Dikes, and possibly too at Ripon where there appear to be traces of another villa. Pre-Roman occupation of the lowlands is likewise attested at a number of sites including the iron-age fort overlooking the river Nidd at Scriven. For present purposes, however, the most instructive site is that of the iron-age settlement at an altitude of about 450 feet on Horn Bank. This former settlement with its numerous corn-drying hearths occupies a site almost identical with that of the neighbouring settlement at Walton in its physical attributes, including altitude and even soil quality. Like Horn Bank, therefore, this particular Walton could have originated in the iron age, and appropriately the early forms of the name reveal that it was a *tūn* of the Welsh. In 1086 this *tūn* and Barrowby were sokelands of the small multiple estate centred at Kirkby. The other component of this multiple estate was the berewick named Tidover, which the late A. H. Smith identified with a settlement site near Kirkby now lost save for its well (Smith 1961–3, V, p. 43). Smith also identified this site with the vill called *On Tiddanufri* recorded by Eddius Stephanus in his *Life of Bishop Wilfrid* which was written at Ripon *c.* 715 (Colgrave 1927). Here, according to Eddius, Wilfrid in the late seventh century brought an infant boy back to life, and, after so doing, bade the mother give the boy when he had attained the age of seven years to the service of God. But, by the appointed time, the mother had fled so as to conceal herself and her son. Their flight, however, was to no avail because they were sought out by Bishop Wilfrid's reeve, and the boy was taken by him to serve God at Ripon. In recounting this miracle Eddius reveals, in a phrase used only incidentally, that the mother had attempted to conceal herself and her son 'among others of the Britons [*sub aliis Bryttonum*]'. Unlike Tidover and Kirkby, which are both sited on a single large expanse of well-drained brown-earths suitable for cultivation, Walton occupies only a small island-like expanse of such soils (Jones 1966). It was therefore a suitable settlement for purposes of concealment. Given the recorded status of both Tidover and Walton in Domesday Book as components of the same multiple estate it is highly probable that the latter was the actual place of concealment, especially as there is no other *tūn* of the Welsh known to have been located nearer to Ripon. The role of the reeve suggests that Bishop Wilfrid exercised juridical rights at the place of concealment. Moreover the mother was probably impoverished for her infant was clothed in rags so that, although she was said to have fled *de terra sua*, this phrase is probably meant to convey the belief of Eddius that she had departed from the bishop's land. Tidover as a berewick in 1086 was part of the demesne of the significantly named Kirkby, literally the village with a church. It is therefore possible that already in the seventh century Kirkby was the *caput* of a multiple estate comprising sokeland at Walton, and Wilfrid's 'own land' or demesne in his berewick at Tidover. Certainly the phrase 'own land' was used *c.* 1030 to describe land belonging to the archbishop at Ripon and also hides in some outlying components of his multiple estate of Ripon. The same phrase was used of some of his ploughlands at Otley, just beyond the southern boundary of Burghshire, and of ploughlands in some of the appendages of Otley, including a few of those known as berewicks of Gereburg in 1086 (Farrer 1914, pp. 21–3).

Walton was so named by the English presumably because, when named, it was inhabited predominantly by Britons. But Tidover, too, despite its Old English name, meaning Tida's bank, had housed at the very least the British mother and her son. It follows, therefore, that in the late seventh century, and possibly also the early eighth century, settlements bearing Old English names could nevertheless still house Britons. This was probably the case also with Kirkby, despite the Scandinavianized form of its name. Conveniently placed between Walton and Tidover, it occupied a site almost identical with that of the latter. By 1086 both Kirkby and Tidover were assessed at three carucates each whereas Walton was assessed at only one carucate. In other words, the settlements taken over from the Britons, and later, possibly, by the Scandinavians, were potentially and in practice the most successful.[4] But the very take-over of such settlements usually brought about changes in their place-names, thus effectively concealing the British origin of many a settlement. That villages in England bear English or Scandinavian names is no proof of an English or Scandinavian, and thus relatively late, origin.

The renaming of settlements is frequently likely to have taken place when the bonds linking the components of any multiple estate to its *caput* were loosened or severed. In general, such fission of multiple estates is likely to have been more advanced in the richer areas. Thus, for example, it had proceeded much further in Burghshire, where over 10 per cent of the land today is classified by the Agricultural Development and Advisory Service as being of grade II, than in the hundred of Aberffraw where much less than 1 per cent of the land is of this high grade (Ministry of Agriculture, Fisheries and Food 1968). In England fission was more advanced by 1086 in the richer lowlands, hence the predominance there of villages bearing English or Scandinavian names, and the more frequent survival of place-names indicative of British settlement in the uplands. The topographic dispositions of place-names viewed in simplistic fashion with scant regard for the organization of society and the functioning of the economy did, it is true, provide some basis for the ethnic interpretation of settlement history. Nevertheless the models, and actual examples of territorial organization presented in this paper would appear to provide a better alternative. This, however, is not to claim that every multiple estate as such is of considerable antiquity. In England, as in Wales, fission could result in small multiple estates where formerly there had been large ones and, as a result, in counties like Yorkshire a hierarchy of multiple estates can be discerned (Small 1965, p. 82). For the large multiple estate with its *caput* near an iron-age fort or a Roman settlement a considerable antiquity can reasonably be inferred; and the same is true of the hundredal manor (Cam 1944). But when it is considered that the hundreds of Domesday Sussex, for example, ranged from $1\frac{1}{2}$ hides to 265 hides, this inference manifestly cannot be applied to all hundreds or to all multiple estates. With regard to antiquity, however, a distinction should perhaps be drawn between the multiple estate and its components. The former need not be as old-established as the latter. This qualification notwithstanding, to arrive at an adequate understanding of the colonization of England it is essential to look beyond unitary settlements. Rather it is necessary to adopt as a model the multiple estate; for this provides the most meaningful of all frameworks for unravelling the complex interrelationships between society, economy and habitat involved in the process of colonization.[5]

[4] The sites of both Kirkby and Tidover are a little lower, less exposed, and therefore slightly better than those of Walton and Horn Bank. Kirkby and Tidover were said to contain together fifteen tenants in 1086. No tenants were recorded for Walton, but there were five tenants in the Kirkby sokeland at Barrowby. The latter, like Walton, was assessed at one carucate, so that the population of Walton is likely to have been of the same order as that of the Barrowby sokeland.

[5] The author is particularly indebted to the following: the Ministry of Agriculture, Fisheries and Food for permission to use the data published in map form on Provisional Sheets 91, 96, 97, 106 and 183 of the Agricultural Land Classification of England and Wales; the Director of the Soil Survey of England and Wales for permission to reproduce in figures 2.1 and 2.2 data presented on the soil map of Anglesey; the late Sir George Meyrick, Bart, for permitting access to records at the Bodorgan Estate Office on which much of the discussion of the manor of Aberffraw is based; Mr Richard White for discussing in detail his recent findings in the area of Aberffraw fort; and Mr A. A. Dibben, County Records Officer, Sussex, for his assistance in attempting to locate *Walecote*.

3

Chapelries and Rural Settlement: an Examination of some of the Kesteven Evidence

Dorothy Owen

The English parochial system as we still know it seems to have crystallized in the late Anglo-Saxon period and it therefore retains almost intact a picture of the chronology and density of settlement, at least in some areas. Certainly it can be used to demonstrate what were the principal centres of population and which the satellite or daughter communities of the tenth or early eleventh centuries. The laws of Aethelred and Cnut had classified the churches then known in England as chief, that is episcopal, minsters, other old minsters, manorial or private churches with burial rights, and field churches or dependent chapels in outlying settlements (Barlow 1963, pp. 183–95). The Lincolnshire Danelaw and particularly Kesteven, the southwestern portion of it with which we are concerned, contained, so far as can be seen, only one 'old minster', St Mary of Lincoln (Owen 1971, pp. 1–2); the remaining churches were manorial churches with burial rights (our later parish churches), and field churches. It is the distribution and siting of these two classes of church which this chapter will discuss, for in this area the oldest and most populous centres formed parishes, while chapels or field churches occur only where the settlement is recent, or very sparse. In other areas of the country, and especially in the west midlands, or Northumbria, a different sort of ecclesiastical framework and time-scale would almost certainly emerge from such an examination. Any general study of the relation between church provision and settlement must clearly be prefaced by a number of detailed surveys of widely contrasted regions; this small essay is offered as an example of what is possible.

Conclusions can only be made if a full list of all churches, chapels and other ecclesiastical institutions is first compiled, and at the outset it should be realized that this is neither mechanical nor quick. There is no single source which will yield a full list of all churches and chapels. Domesday and the *Valor Ecclesiasticus* of 1535 provide a framework of names at the beginning and end of the period, but gaps must be filled from episcopal institution books, memoranda of tithe and church-rate disputes in court registers, monastic cartularies and private muniments, secular court records, wills, chantry certificates, and even antiquarian notes.[1]

I began to collect the names of Lincolnshire chapels while I was working at Lincoln, as a supplement to Canon C. W. Foster's various lists of 'lost places', and later developed the work as part of the apparatus for *Church and Society in Medieval Lincolnshire*. Some of my results were summarized in that book in a study of three contrasting areas of the county, but now I want to look in more detail at the whole of Kesteven (Thirsk 1954; Williamson 1955). The central limestone ridge which traverses the area from north to south, and which varies in width between two miles in the north and seven or eight miles in the southern half, is its dominating feature. On the west it drops sharply to the Witham–Trent plain; the eastward slope, towards the fens and the lower Witham, is more gradual. The ridge is broken by one east–west gap at Ancaster, where there was a Roman settlement; in the south two

[1] My full list of Lincolnshire chapelries is published in *Lincolnshire History and Archaeology*, 10, Lincoln 1975; I have discussed the uses of ecclesiastical court records in a paper in *Studies in Church History* 11, Oxford, 1975.

parallel valleys, each fifteen miles or so in length, are traversed by streams which turn eastward towards the Wash at the foot of the high land. The ridge is traversed for almost its entire length by Ermine Street, and the Foss Way runs northeastward across the Trent-Witham valley towards Lincoln. A secondary Roman road joins Ermine Street from the southeast at Ancaster, while another follows the fen edge towards Sleaford. The Roman canal known as Cardike runs northwestward to the Witham below Lincoln, along the fen edge.

The surviving parishes form distinctive patterns against this background (figure 3.1). North of the Ancaster gap there is a string of closely set parishes on the western edge of the ridge and a similar row, less closely spaced, flanks it on the eastward-flowing streams of the ridge just below the three-hundred-foot contour. A second, less regular, line of parishes can be seen on the gravel islands and ridges close to Cardike and the fen edge. There are no settlements on the crest of the northern ridge, but south of Ancaster, where there are several eastward-flowing streams, and in the two southern valleys, the parishes lie fairly thick. The whole length of the Witham valley above Lincoln seems to have been well populated, and especially the narrow stretch south of Grantham (where the A1 now runs). As the river turns west and then north below Grantham, in the broad flood plain, there are parishes set fairly closely on either bank of the river, and a secondary line of settlements below the ridge occupies small islands of higher ground on the east bank of the river Brant.

These parishes seem to be almost entirely of the 'private church with burial right' type. Grantham, the centre of a royal manor, had a special relation with neighbouring churches also on the royal demesne (Turnor 1806, p. 67), and Castle Bytham, in one of the southern valleys, was a collegiate church in late Saxon times (Foster and Major 1931–73, I, 81), but there is no evidence for either of these arrangements much before 1050, and nothing to indicate that either was an old minster. For the rest one can only say that most of them were already parishes when written records begin and can perhaps be counted as 'foundation' parishes. Nevertheless there is in the twelfth century a borderline region when certain chapels have already assumed some or all of the marks of parish churches and this suggests some degree of fluidity at an earlier period.

There are at least two stages of evolution; in one case the chapels have acquired fonts and burial grounds and are known as parochial churches, yet they continue to make some token of submission, usually the payment of a pension, to a 'mother' church elsewhere;[2] in the other the chapels are equally parochial, and have font and burial ground, but are still directly subject to a parish church. Disputes about the status of these last-named foundations were frequent, especially in the twelfth and thirteenth centuries, when religious houses tried to establish authority over them as rectors of the mother churches, and it is clear that the distinction between them and the genuine parish churches is very hard to draw. There were four Kesteven churches still paying pensions in 1535—Little Bytham, Old Sleaford, Gunby St Nicholas and Scopwick, the last two of which certainly served upland and prob-ably later, settlements, above their mother churches. The chapels with font and burial rights are more numerous and occupy sites slightly less eligible than the mother parish, even though by the eleventh century there is little difference in size between the two groups of communities. Barkston and Marston, in the thickly settled river plain north of Grantham, are not very much smaller than their mother parishes of Syston and Hougham. The first named had become a parish by the fourteenth century, but the second continued to rank as a chapel until the end of the sixteenth century. Dry Doddington and Fenton were each large settlements on rising ground, two or three miles from their riverside mother churches of Westborough and Beckingham; Dunsby in Brauncewell, and Dembleby in Scott Willoughby each lie upstream of, and slightly higher than, their mother churches in shallow eastward-facing valleys on the northern ridge. The relationship between Allington and its chapelry of Sedgebrook or East Allington, west of Grantham, is more difficult to see. The mother parish and the

[2] Evidence for the payment of pensions has usually been recorded in *Valor Ecclesiasticus*, ed. J. Caley, Record Commission, 6 vols, 1810–34; volume IV contains returns for the diocese of Lincoln.

chapel are on what seem equally eligible sites overlooking the Witham valley.

More obviously dependent chapels display a greater variety of settlement pattern and seem to result from a continuous process of reclamation and settlement, which can be seen still in action even in the twelfth century. Many of them are in areas which are genuinely less eligible or more inaccessible than the parent villages; it seems probable that social and economic pressures led the enterprising to climb higher up the heath or along the river valley, or to venture nearer to the fens. Where a chapel building survives in these settlements, or has been drawn or described, it often seems to be no more than a demesne chapel in the manorial *curia*, although such chapels as this seem always to have served all the inhabitants of these isolated communities. There are a number of examples in the Witham–Brant plain. North Hykeham and Haddington on the left bank of the Witham were each dependent on South Hykeham; Little Stapleford in the low fields of Brant Broughton, Brant in Bassingham, and Stragglethorpe in Beckingham seem to be attempts to prolong northward the line of settlements below the ridge. Fenton in Beckingham, like the larger and more independent chapelry of Dry Doddington, is placed on a slight rise two miles southeast of its mother church; Brandon in Hough is a valley settlement two miles west of the hill-top site of its mother church.

On the ridge north and south of Ancaster there is a range of chapels dependent on mother churches eastward and below them. Washingborough, on the Witham close to the end of Cardike has a chapel at Heighington, a mile south up the hill. Leasingham, on a spur of higher ground protruding eastward of the main ridge, had from the twelfth century and probably earlier a chapel at Roxholme, a mile north. On the mid heath, at the eastern end of the Ancaster gap, Rauceby and its chapel of South Rauceby lay half a mile apart in identical conditions, though Silkby, west of its mother church of Willoughby, is on rising ground. The complicated parish of Heydour lies at the head of a shallow eastward-facing valley, with two hamlets, Oasby and Aisby, on the slope half a mile south and a manorial chapel at Culverthorpe two miles east down the valley. One and a half miles north of Heydour is its old and substantial chapel of Kelby, at the western head of a smaller parallel valley. Further south, Avethorp in Aslackby, Stainfield in Hacconby, and Hanthorpe in Morton all lie west of their mother churches on rising sites.

The southern end of the ridge is a well-wooded area where the place-names suggest that many of the settlements were clearings in the woods, and where the Cistercians were able to find a remote and uncleared site for their house of Vaudey even in the twelfth century. Edenham was a characteristic parish where, during the twelfth century, four separate manorial chapels for the households of Huntingfield, Baiocis, Neville and Amundeville were in existence in the hamlets of Southorpe, Elsthorpe, Grimsthorpe and Scottlethorpe. North of Edenham is the equally large parish of Irnham, where in less heavily wooded country (probably therefore cleared earlier) there are two well established and substantial chapelries at Bulby and Hawthorpe. These two settlements seem to have resulted from early colonization of the east bank of the river valley facing the mother village. In Witham on the Hill, where the mother church and village lay on high land west of the river Glen, there are three hamlets across the river and in small valleys opening on it, at Toft, Lound and Manthorpe; Lound had a parochial chapel from the first, at Toft there was a manorial chapel, but at Manthorpe no chapel of any sort. In the large parish of Castle Bytham, besides the collegiate arrangements to which reference has already been made, there was a parochial chapel at Counthorpe, which was later assigned to Creeton, besides a group of four chapels in and around the castle.

Something of the same sort can be seen in the southern valley of the Witham and on the high ground south of Grantham. Casthorpe in Barrowby lies half a mile downhill from its mother church, on a rather constricted site; Woolsthorpe in Colsterworth is a hillside chapel above a mother church in the valley, where Ermine Street comes down into the valley. There is an interesting complex in the area south of Ponton Heath which is dominated by Skillington. Here two small tributaries flow east and north to join Cringle Brook, which itself falls into the Witham at Great Ponton. Until the thir-

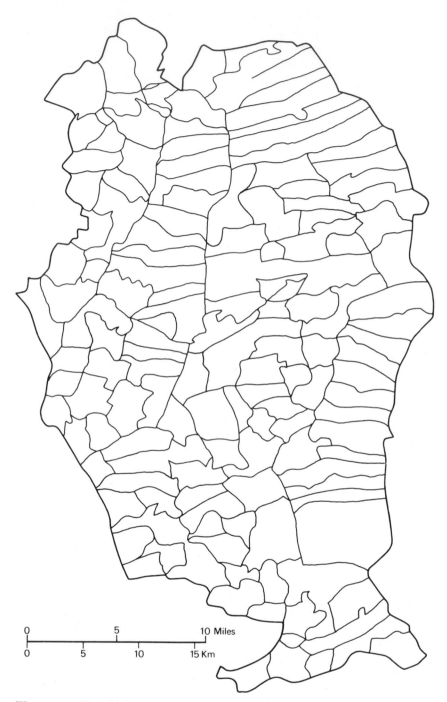

Figure 3.1   Parochial boundaries in Kesteven *(after J. Thirsk 1954–5).*

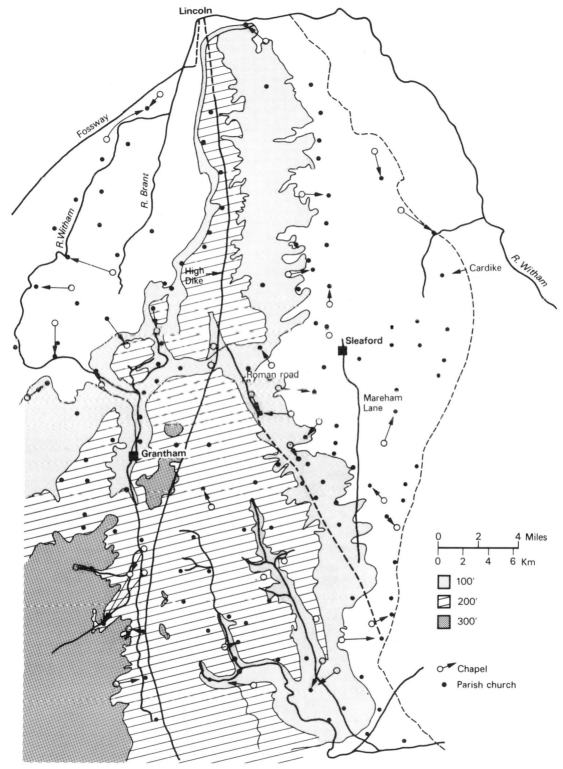

Figure 3.2 Chapels and parish churches in Kesteven.

teenth century, Skillington was spoken of as the mother church of Stoke (that is, South Stoke) which lay a mile and a half downstream and of Easton, on the eastern side of the valley where the land rises towards the line of Ermine Street. Assarting was in progress in this area in the later eleventh century; settlement was pushing northward, and there was a chapel among the assarts of North Stoke before 1100. Due west of South Stoke in the valley of the northern tributary of Cringle Brook lay Wyville, a parish with a still higher chapelry at Hungerton at the very limit of the valley.

The pattern so far has been of mother churches in valleys or on flat accessible sites, with chapelries less favourably situated in clearings in the woods or on the upper slopes of the hills. There is a similar process at work in the area between the northern ridge and the lower Witham, where a strip of fen-land borders the lower slopes of limestone. Here the main settlement was at Timberland, half-way along a narrow gravel strip which runs north and south on the west bank of the river. There is a small hamlet at Thorpe Tilney without chapel, and a larger chapelry at Martin, where a spur of gravel runs out into the fen. Four miles south of Timberland, where Cardike crossed a tributary of the Witham, lay Billinghay with a chapel at Walcott on another narrow spur of gravel. There are also a number of chapels on the southern fen edges and here a pattern is not easy to see. Laythorpe, a lost hamlet in Kirkby, was close to the mother settlement; Birthorpe, said to be a chapel of the lost mother church of Stow by Threekingham, lay west of it, but not much higher; Spanby lies westward of and higher than its parent settlement of Swaton. Other supposed chapelries, such as Pointon once assigned to Sempringham, before the Gilbertine foundation there, are very uncertain in status and the relations between them and their mother parishes are completely obscure.

We have already seen that manorial or demesne chapels seem to be associated quite frequently with the establishment of communities in newly opened land. There are probably many such small establishments which, from lack of record, have gone completely unnoticed, and cannot now be recovered. When they served a monastic grange and its lay dependents, like the chapel at Thetford, on the fen edge south of Bourne which Crowland founded in its own parish of Baston, Shelford Priory's chapel in the eastern end of Dorrington, or the Templar and Hospitaller chapels at Temple Bruer on the northern ridge, and Eagle and Swinderby in the sandy wastes between Fossway and the Trent, they survived at least for a time, and have left record of themselves, but it is difficult to believe that there were not similar, but unrecorded, lay foundations in such 'new' hamlets as Manthorpe or Thorpe Tilney.

On the whole the picture presented by the Kesteven parishes and chapels is of single secondary settlements on relatively marginal land or narrow constricted sites (figure 3.2). There are, however, one or two cases where the original parochial area has been so large that two or three subordinate chapels are supported within it, as at Edenham, Lenton, Witham on the Hill and Irnham, which lie perhaps significantly within the heavily wooded areas, and in the Witham–Trent valley between Grantham and Lincoln, where the enormous parish of Beckingham supports two parochial chapelries and a manorial chapel. South Hykeham also has two parochial chapels at Haddington and North Hykeham. Such divergences from the general pattern can probably be 'explained' by geographical or geological features; an originally thin settlement due to poor soil or heavy woodland has given such parishes considerable areas which were not encroached on until much later.

4

Early Boundaries and Estates in Southern England

Desmond Bonney

Elsewhere the writer has put forward the view that elements of the pattern of estates and parishes, familiar from later Saxon times onwards in Wessex, may be discerned in the pagan Saxon period and even earlier (Bonney 1966; 1972). It is the purpose of this brief essay to develop one aspect of this theme, largely ignored until now, in an attempt to further discussion of the origin and evolution of estates. The initial argument was based chiefly on the observable fact that a considerable proportion of the pagan Saxon burial sites that may be located with accuracy, both cemeteries and isolated burials, in flat graves and in barrows, lay on or very near (here defined as within five hundred feet) the boundaries of the ancient ecclesiastical parishes. Most of the latter, except in and around expanding urban centres, remain unaltered to this day, fossilized in their modern civil counterparts. In Wiltshire, for example, of sixty-nine burial sites twenty (29 per cent) lie on ancient parish boundaries and a further fourteen (20 per cent) within five hundred feet, many of them much nearer. In Dorset of eight certain burial sites two are on parish boundaries and five within three hundred feet. Preliminary work in Hampshire, Sussex, Berkshire, Cambridgeshire and Lincolnshire lends substantial support to this observation.

Examples of such occurrences are shown in figures 4.1 and 4.2. On Tarrant Launceston Down five miles northeast of Blandford, a group of round barrows was examined in advance of probable damage by the War Department who had recently acquired the area for training purposes (Piggot 1944). Time did not allow total excavation but all the barrows were examined, some extensively. All proved or appeared to be of prehistoric date except one, (a) on figure 4.1, which was considered by the excavators to be of pagan Saxon date. It lay on the parish boundary between Tarrant Launceston and Long Crichel. A second barrow (b), also adjoining the parish boundary, yielded an inhumation burial undated but possibly pagan Saxon. On Roundway Hill, northeast of Devizes, is a scatter of barrows nearly all of which have been excavated or dug into in the past. Only two are known to have had pagan Saxon associations. One, on the boundary between Roundway and Bishops Cannings, was of pagan Saxon construction; another, some two hundred feet from the boundary with Bromham, contained an intrusive burial of the pagan period. A more complex example is that shown in figure 4.3. Many of the barrows in the well-known group at Winterbourne Stoke crossroads just west of Stonehenge were dug into in the early nineteenth century, though none has been completely or scientifically excavated. Only one, (a), has so far yielded what is generally regarded as a pagan Saxon intrusive burial. It lies at a junction of boundaries, at the point where the parish boundary is met by the boundary between the manors of Wilsford and Normanton, itself formerly a parish boundary when Normanton was a detached part of the parish of Great Durnford.

In addition to the archaeological evidence there is some documentary evidence to suggest the presence of yet other pagan Saxon burials on boundaries. Certainly references to 'heathen burial(s)', and perhaps to just 'burials', which occur in the description of the boundaries of a number of estates granted by charter in the later Saxon period, invite such a conclusion. The term 'heathen burial(s)'

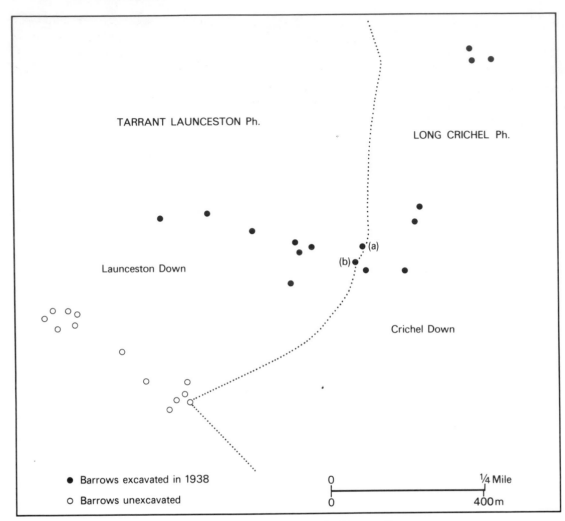

Figure 4.1   Barrows and boundaries on Launceston and Crichel Downs, Dorset.

occurs thirteen times in charters relating to Wiltshire, eight for Berkshire, seven for Hampshire and one for Dorset. It has also been suggested that the term *hlaew* (*hlaw*), generally meaning 'barrow' or 'burial mound', and which occurs only infrequently in charters relating to estates in southern England, is used to indicate a barrow with pagan Saxon associations and that the far commoner *beorg* was used of prehistoric barrows. Should this be so, then in Wiltshire a further ten burial sites occur on boundaries, in Hampshire five and in Berkshire thirteen. Figure 4.4 presents the provisional overall picture of the relationship between pagan Saxon burials, certain and probable, and boundaries in Wessex.

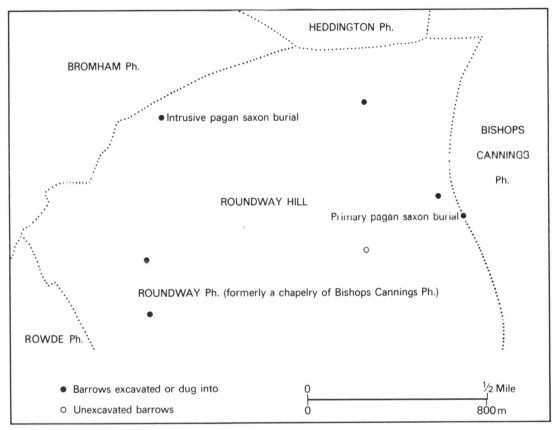

Figure 4.2 Barrows, boundaries and pagan Saxon burials on Roundway Hill, Wiltshire.

Since the pattern of ancient ecclesiastical parishes and churches was established largely on the basis of secular estates, many of which are known from charters to have been in existence by the later Saxon period, it is clear that many boundaries and the areas of land they define have been recognizable and valid entities for a thousand years or more. The apparently deliberate associations of pagan Saxon burials with such boundaries suggests that this pattern existed, or was coming into existence, somewhat earlier than has been generally supposed and certainly within the pagan period. It is not the purpose of this paper to press the argument in favour of a pre-Saxon origin for some boundaries, and by implication estates, but it is an observable and presumably significant fact that in Wessex and elsewhere (e.g. Taylor 1974, pp. 6, 7) the pagan Saxons generally chose to settle in areas which can be shown to have had a substantial rural population in the Romano-British period. The map for Wiltshire

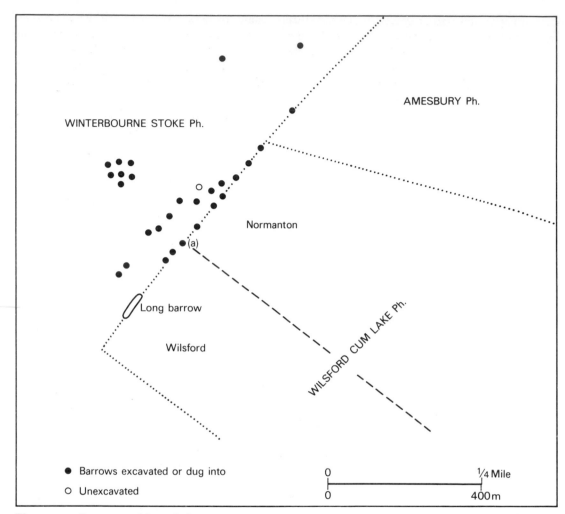

Figure 4.3   Barrows and boundaries near Winterbourne Stoke crossroads, Wiltshire.

(figure 4.5) demonstrates this clearly. In such areas the countryside had long been farmed and managed and was essentially man-made, not just a scatter of cultivated islands in a sea of waste. In these conditions clearly defined and well understood boundaries were not only possible but highly desirable.

So far, however, discussion has centred on boundaries which in time also became ecclesiastical parish boundaries and no account has been taken of any burials on or near estate boundaries which lie within parishes, i.e. where the estate does not coincide with the parish but forms a constituent part of it. The existence of such estates is well known and widespread (for Wessex, see RCHM *Dorset II* (1970), xxxviii; *Dorset III* (1970), xliv, 60). Their boundaries, though often more elusive

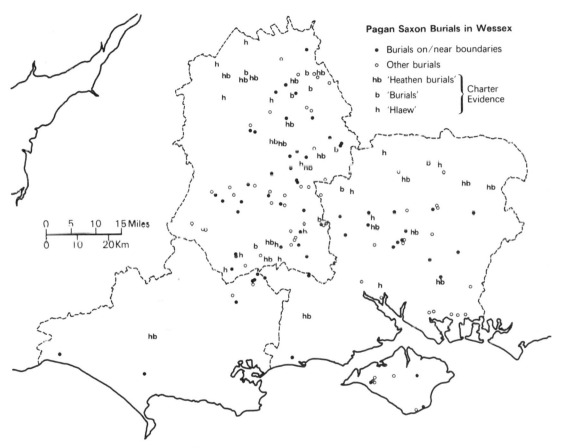

Figure 4.4 Pagan Saxon burials in Wessex.

than those of the ecclesiastical parishes, may frequently be recovered from early maps—estate, tithe, inclosure, etc.—and surveys, and many have survived to the present day. They are often discernible as continuous lines of hedge or fence, sometimes followed by a road or track, and largely unaffected by the pattern of enclosed fields on either side which in most cases is of much more recent date. In a number of instances in Wiltshire, which has been studied in detail, pagan Saxon burials or charter references to 'heathen burials' are associated with such boundaries. Perhaps the best example is an inhumation burial in a wooden coffin with iron nails and clamps found during construction work on the airfield at Netheravon. Though now in an area devoid of all but modern features it is clear from the tithe map and award for Figheldean parish that it lay on the boundary between the manors

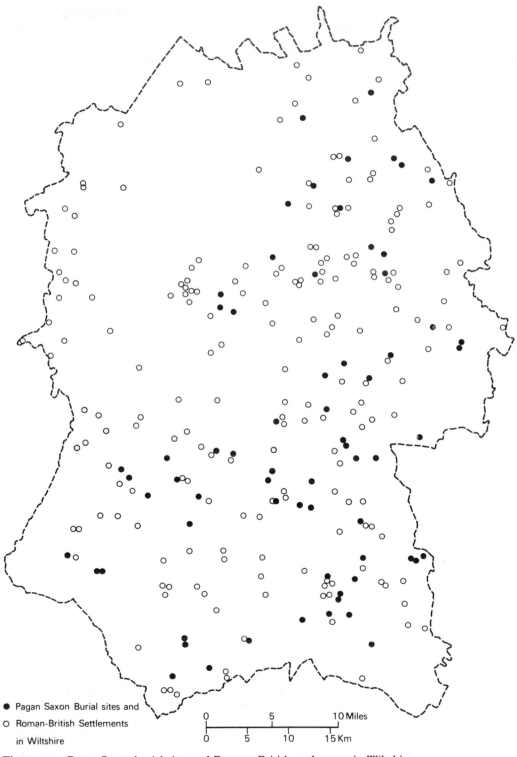

● Pagan Saxon Burial sites and
○ Roman-British Settlements
  in Wiltshire

| 0 | | 5 | | 10 Miles |
| 0 | 5 | 10 | 15 Km |

Figure 4.5   Pagan Saxon burial sites and Romano-British settlements in Wiltshire.

of Choulston and Figheldean (see figure 4.9), both Domesday estates (Victoria County History, Wilts. 1955, 131, 163) but probably of much earlier origin. The small cemetery just north of West Chisenbury in the parish of Enford lies on the edge of a low gravel terrace above the flood plain and two hundred feet from the river Avon which here forms the boundary between East and West Chisenbury (figure 4.9). A cemetery, discovered very close to the boundary between the tithings of Crofton and Wilton

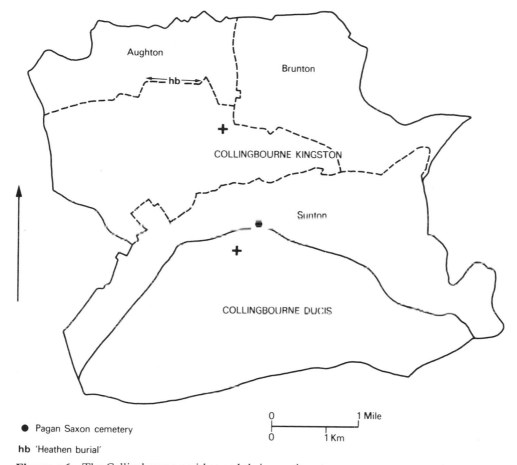

● Pagan Saxon cemetery

hb 'Heathen burial'

Figure 4.6 The Collingbourne parishes and their constituent manors.

in Great Bedwyn, though lacking grave goods included a number of burials radiating from a common centre like the spokes of a wheel and which by analogy with such arrangements elsewhere are probably of late sixth- or seventh-century date. Charter references to heathen burials occur on the boundaries between Wroughton and Elcombe within the parish of Wroughton (Sawyer 1968, no. 585), Aughton and Collingbourne Kingston (Sawyer 1968, no. 379; figure 4.6), Shaw and West Overton (Sawyer 1968, no. 547; figure 4.7); and on the boundary between Smithcot and Dauntsey in the latter parish the Dauntsey charter twice refers to heathen burials, apparently physically separate, and also to *Strengesburiels* (Sawyer 1968, no. 1580; Grundy 1919, 165–9).

If the explanation advanced above of the presence of burials on boundaries is accepted then it would appear that some small units or estates, of considerably less than parish dimensions, were recognizable entities in pagan Saxon times, e.g. those based on Aughton, Shaw, Choulston and West Chisenbury. There is no reason to regard these as exceptional either on account of their size or in any

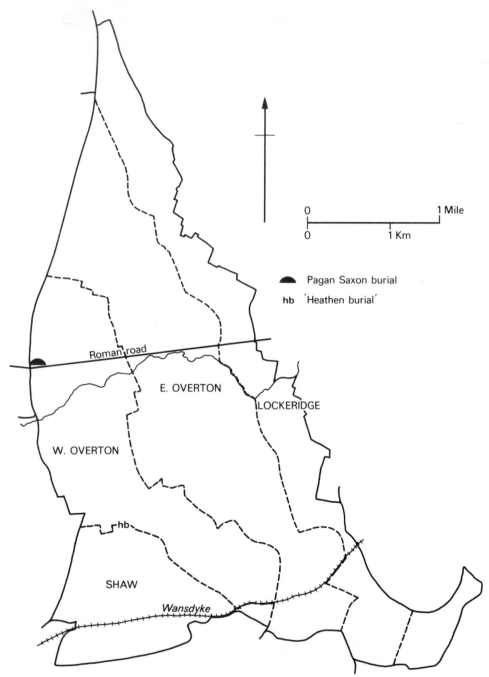

Figure 4.7 The parish of West Overton and its constituent manors.

other way. Each unit comprises the land associated with a single settlement or community which farmed and obtained a livelihood from it; and certainly from the later Saxon period onwards there is abundant evidence that these were the basic units of settlement and land utilization over much of England, especially the more densely settled parts of the lowland zone. If the estate or unit of land in

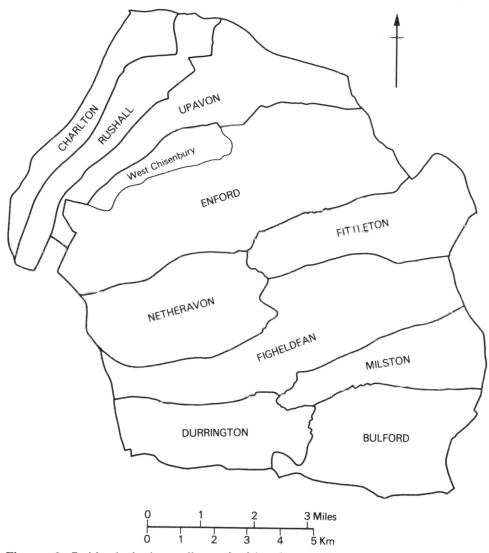

Figure 4.8   Parishes in the Avon valley north of Amesbury, *c.* 1840.

Collingbourne Kingston which later came to be known as Aughton was an entity in pagan Saxon times, then perhaps the other units within the parish—Brunton, Sunton and Kingston itself—are of comparable date. The same may also be argued of the estates or units which comprise West Overton parish and the parishes of the Avon valley illustrated in figures 4.8, 4.9 and 4.10.

The large multiple estates, to which Glanville Jones has drawn attention in a notable series of papers (e.g. Jones 1971), normally consisted of a number of such smaller units. Because of the distances

Figure 4.9 Boundaries and pagan Saxon burials in the Avon valley.

involved large estates could not be worked efficiently and economically, and certainly not intensively, from a single administrative centre, and were, of necessity, divided into a number of smaller estates or units each worked from its own settlement. What remains uncertain is how the known pattern evolved. In a recent paper Peter Sawyer (1974) has suggested that the settlement of Anglo-Saxon England is best understood in terms of the fragmentation of large multiple estates implying a division of something that was once whole. But how early are the constituent parts of such estates? It is possible that some multiple estates, at least, emerged through the amalgamation of their component parts.

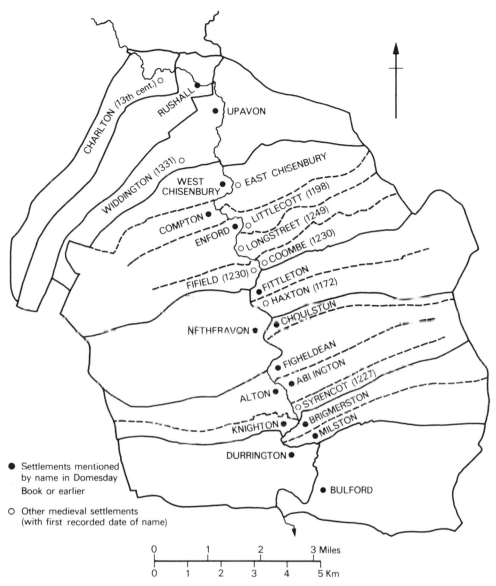

Figure 4.10 Medieval settlements and their lands in the Avon valley.

5

Wharram Percy: a Case Study in Microtopography

M. W. Beresford and J. G. Hurst

M. W. BERESFORD

Marc Bloch once wrote that history has all the excitement of an unfinished excavation. This joint contribution to the symposium will try to show that an unfinished excavation is itself now part of history. It is, however, appropriate that the major part of the paper should be presented by and in the words of John Hurst. We have already collaborated in the production of a long book summarizing the progress of village studies in general (Beresford and Hurst 1971) but our collaboration began by a chance encounter and the discovery of a common interest in and curiosity about the fabric of medieval villages. At that time my interest and researches were just moving from the documentary to the archaeological. The identification of sites in the Midlands by W. G. Hoskins in Leicestershire and by myself in Warwickshire and Northamptonshire had included field work and the search for characteristic earthworks, and that work was complete before I came to Leeds in the spring of 1948. In my last winter at Rugby I had been offered some help from interested staff and boys at Hinckley Grammar School and had dug one or two trial trenches on or near the church site at Stretton Baskerville (Warwickshire).

I had no excavation training, and this form of 'excavation' was simply the confirmation that earthworks of a house-like shape did conceal stone walls, the tracing of these walls and the measurement of house sizes. The church at Stretton Baskerville and three house sites at Wharram were susceptible to this rough investigation but similar methods at Wilstrop and Steeton (Yorkshire, West Riding) and East Lilling (Yorkshire, North Riding) had failed to reveal houses; with hindsight, I realize that my trial trenches were on house platforms with former timber structures, not stone buildings, and neither the technique nor my own knowledge was capable of identifying former structures not made of stone.

Nor did the uncovering of one set of walls just below the sod reveal the complexity of earlier house building that J. G. Hurst's contribution to the symposium will illustrate. However, as it happens, the excavation of house 5 at Wharram which was in progress when he first came to see me at work had reached a stage, recorded in one of the few photographs then taken (plate 5.1), where I had gone beneath the floor level of the house, puzzled by the occurrence of solid stones there, only to find a whole line of large stones out of alignment with the excavated walls and running out of sight underneath. It was an opportune moment to meet a partner who had been trained in archaeology and who was prepared to throw aside trench excavation for the patient innovation of area excavation.

Thereafter my role over the successive seasons at Wharram has been labour recruiting, organizing the food supply and cooking, public relations and historical research. Wharram Percy was not a village with very extensive documentary cover; had this existed, there might have been less temptation to begin the other forms of enquiry when the suggestion was first made to me by a local schoolmaster, Mr Winstanley of Settrington, in 1949. In the nature of medieval village documents, even when they survive, the matters which concern us today, the microtopography of houses, crofts, tofts, streets and minor village buildings, are never well delineated, and Wharram was not one of that handful of villages where elaborate surveys or maps were drawn in the years before its destruction.

Plate 5.1 Wharram Percy area 5, southwest corner showing two courses of latest chalk-built house with an earlier wall obliquely underneath and fill of chalk quarry below 1952 excavations (*photograph by courtesy of the Hull Daily Mail.*)

If we were dependent only on documents we would not know of a Wharram earlier than its 1066 valuation in Domesday Book (1086); we would know of a manor house at the time of the Percy purchase from the crown, but not whether it was the same manor that served the two insane female members of the Percy family who died here, nor whether it was the manor house mentioned in the fifteenth-century inquisitions post mortem. From an isolated deed we know that there was a little park alongside the manor. From four surviving inquisitions post mortem we know that there was a kiln and two watermills, and the language of one inquisition post mortem suggests strongly that there was a form of *solskift*, the regular distribution of a particular peasant's selions throughout the furlongs of the open fields. From documents we know that it was the Hiltons and not the Percies who depopulated the village, and from litigation in the church courts we know of mid sixteenth-century vicars with no congregations other than folk from Thixendale across the Wold top, and of the burning of the medieval vicarage which was inadequately replaced. The villagers had gone, and only the shepherd and his dog remained. In the late seventeenth century the hearth tax collection reveals the same strange neighbours, the vicar and the shepherd, in the empty township, and the evidence of early nineteenth-century plans, after the Middleton purchase of the estate, shows that a quite extensive vicarage was still surviving then. The first edition of the 6-inch ordnance survey map indicates that the vicarage had been pulled down, probably after the amalgamation of the living with that of Wharram le Street. It was the surveyors for that map who paused to notice and to delineate the earthworks of the village in the field above St Martin's church, and to record the local tradition as 'site of ancient village'. How ancient a

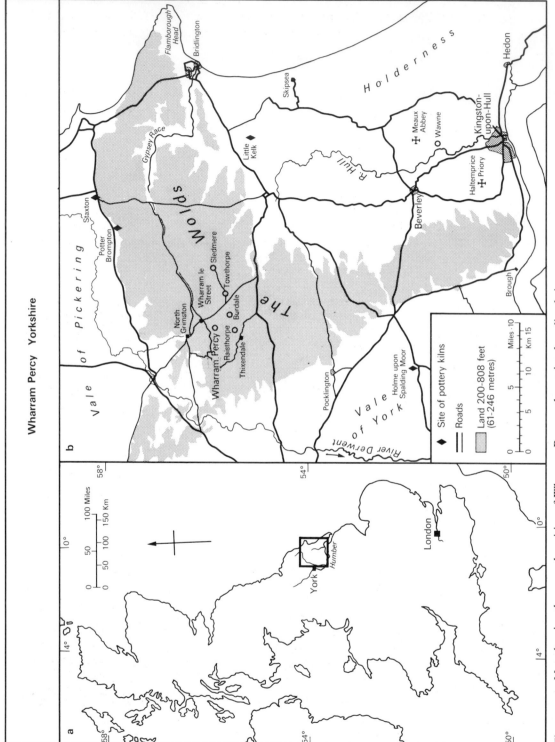

Figure 5.1   Map showing the general position of Wharram Percy and associated medieval sites.

village they did not say, but it was the conjunction of an isolated church and earthworks, the classic pattern of Midland medieval village desertion, that first aroused my interest in 1948 when I was examining the maps of my new home county to see whether Yorkshire had its deserted villages too. It did not disappoint.

J. G. HURST

Wharram Percy is situated towards the western edge of the Yorkshire chalk wolds, eight miles south of the twelfth-century market borough of Malton and about half-way between York and the port of Scarborough. It comprises a large parish of 9,500 acres in which there were five nucleated settlements in the medieval period: Wharram Percy, the main settlement with 1,500 acres; Raisthorpe, Burdale and Towthorpe of similar size, with Thixendale of 4,000 acres (figure 5.1). These demonstrate the extensive settlement and agrarian exploitation of the high wolds in the medieval period as is shown by the large amount of ridge and furrow visible on air photographs. With the economic changes of the late fifteenth century, when it became more profitable to keep sheep than to grow crops, four of these settlements were deserted, only Thixendale surviving. The village earthworks survive fossilized in small pockets of grassland, but in the eighteenth century the wolds returned to arable and now there is hardly any surviving permanent pasture. We therefore have a return to the medieval situation—

Plate 5.2 Wharram Percy oblique air photograph looking northwest, showing valley and Nutwood in the foreground with church on left and cottages in centre. Beyond main row of tofts 4–18 with late manor house on the right and Romano-British enclosure beyond. Taken February 1967 with area 6 in process of excavation behind the church (*Cambridge University Collection, copyright reserved*).

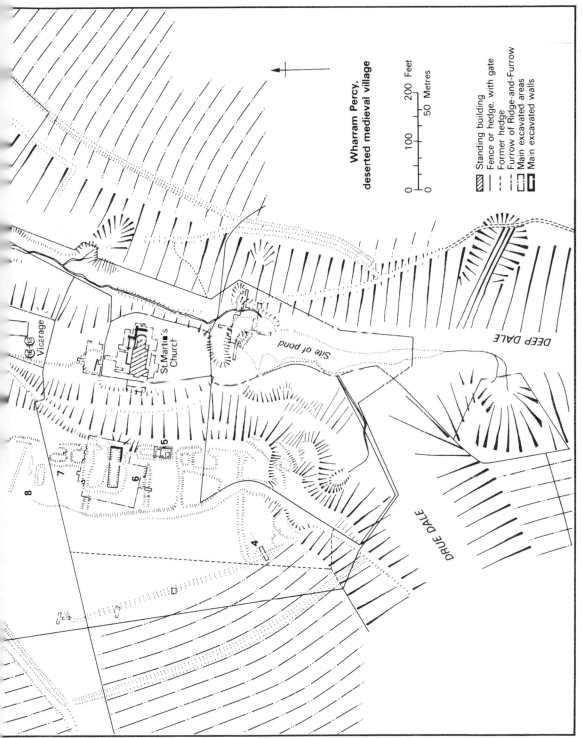

**Wharram Percy,
deserted medieval village**

Standing building
Fence or hedge. with gate
Former hedge
Furrow of Ridge-and-Furrow
Main excavated areas
Main excavated walls

Figure 5.2   General plan of Wharram Percy showing earthworks and excavated areas.

an arable landscape—but with the significant difference that the land is now cultivated from a few large isolated farms; there was no return to nucleated villages. Wharram Percy is now run from Wharram Percy farm (1,000 acres) and Bella farm (500 acres). The only surviving medieval building at Wharram Percy is the ruined church which served all the five settlements and remains because it was used by the inhabitants of Thixendale until a separate church was built there in 1870. Since then it has gradually fallen into decay.

Plate 5.3 Wharram Percy oblique air photograph looking south with main block of tofts 18–19 in the foreground and area 6 in course of excavation beyond. Valley to left with corner of Nutwood, cottages and church. Taken February 1967 (*Cambridge University Collection, copyright reserved*).

The earthworks of Wharram Percy village comprise rectangular mounds left by individual peasant houses, set in their tofts and crofts, and a network of sunken roads between; all are clearly visible on the ground (figure 5.2) and, as can be seen better from the air (plates 5.2, 5.3), form a very regular pattern of a village as it was at the time of its desertion about 1500. During the past twenty-five years the excavations by the Deserted Medieval Village Research Group (DMVRG) have uncovered two complete tofts (areas 10 and 6), the twelfth-century Percy manor house, the church and part of the churchyard; other sites and boundary banks have been sampled.[1] Work is currently in progress at the vicarage and the mill. As the site covers some thirty acres, and there is only a three-week season each

[1] Annual interim reports in *Annual Reports Deserted Medieval Village Research Group*, I–XXIII (1953–75); also from 1956 onwards shorter interims with plans in the 'Medieval Britain' section of *Medieval Archaeology*, vols. I–XIX (1957–75).

year, a very small portion of the site has been investigated—as can be seen from the areas of excavation marked on the plan.

In the 1950s, area 10 was excavated. Before excavation the remains comprised a rectangular earthwork fifty feet long and twenty feet wide set in a rectangular toft. When the turf was removed it was seen that the earthwork was made of rubble which, when cleared, exposed a series of chalk wall foundations. These did not, however, come from a single rectangular building, but a whole series of small lengths of wall on differing alignments, each cut into the other in a series of frequent rebuildings (plate 5.4). The whole deposit was only about one foot deep but, fortunately, the ground sloped to the

Plate 5.4 Wharram Percy area 10, showing west end of main site with complex series of walls of different periods looking north. Behind are earthworks of tofts 12 and 13 (*copyright MVRG*).

east so that here there were superimposed walls where the ground had been levelled up over the centuries. This made it possible to work out a sequence of building plans, but it was immediately apparent that there was not one building rebuilt on the same site; rather the whole toft was covered in buildings, as rebuilding took place not only on different alignments but in different positions. The whole toft was therefore excavated to produce a very complex pattern (figure 5.3).

Figure 5.4 is an interpretation which shows that in the twelfth century this was the site of the Percy manor house with an impressive undercroft (figure 5.5; plate 5.5). There is remarkable agreement in the dating of this building between the finding of architectural fragments datable from 1180–90 and the documentary evidence which suggests 1186–8. In the thirteenth century the manor house was demolished and a new one built at the north end of an extension to the village area. Area 10 was then used for two small peasant houses set sideways on to the street and parallel with the slope. In the fourteenth century, possibly as part of the general reduction in population, the two tofts were made into one, with a similar house on the same general line straddling the position of the previous two. Finally, in the fifteenth century, a series of long-houses were built at right angles to the street and the slope.

The Percy manor house had been built of chalk obtained from a quarry which then formed the site

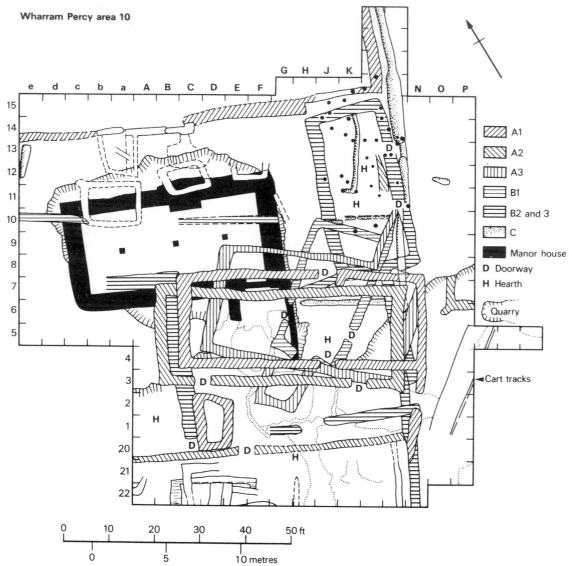

Wharram Percy area 10

Figure 5.3   Wharram Percy, area 10, showing the complex sequence of superimposed buildings (see figure 5.4).

for the undercroft, with quoins and dressings of sandstone from quarries at North Grimston about three miles to the north. The earliest peasant houses in the thirteenth century were built of timber; chalk was not used until the later thirteenth or early fourteenth century. In the fourteenth century there were solid three-feet wide walls built to full height (plate 5.6), but in the fifteenth century the area 10 houses were again timber-built on narrow eighteen-inch chalk foundations. The building stone was excavated from a series of individual quarries in the toft, six feet across and varying in depth from six to fifteen feet. The frequent rebuilding, which seems to have taken place about every generation, suggests that the roofs were not properly carpentered but flimsy do-it-yourself structures of undressed timber and branches. It is not clear whether this was because of a shortage of timber, or its unavailability to the peasant, or whether it was the fashion to build impermanent dwellings on the assumption

12th century

13th century

14th century

15th century

0   40 ft

0   15 metres

Figure 5.4   Wharram Percy, area 10, showing the main sequence of buildings.

that each time a peasant took over from his father he would want to rebuild. The latter is suggested by the evidence of complete rebuilding on a new site, as if the new owner often wanted to do something quite different.

In the 1960s toft 6 was completely excavated. It was confirmed that in the early medieval period this area was cultivated and that the settlement did not expand up on to the west plateau until the twelfth century. As with area 10, the first peasant houses were of timber (figure 5.6) and were replaced by small stone houses in the late thirteenth century. But there were then two differences: firstly, that in the fourteenth century a long-house was built; and secondly, that in the fifteenth century

Wharram Percy Manor House

Chalk
Sandstone
Flint
Overhanging
Quarry face

Figure 5.5 Wharram Percy, plan of the twelfth-century Percy manor-house.

Plate 5.5 Wharram Percy area 10, general view of the undercroft of the Percy manor house built in the 1180s, looking to the northwest. In foreground, threshold with three central pillar bases and foundations of fireplace in sandstone with the main walls chalk-built set into a chalk quarry *(copyright MVRG)*.

there was no change in building technique (figure 5.7). A large ninety-foot long-house with a central row of posts was rebuilt and repaired several times in the same general position (plate 5.7), losing its central posts and being shortened. Throughout it continued as a stone-built house. We therefore have two major differences between areas 6 and 10: long-houses starting at different times and differing building constructions. This suggests that, after the almost universal change from timber to stone-built houses, the types of plan and, later, building methods depended on the status and needs of the peasant concerned. It is therefore very dangerous to generalize from these two tofts when the other twenty might each produce different results.

At the time of desertion, about 1500, as can be seen from the plan (figure 5.2), each toft contained a single long-house or a simpler building. Excavation has shown that long-houses go back to at least the thirteenth century and that simple two-roomed houses, and long-houses in which the farming activities took place under the same roof as the living accommodation, were in use at the same time. It is suggested that the choice depended simply on the prosperity of the peasant and whether or not he had a number of animals. House 10 was never longer than fifty feet while house 6 was ninety feet long in the early fifteenth century, but reduced to seventy feet by the end of the century. It is tempting to link this reduction in size to economic contraction, but it could be simply a change in emphasis on animals. The only courtyard farm at Wharram, in which the various activities were separated out into different buildings, was complex 20–22. This was situated in the manorial enclosure so it was pre-

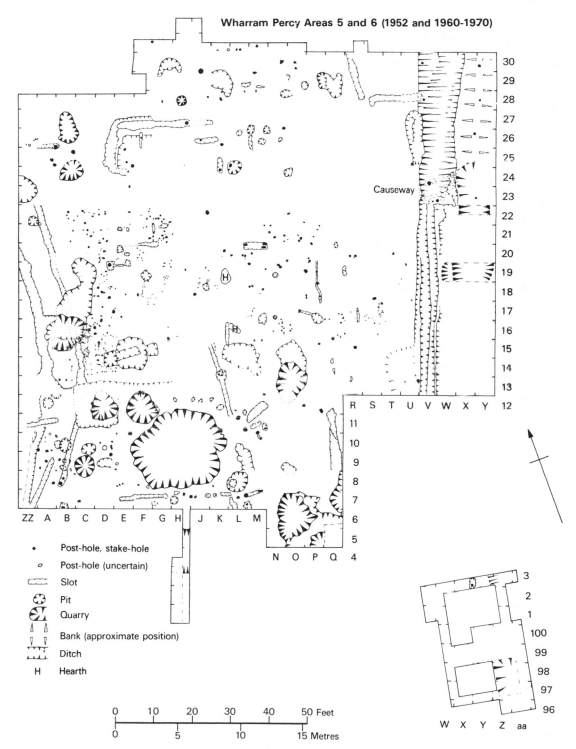

Figure 5.6 Wharram Percy, areas 5 and 6, showing post-holes cut into by later quarries.

Plate 5.6   Wharram Percy area 10, northeast part of site looking north showing post-holes and slots of timber buildings cut into the natural chalk with chalk-built walls of peasant house above (*copyright MVRG*).

sumably the demesne farm and should be considered in seignorial rather than peasant terms. In other parts of the country peasants were already building courtyard farms by the thirteenth century, at Gomeldon for example (Beresford and Hurst 1971, fig. 22). In the East Riding this does not seem to have occurred until the sixteenth century, later than the desertion of Wharram. At Towthorpe and near-by Duggleby, where desertion or shrinkage was post 1500, there are surviving earthworks of both long-houses and courtyard farms (plate 5.8).

The last service at Wharram Percy church was held just after the second world war and, when excavations started, the roof was still complete and the fittings intact (plate 5.9). After thieves stole the lead fittings from the roof there was rapid deterioration and birds soon dislodged slates which let in the rain and brought down the plaster ceiling. The bells, pews and monuments were removed, and the west face of the tower collapsed in 1960, so that over as short a period as ten years an intact church became a dangerous ruin (plate 5.10). It was readily apparent that there had been many changes in the architectural history of the church; they were demonstrated by the blocked-up north and south aisles and the scar of a larger chancel. The Royal Commission plan of the 1950s showed six periods between early Norman and the nineteenth century. There is no tradition in England of church excavation such as has taken place on the continent during the last thirty years. This is partly because of the fact that there is much more opposition to the excavation of churches still in use and partly because of problems of recent burial. A deserted village church, where these restrictions do not apply, is therefore ideal and it was for this reason that the DMVRG decided in 1962 to start a complete excavation of Wharram Percy church; this was completed in 1974. It produced even more remarkable results than had been expected and a plan as complex as that for the peasant houses, though spread

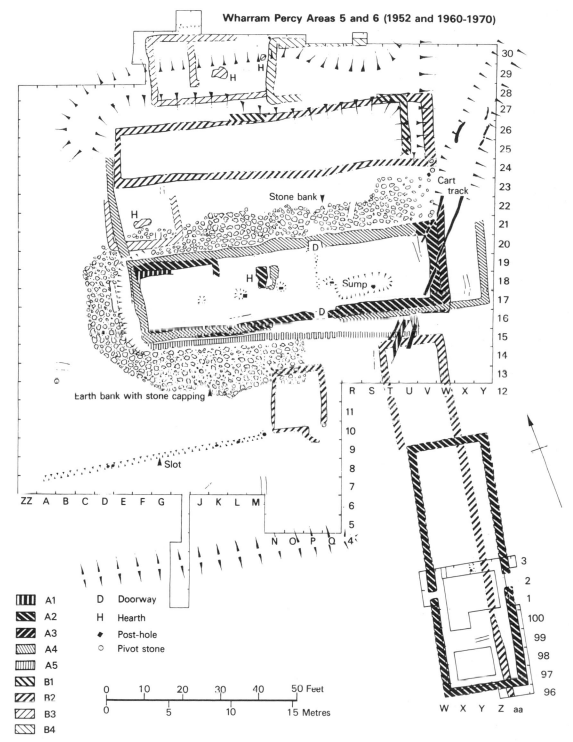

Wharram Percy Areas 5 and 6 (1952 and 1960-1970)

Cart track

Stone bank ▼

Earth bank with stone capping ▲

Slot

Sump

▦ A1	D	Doorway
▨ A2	H	Hearth
▧ A3	◆	Post-hole
▨ A4	○	Pivot stone
▥ A5		
▨ B1		
▧ B2		
▧ B3		
▨ B4		

0   10   20   30   40   50 Feet

0   5   10   15 Metres

Figure 5.7 Wharram Percy, areas 5 and 6, showing the succession of thirteenth- to fifteenth-century peasant houses.

Plate 5.7   Wharram Percy area 6, looking east showing the fifteenth-century long-house with central hearth and series of rebuilt sections of wall on the same general alignment (*copyright MVRG*).

over a longer period (figure 5.8). This doubled the number of major periods to twelve with many other subphases (figure 5.9). The earliest building was a small timber structure, possibly of more than one period, which was replaced by a larger substantial church built of sandstone ashlar and set in a deep and wide foundation trench (plate 5.11; figure 5.10). This was in turn replaced by a large church comprising a nave fifty by twenty-five feet and chancel forty by twenty feet, built on a large chalk rubble foundation over the sloping valley side. The date of these first periods is a matter for debate, and it is hard to decide if the sequence starts in the eighth or ninth century or if all the buildings post-date the Scandinavian invasions and date from the tenth century onwards. There is no datable evidence from the buildings themselves but there is clearly eighth- and ninth-century activity, with a cross-fragment of the late eighth or early ninth century and five *sceattas* and *stycas* datable between 750 and 850. Unfortunately none of these are stratified in significant contexts. It could therefore be argued either that these objects are associated with the early timber and stone buildings, or, if the buildings are later, that there was only a freestanding cross in the earlier period.

To the large late Saxon or early medieval church was added an unusual Saxo-Norman overlap tower partly inside and outside the west wall. The Percies added a south aisle and changed the earlier square chancel into an apse in the 1180s (plate 5.12). In the early thirteenth century a north aisle and northeast chapel were added and finally, in the early fourteenth century, a top stage to the tower. The development of the church plan therefore clearly shows the expansion of the village from a small Anglo-Saxon village to a large medieval settlement including accommodation for the parishioners from the four other settlements. From the later fourteenth century onwards decline is shown by the

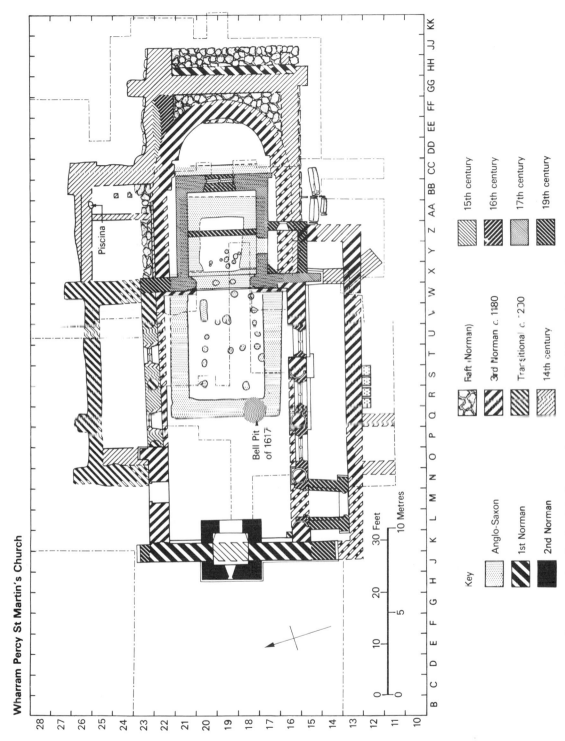

Figure 5.8 Wharram Percy church, showing the complex sequence of building periods (see figure 5.9).

Wharram Percy St Martin's Church

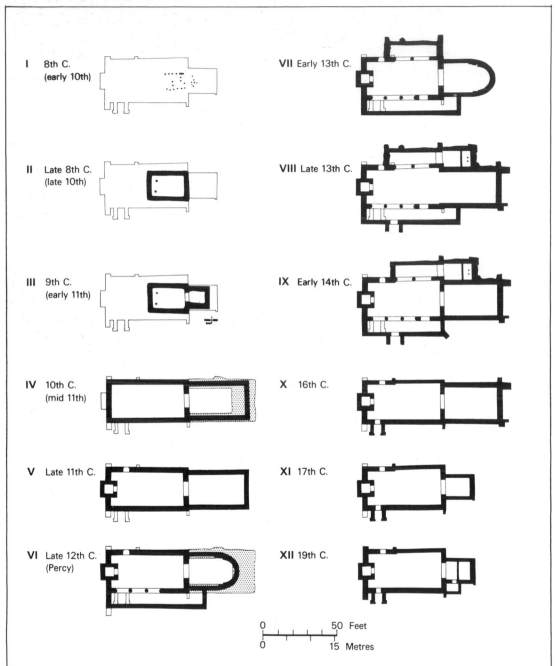

Figure 5.9 Wharram Percy church, interpretation of the building sequence.

Plate 5.8 Duggleby, North Yorkshire, a few miles northeast of Wharram Percy showing earthworks of alternate long-houses and courtyard farms on either side of the stream (*Cambridge University Collection, copyright reserved*).

pulling down of the aisles and the reduction of the chancel. The remains of the church therefore epitomize the whole expansion and contraction of medieval settlement and are a visual reminder of the effects of these changes.

The excavations inside the church located fifty-two burials (figure 5.10) but these were post-medieval and all earlier burials had been disturbed. A programme of excavation was therefore started in the churchyard to obtain a sequence and series of medieval burials. The earliest cemetery consisted of burials laid out in rows to the east of the first timber church. One of these had wood associated with it but was not a proper charcoal burial. In the southeast corner of the nave and chancel of the first stone church was found the main nucleus of the next series of burials—three graves with limestone grave slabs, head and foot stones. Two slabs had simple ridges and the third a simple expanded cross (plate 5.13). One burial contained a dress fastener, but unfortunately neither this nor the slabs help the dating problem. There were other similar graves including at least one stone coffin, since fragments were built into later periods. Sample areas excavated to the north of the church (200 burials) and west (168 burials) (plate 5.14) showed that the graveyard was laid out with burials at a uniform two-foot depth. There was very little disturbance but, as the churchyard became full, another round was started and, as the ground built up, there accumulated four layers of burials. Important burials included two vicars with pewter chalices and pattens. Unfortunately, in these areas north and west

Plate 5.9   Wharram Percy, St Martin's church, general view of the nave looking north before the taking out of the pews and other furnishings in 1952. (*Photograph by courtesy of the Hull Daily Mail.*)

of the church it is not possible to date the earliest burials as they cannot be linked with the building periods and there are no datable grave goods. It is therefore hard to say how long it took to fill the graveyard and how often a new series was started. Now that the excavation of the church is complete, further work will be aimed at determining the limits of the churchyard and an estimate of the total number of burials. The skeletons themselves will produce important information on the physical anthropology, disease and nutrition of a medieval rural population. Preliminary work has already been reported (Brothwell 1972), but the final account will take some time to prepare.

This work on the church, coupled with the excavations of areas 10 and 6, enable us to suggest that

Plate 5.10 Wharram Percy, St Martin's church, general view from southeast before the fall of the tower and removal of the roof and vestry (*copyright MVRG*).

there was originally a small Anglo-Saxon village, with its associated church and, presumably, manor house, on the lower terrace west of the stream. In the twelfth century the village expanded up on to the higher ground to the west which was originally fields (figure 5.11). The Percies constructed their manor house in the 1180s at the northern limit of this extension, and laid out a northern boundary bank of earth with a stone wall on top. In the thirteenth century another furlong of the common fields was taken in and laid out in a regular pattern of tofts and crofts. To the north of this extension a new manor house was laid out in the same relationship to the village as before, but on a larger scale. This included a small park, recorded in 1324. The present earthworks, however, including the main manorial buildings round a series of courtyards and the great barn (figure 5.2, N), are likely to date from the Hilton occupation of the fifteenth century. Excavation of this vast complex is beyond present resources either of time or money but it is hoped over the next few years to carry out a series of limited excavations to date the various main features.

A most important recent development, which has changed the whole course of the work, is that the village site has been placed in the guardianship of the Department of the Environment, thanks to the generosity of the owner, Lord Middleton of Birdsall and of the farmer, W. Midgley of Wharram Percy farm, to both of whom a debt of gratitude is owed for their patience and interest over the years in which the excavations have taken place. A fence has been put round the site and it is hoped to mark out areas 10 and 6 with explanations for visitors. The Church Commissioners have also placed the church in guardianship, and work is now nearly complete on the consolidation of the stonework, after which the main periods will be laid out. After twenty-two years as a voluntary excavation, the Wharram excavation has been, for the past three years, a joint project between the (renamed) Medieval Village Research Group and the Department of the Environment—with limited financial assistance. This has made it possible to pay supervisory staff and more than one project can now be undertaken at a time. There are not sufficient funds to pay volunteers but there is enough to pay for their food so that no charge has to be made. More sophisticated equipment can now be purchased or hired. This has improved the catering arrangements and enabled backfilling to be done by machine. Pumps have allowed us to excavate the pond and we have Flymo experiments in grass management. Finally it has also been possible to expand the three-week season by four working weekends during the year enabling other projects which are not practical in July to be started.

The aim of the MVRG is to study the whole topography of the village, so that after the complete excavation of two tofts (areas 10 and 6), the twelfth-century manor house and the church, there are

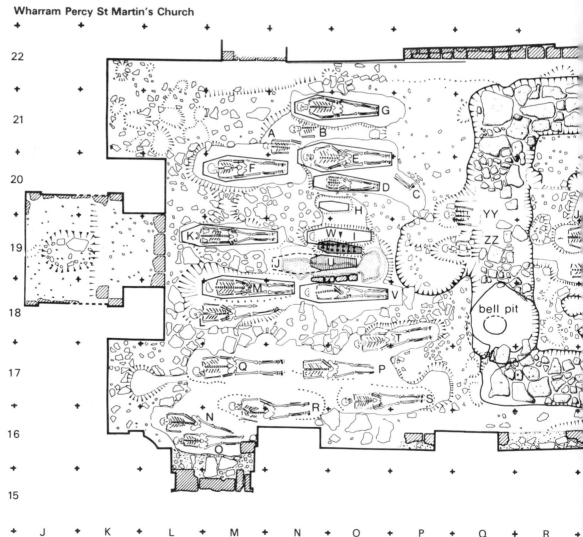

Figure 5.10 Plan of Wharram Percy church, showing the totally excavated nave and chancel much mutilated by post-medieval burials.

four main aims over the next five years. Firstly, the investigation of the glebe terrace, the area between the churchyard and the nineteenth-century cottages at the site of the eighteenth-century vicarage. Trial excavations here have shown massive traces of sandstone ashlar walls of a major thirteenth- and fourteenth-century building which is thought to be the vicarage. This is a high priority as there has been no major work on this type of site. First, however, the rest of the terrace, forming the courtyard and outbuildings of the vicarage, will be excavated since it is hoped to find remains of the Anglo-Saxon village here. In the churchyard all traces have been disturbed by graves, making this the last possible area. Fourteenth-century levels have been reached and it is hoped that earlier levels will be intact underneath. A trial trench has located a Saxo-Norman ditch and undated post holes of timber building.

Secondly, a limited programme of excavation will be aimed at determining the limits of the grave-yard at different periods, as well as producing further burials for analysis. Thirdly, further south a start has been made on the south watermill and fishpond. It is too early to draw firm conclusions as

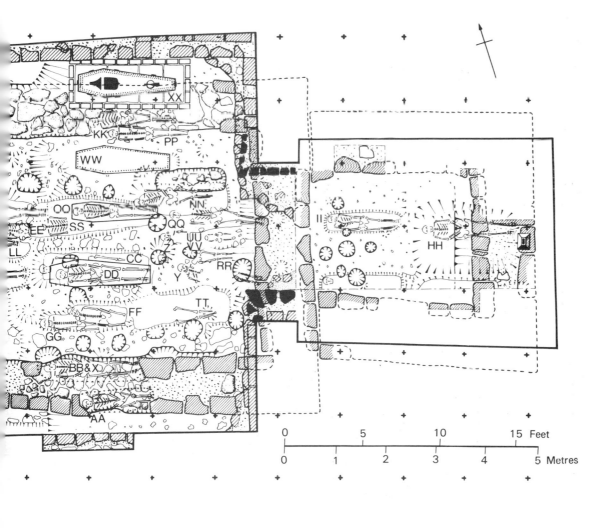

Plate 5.11 Wharram Percy, St Martin's church, general view of the fully excavated nave looking west to the tower. In foreground chalk foundations and the few remaining ashlar blocks of the first stone church enclosing post-holes of the timber church. The centre and far end are much disturbed by post-medieval burials. Nineteenth-century lead coffin and brick vault are on right (*copyright MVRG*).

Plate 5.12 Wharram Percy, St Martin's church, the large chalk raft with square east end, and Percy apse of the 1180s, looking northeast with the valley and stream beyond (*copyright MVRG*).

yet, but the results to date are most encouraging in showing two possible earlier periods underneath the thirteenth-century chalk rubble dam which was landscaped in the eighteenth century and became a sheepwash in the nineteenth century. The actual mill has not yet been located but it is hoped it will be found, as we know almost nothing about how watermills worked in the medieval village, surviving examples having been radically changed in post-medieval times. Of prime importance will be the environmental evidence from the waterlogged deposits. Previously little work on this aspect has been possible at Wharram because of the dryness of the chalk and the difficulty of obtaining pollen from calcareous soils. When the area has been excavated it is proposed to reconstruct the dam and refill it with water to recreate more of the medieval landscape. This area, and the length of the stream to the north, will become a small nature reserve in which the surviving flora and fauna will be preserved. A programme of planting and management is already in progress.

Fourthly, a programme for trenching boundaries has been in progress for the last five years on the west plateau. The original aim was to check the dating of the expansion of the village up from the lower terrace but the interesting results of this have been completely overshadowed by earlier finds from the Romano-British period. As early as 1961 the site of an early Romano-British building was found in a trial trench under the late manor house, and in 1965 aerial photography located another Romano-British enclosure just to the northwest of the village. Throughout the excavations of areas 10 and 6 a scatter of Romano-British pottery has been found, suggesting that this area had been under cultivation and manured at that early time. In 1971 the south boundary of the northwest Romano-

Plate 5.13   Wharram Percy, St Martin's church, the three late-Saxon limestone grave slabs with head and footstones broken off at ground level, looking west. The child and adult burials are in background with simple rib, and the slab in foreground with expanded cross (*copyright MVRG*).

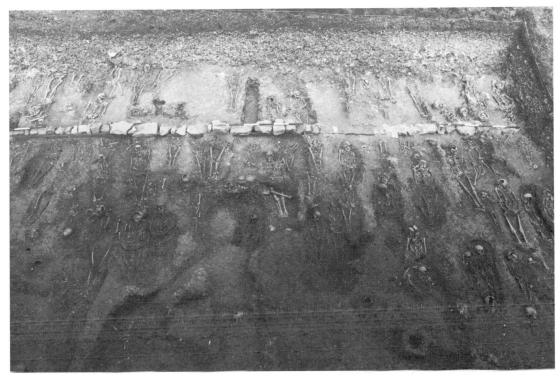

Plate 5.14 Wharram Percy, St Martin's church, burials west of the church looking west. The eighteenth-century conduit taking water from a spring to the vicarage runs across the centre. (*Copyright MVRG*).

British enclosure was sectioned, showing it to date to the second half of the first century AD with a ditch fifteen feet wide and eight feet deep. This was filled in about AD 100 and buildings constructed over it with a nucleus further to the west where there was an extensive scatter of Romano-British pottery in a ploughed field.

In this area the main medieval road westwards from the village turns sharply north (figure 5.12). Excavation showed that this was due to a bank several feet high running north–south at that point, a lynchet formed by Romano-British ploughing. This discovery led to a re-examination of the major earthwork which runs north–south across the whole village site, dividing the tofts from the crofts. This earthwork is also several feet high and is clearly more than a simple division within each peasant property. Examination of the ground and of air photographs shows that in fact it was once continuous across the site but was cut through or levelled by medieval features. In view of its size, this earthwork can only be a lynchet formed by ploughing over a very long period. As it does not extend north across the late manorial enclosure it is possible that the main road west out of the village is on the line, not only of another Romano-British field boundary, but also on the line of the Roman access from the valley.

It is therefore beginning to look as though the basic plan of the medieval village was determined by the layout of the Romano-British fields. This immediately raises the question of continuity. The main objections to this are the lack of late Romano-British pottery of the third and fourth centuries and of datable early Anglo-Saxon finds. So far no structures of this date have been located. There are therefore two possibilities: either there was continuity from some, as yet unlocated, centres with the fields maintained under cultivation; or, when settlers returned after an interval, the outline of the

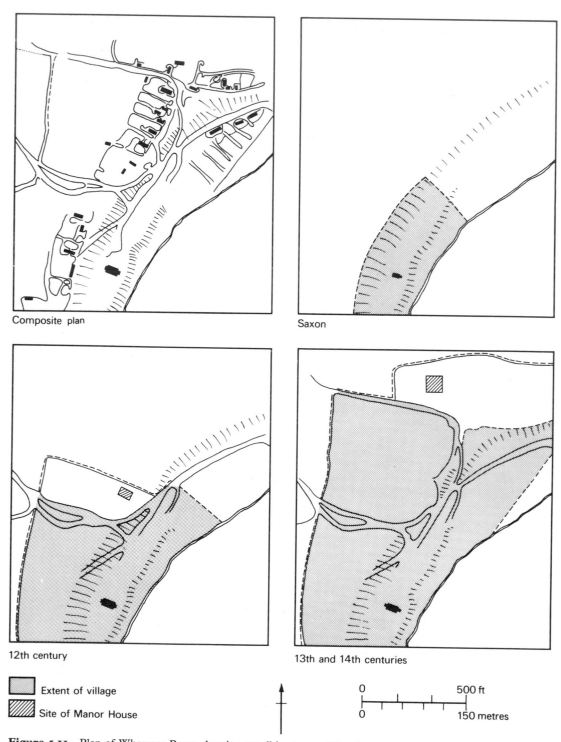

Composite plan

Saxon

12th century

13th and 14th centuries

Extent of village

Site of Manor House

0   500 ft

0   150 metres

Figure 5.11 Plan of Wharram Percy showing possible stages of development.

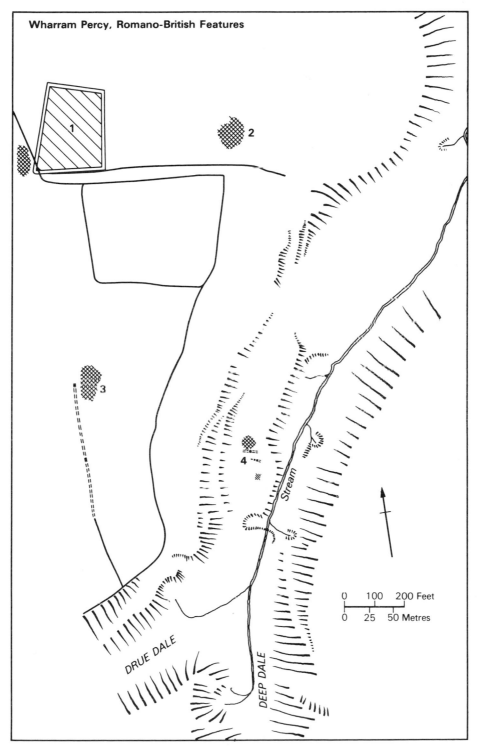

Wharram Percy, Romano-British Features

1

2

3

4

Stream

DRUE DALE

DEEP DALE

0   100   200 Feet
0   25   50 Metres

Figure 5.12 Plan of Wharram Percy, showing Romano-British features which determined its later medieval development.

Romano-British fields, and particularly the major lynchets, were still visible. If they had reverted to scrub it may have been less dense here than elsewhere. The siting of the village is due to the presence of six major springs along the junction of the chalk and clay over a length of half a mile in the valley; it would be a natural place to resettle.

Excavation in 1974 across the northern boundary of the twelfth-century manorial enclosure and the western boundary of the extended crofts showed that underneath the medieval earthworks, and on the same line in the same direction, were Romano-British ditches. It almost begins to look as though even smaller subdivisions of Romano-British fields may be perpetuated in medieval features. On the other hand, other Romano-British ditches have been found elsewhere and it may be only a coincidence. It is hoped a geophysical survey may be carried out to determine if these ditches follow the medieval line or are just passing here by chance where the trenches have been placed. Even more remarkable was the finding of another Romano-British ditch on the same line as, and only a few feet away from, the northern boundary of the medieval churchyard and vicarage. Whatever the continuity, there was clearly an extensive network of Romano-British cultivated fields as shown by the scatter of pottery from manuring. There was not a nucleated settlement but apparently a series of scattered farms set among the fields, of a type which is well known from the East Riding from air photographic evidence.

So far, at least four farms (or more precisely, suggestive evidence for buildings) have been located (figure 5.12). Firstly, the first-century ditched enclosure to the northwest of the village where there is firm evidence of an enclosure with later stone foundations; secondly, the finds from underneath the late manor house (not very far to the east), comprising post holes, slots, ditches and a burial; thirdly, and perhaps significantly in the angle west of crofts 8/9, a second-century ditch containing a large quantity of pottery and a dragonesque brooch, suggesting that a building was near by; finally, the ditch to the north of the churchyard containing a large amount of second-century pottery and another brooch, while under the chancel of the church was found a large quantity of first-century pottery and the disturbed burnt stones from a hearth. The lack of third- and fourth-century pottery from these settlement sites, combined with the presence of pottery and coins in fields which had undergone third- and fourth-century manuring, suggests that in the late Roman period the estate may have been consolidated into one holding, run from a centre as yet unlocated (though it might be the northwest site where little investigation has so far taken place).

We have been asked how anything new of significance can be found after twenty-five years, but we hope it has been demonstrated that with each season new horizons have been opened up and that simply to excavate a toft or two without looking at the other major components of the village, the manor house, church, graveyard, vicarage, mill and boundaries, would have been very misleading. Wharram Percy has turned out to be a life's work for both of us, though it is only one of our very many activities, and it is impossible to envisage in the foreseeable future either the money, personnel, or, in some ways most important, the patience required to launch a similar project elsewhere. We hope that the results have justified the decision (taken by the DMVRG more than twenty years ago) that the group should concentrate its research excavation on one site while others were sampling single tofts or specialized aspects on a multitude of sites. The overall results have recently been summarized (Beresford and Hurst 1971, chapter 2) and show that many of the special features of Wharram Percy— the change from timber to stone building construction, the constant rebuilding of peasant houses on new sites and alignments and the more fundamental changes of land use within the village—are repeated all over the country. This work has thrown unexpected light not only on how the medieval peasant lived but also on the fluidity of medieval settlement previously unappreciated. By studying the microtopography of Wharram Percy for the past twenty-five years we hope that we have contributed to this subject. There is still a great deal to be done—not only within the village. In 1974 a programme of fieldwalking to study the common fields and obtain evidence for manuring was initiated. We are now moving into the macrotopography of our medieval village.

The Wharram Research Project: recent results (1974–8)

When this chapter was written, four main topics were listed for investigation during the next five years (pp. 74 ff). The results of these excavations have been of great significance for the history of the village. First, work on the glebe terrace by Charlotte Harding has shown that in the thirteenth century the graveyard extended at least 50 feet further north than the fourteenth- to eighteenth-century boundary, for when the Parsonage was built in the early fourteenth century its courtyard, defined on the south by a stone wall (see figure 5.2) encroached on earlier burials. The graveyard had not always extended so far north, however, as below the burials were postholes of a possible twelfth-century building. Before this there seems to have been a gap in occupation, but there is evidence for a Romano-British settlement underneath. The problems raised by this expansion and contraction of the graveyard will be investigated by extending the excavation further north in 1979. Secondly, the limits of the graveyard: to the north these are still uncertain in view of the above new evidence, but to the south they have been defined by G. Foard as having been on the present boundary since medieval times. The southwest corner has also been confirmed by D. Andrews as extending up the steep west hillside to the terrace-way coming down to the dam from the western plateau. The eastern limits have not yet been further investigated, owing largely to the great depth of deposits there and the fact that the results elsewhere have been much more complicated than had been expected. It has been decided not to excavate any more burials as a further sample until the scientific analyses of the first 500, which are still awaited, have been obtained. Nevertheless, a further 150 skeletons have been found over the last five years in the areas excavated north and south of the graveyard.

Thirdly, extensive excavation by C. Treen has taken place on the south water mill and fishpond but the results have been very complex and are still not fully elucidated. The valley seems to have been dammed with a timber-supported structure in middle Saxon times (uncalibrated C14 dates of AD 650 and 750). There was a sequence of channels and leats during the late Saxon and early medieval periods but the actual mill site has not yet been located. In the thirteenth century, with the amalgamation of the two Wharram manors, the south water mill was abandoned and a chalk dam was built over the earlier sequence to form a fishpond.

It has, however, been the continued trenching of the boundary earthworks at Wharram Percy that has had the most significant and far-reaching results. The whole assumption that the northern end of the village was a late accretion was changed in 1975 with the discovery by G. Milne of a mid eighth-century *Grubenhaus* to the northeast of the north manorial earthworks, a good hundred yards east of the manor and 500 yards north of the church—which had been assumed to be the Anglo-Saxon nucleus. Subsequent excavation has shown that the northern manor house is not only on the site of a Romano-British farm, but that there is clear pottery evidence for continuity of occupation through Anglo-Saxon times. In the 1950s it had been assumed that the Area 10 manor house (Andrews and Milne 1979) was built on virgin ground in the late twelfth century, as there was only a handful of Romano-British and Anglo-Saxon pottery which was interpreted as manuring from agriculture of this period. In 1977, however, further excavation by D. Andrews, immediately to the west of the area previously excavated, produced a large number of Romano-British and Anglo-Saxon sherds. There now therefore seem to have been two Romano-British farms on the western plateau showing continuity through Anglo-Saxon times to form the two manors recorded in Domesday.

The main work of the next five years will be to open up larger areas in these enclosures to determine the nature of this continuity and to what extent the Romano-British field boundaries survived to form the basis for the medieval village layout. There is now increasing evidence for this survival elsewhere in England (Rodwell 1978, and Taylor and Fowler 1978). It must also be resolved why on the valley terrace the Anglo-Saxon church was sited by and over earlier Iron Age and Romano-British farms when there is as yet no evidence for Early or Middle Saxon domestic settlement in this area before the late Saxon period. It follows that the interpretation put forward in the 1950s and 1960s, and set out in this chapter (above pp. 59, 73 and Fig 5.11) was too simplistic, with its idea of a single Anglo-Saxon nucleus by the church expanding up on to the plateau to create a large nucleated village. It is now possible that the long line of village houses with so much regularity in their layout, known to override a manor house built *c.* 1180 and occupied until about the middle of the thirteenth century (Andrews and Milne 1979), was planned as a whole, probably after the Percies obtained control of all the holdings in 1254. Current work therefore strongly suggests a progression from a number of separate settlements to one nucleated polyfocal settlement (Taylor 1977). This new evidence is fully consistent with similar suggestions made from many other parts of England for the full opening up of the countryside by Roman times, if not before, followed by a setback in the early Anglo-Saxon period (Taylor 1975), but with renewed exploitation by middle or late Saxon times. In this interpretation the surviving medieval earthworks are to be seen as a consolidation of scattered settlements rather than progressive expansion from a single nucleus.

As foreshadowed above (p. 82), work at Wharram has moved over the past five years from a study in microtopography of the medieval nucleated settlement of Wharram Percy and its antecedents to a macrotopographical study of the two ecclesiastical parishes of Wharram Percy and Wharram le Street, comprising an area of 11,165 acres. Programmes of fieldwalking directed by C. Hayfield, and of air photography by A. Pacitto, have so far located only one Mesolithic site, but produced considerable evidence for Neolithic and Bronze Age clearance of the Wolds tree cover. There is a scatter of type VI stone axes and several flint spreads denoting occupation. The intensity of Bronze Age settlement is shown by the large number of barrows along the ridgeway which forms the south boundary of Wharram Percy township. Far more tumuli are visible on the air photographs than on the ground in the nineteenth century when Mortimer opened a number of them (Mortimer 1905). On the valley terrace south of the church, excavation by G. Foard has located a remarkable late-glacial hollow filled with hillslip which contains stratified levels of Neolithic, Bronze Age, Iron Age, Roman and Medieval date. The earlier levels do not seem to be *in situ*, but by the Iron Age there was a series of ditches, gullies and postholes here. This provides important evidence for early settlement since on the plateau above the valley the gradual lowering of the chalk by erosion and ploughing means that prehistoric features are preserved only under later earthworks, such as the Bronze Age gully beneath the Iron Age lynchet in Area 13.

By the time of the Roman occupation this area of the Wolds seems to have been fully exploited. There were Romano-British farms at approximately half-mile intervals over most of the area of the parishes of Wharram Percy and Wharram le Street. These settlements comprise patterns of rectangular enclosures set by the sides of trackways in a manner typical of the Yorkshire Wolds, as has been shown by recent work by the Royal Commission on Historical Monuments. This important new evidence, together with the discovery of at least three Romano-British farms under the medieval village of Wharram Percy and a scatter of Anglo-Saxon settlement sites over the parishes, suggests that the Romano-British pattern of dispersed farms continued through the Anglo-Saxon period. Other parish surveys are producing similar evidence for Anglo-Saxon scattered settlement (Foard 1978).

In addition to Wharram Percy, other Romano-British settlements, for example at Burdale, also gave rise directly to medieval villages, but others were deserted at the end of the Romano-British period so that some of the Anglo-Saxon settlements appear at new sites. The full process by which these scattered and sometimes mobile settlements could have become nucleated into discrete medieval villages will be the main study in the parishes after the completion of the initial parish survey.

D. Hall's survey of the medieval field systems from fieldwalking and aerial photography has shown that almost all the flat plateau areas were ploughed, with only the steep valley sides remaining under grass, scrub or wood. Some of the selions are very long, from 500 to 1,000 yards, typical of others on the

Wolds and in Holderness as current work by Mary Harvey is showing (Harvey 1976; 1978). This suggests regular planning at the time of the original nucleation in late Saxon times or a later re-organization. The presence of these long selions in the other Wharram townships, however, suggests a more general origin, with the open field planned at the time of nucleation, though it is hard to prove that one was caused by the other. It is very suggestive that the archaeological evidence for nucleation and the historical evidence for the development of common fields both seem to centre on the late Saxon period, as was shown at the 1979 Oxford seminar on open fields.

Each new area excavated in the main village site has raised fundamental new questions and the current reinterpretation shows the danger of drawing wide conclusions from even large area excavations. At the same time, the extension of research into the fields of the Wharram parishes has enabled the village site to be put in its landscape setting and has helped us to begin to understand how the whole area developed from the original forest clearance to the present day.

The most recent report on the total research project will be found in the forthcoming publication, *The Changing Past*, edited by G. D. B. Jones. More detailed annual reports are to be found in the duplicated Interim Reports, with shorter summaries in the Medieval Village Research Group, Annual Reports, and the 'Medieval Britain' section each year of *Medieval Archaeology*. The first monograph on the peasant houses in Areas 10 and 6 has now been published (Andrews and Milne 1979) and the second volume on the church is in preparation.

6

Pottery as Evidence for Social and Economic Change

H. E. Jean Le Patourel

The suitability and limitations of pottery as evidence

If any artifact is to be singled out as of special significance in demonstrating change in the social and economic fields, it will need to have certain qualities. It is essential that it should be an article in common use in all or most social contexts and it is necessary that it should be a 'good survivor' so that it can be expected to be present in all phases of an archaeological site in some quantity. It needs also to be culture-specific, that is to say it must be possible to recognize qualities in any artifact that make it characteristic of a restricted period and a defined area. But while it must be specific to one culture phase only, it must also be sensitive to changes in the culture that produces it. There is a further requirement. Excavated material must be reported in such a way that the reader knows exactly how much and what kind of material has been recovered and its precise relationship to each phase of the excavation.

As far as pottery is concerned there is no difficulty about the first of these requirements. Although there have been exceptional a-ceramic periods, it is generally true to say that it is far and away the most common artifact on any site. It is cheap to make and no great skill or equipment is needed for its manufacture. It also survives well. When a pot is broken the resulting sherds do not decay and are very little affected by soil conditions. The pot itself is fragile and therefore has a short life and is quickly replaced, so adding to the quantity available for study. Its cheapness ensures that it is not hoarded, nor does it normally outlive the generation that produced it. Very occasionally pots are found that have been repaired (Charleston 1965, p. 16; Myres and Green 1973, p. 60; or the pot found at Wharram Percy repaired with lead), but these are exceptions. In most circumstances it should be contemporary with the material with which it is found. Again, provided the limits are not unduly narrow, pottery is highly culture-specific. The limitations imposed by the state of technology reached, the methods of finishing or of glazing and the firing temperature that can be attained, together with shape and decoration all combine to make most pottery readily recognizable. Wheel-made pot can be easily distinguished from hand-made pot, Roman from Saxon pot and both from their medieval or post-medieval successors. Though there can be difficulties with small amorphous sherds, the increasing availability of scientific aids such as petrological identification, neutron activation analysis and thermo luminescent dating may eventually make it possible, always supposing the time and money are available, to establish the provenance and approximate date of most sherds. Even without such sophistication, it is to the pottery that an excavator looks for evidence of the date range of his site. Without it there are times when he would not know whether he is dealing with the ninth or the nineteenth century. Because pottery is culture-specific, it is also sensitive to cultural change. If an incoming culture is at a different social or economic level, these facts will be reflected in the pottery and its distribution. In certain circumstances it may also demonstrate development within the same culture.

When all this has been said, there are a number of factors that limit its value, some intrinsic to the pottery itself and the circumstances in which it is made, others inherent in those that surround the deposition, excavation and reporting of archaeological material. It is necessary to state these briefly since scholars in other disciplines are not always aware of these limitations.

Discarded pot may be subjected to various processes that mix up and disperse sherds from different periods so that it is difficult to build up an accurate sequence. An example will demonstrate the process by which this occurs. Sherds from a very distinctive imported French pot were found in the make-up material below floors in three different parts of Kirkstall Abbey (Le Patourel 1967, p. 45) (figure 6.1). Clearly their immediate origin was a near-by rubbish dump of unknown longevity. They need not all have been redeposited at the same time. In other cases make-up material may come from further away, as in the case of Thomas of Bayeux's rebuilding at York Minster (information from D. Phillips). By a somewhat different process, disturbance of earlier levels during building operations in antiquity or the digging of rubbish pits also tend to disturb the natural sequence. Residual material thus churned up complicates both typology and chronology, for the 'single period' site is very unusual. Until recently many archaeologists failed to recognize the extent of the problem posed by residual material, especially in the later phases of a site, and indeed it is difficult to see a satisfactory solution to it.

A different problem, but one that puts considerable limitation on the usefulness of ceramic evidence in our context is that we just do not know the precise importance of clay pottery within a normal household economy. There have always been substitutes. Soapstone, wood, leather, iron, silver, bronze and brass can each be used for one or more of the functions of pottery. Some of the substitutes are more efficient, as, for example, brass or iron pots for stewing over a fire, or more durable in use, like metal-bound wood for carrying or storing liquids, or more beautiful, like silver for tableware. But silver and brass apart, and they were too valuable to be casually abandoned, none of the substitute materials survives well in soil and in consequence the environmental picture is seriously distorted. In the one case where the whole range of articles in contemporary use is known by excavation, pottery plays a very small part. The excavation at Sutton Hoo produced thirteen bowls and a cup in silver, over a dozen wooden vessels, seven bronze bowls, three drinking horns and one solitary clay pot (Bruce-Mitford 1972). There is nothing else in the post-Roman archaeological record to show how common such a proportion would be. Examination of a household account nearly eight centuries later, however, is suggestive. At Methley in Yorkshire the Waterton household between 1417 and 1418 shows expenditure on the repair of silver, wooden and lead vessels, eight dozen wooden cups and two brass pots purchased and twenty-five earthen pots bought, but for the specific use of the stews or baths (account of Thomas Clerk for the Waterton household, archives of the earl of Mexborough, Leeds City Archives). Making allowance for the greater use of precious metal in a princely household and for the increase in domestic cleanliness in the fifteenth century, the picture has not changed very much and did not change for some centuries. M. Pickles kindly made available the results of her analysis of over a hundred seventeenth-century Wharfedale inventories, which indicated only one per cent of clay pot. Briefly, then, pottery on an excavated site forms an overwhelmingly high proportion of the artifacts found, yet when chance enables us to see the relative part played in the social environment by other materials, it becomes clear that judgements based on ceramic material alone produce a distorted picture.

So far we have looked at factors inherent in the deposition and survival of archaeological material that limit the value of pottery as evidence. We must now consider certain relevant aspects of pottery manufacture. The first is that, although in a broad sense culture-specific, pottery styles change extremely slowly. The craft is remarkably conservative. This is true of the fabrics used, of shapes and rim forms, of decoration and of the techniques of production. The fabric of a pot is determined by the clay, which usually needs an additive to assist its plasticity and to increase its refractory powers. Several sources of clay were known that needed no such backing, but only that found near Stamford

Figure 6.1   Map to show places mentioned in the text.

in Lincolnshire was fully exploited in our period, and that for some three hundred years. No fabric mixture had a life of less than two centuries and most were in constant or intermittent use. If shapes and rim forms cannot offer quite such long periods without change, yet they were disturbingly persistent. The pitcher form that preceded jugs lasted in eastern and southern England from the ninth to the twelfth century. The tall, narrow-mouthed cooking pots in use from the mid-ninth century saw no development in nearly three hundred years. Kiln complexes such as those at Brandsby or West Cowick in Yorkshire showed remarkably little change over a century or more. Duration of decoration is a more complex subject for there are some motifs that are so widespread in time and place that they seem imposed by the nature of the material. Others are intimately related to the use of the potters' wheel, particularly such decoration as rouletting and combing, executed while the pot is in rotation. Others again, such as applied strips, decorative treatment of handle joints and thumbing of the pot base, were functional in origin but continued in use as pure decoration. Over and above these common motifs that show little development over long centuries, there is ornament copied from pots imported from other regions or countries and decoration related to different art forms, such as the Ipswich pot of middle Saxon date (Smedley and Owles 1970, pp. 84–7), whose incised human faces echo the Sutton Hoo sceptre, or the anthropomorphic and zoomorphic plastic decoration of later years which seems to derive from decoration common among masons and carpenters. The difficulty is that once adopted into the repertoire of a given industrial group, such ornament tends to become stereotyped in much the same way as archaic forms are fossilized in documents. The rate of change is very slow. Production techniques concern us here only in so far as there is always a very long time-lag before a new skill is universally adopted. The slow wheel or turn-table, known in East Anglia and parts of Northumbria in the seventh century, was not overtaken by the technically superior fast wheel for a couple of centuries. The latter spread so gradually that it did not reach Wales until the twelfth century, leaving behind pockets where for a further century or more its use was confined to a final trueing up of the rim (as at Lyveden, Northamptonshire, where recent work indicates that the change came in the fourteenth century, though earlier the pot was thought to be wheel-made), (Bryant and Steane 1969, p. 19).

The second factor is that pottery is strongly regional in character. To a certain extent this was so in the Roman period. True, there were large-scale industries such as that at Lezoux which served the whole empire and penetrated beyond its boundaries, while in Britain itself industries not much smaller supplied the towns and the legionary market. But from at least the second century there were also many small local industries whose products varied considerably from one part of the country to another. When we can again speak of a pottery 'industry', it is the difference in pottery styles between the various regions that is most striking, and such differences continue throughout the middle ages. Middle Saxon wares thrown on a turn table had a restricted distribution round the town of Ipswich, or such monastic sites as Monkwearmouth, Jarrow or Whitby. Lincolnshire had its tradition of shell-gritted fabrics spreading only into the neighbouring counties (Addyman and Whitwell 1970, pp. 96–102). In the south and southwest handmade pottery was strongly influenced by the local iron age tradition. But there is some fluidity in the situation. Saxo-Norman cooking pots showing an astonishing homogeneity in shape and rim form tend to be confined to eastern England north of the Thames, though there is a westward spread by the tenth century, with similar pot at Chester (Petch and Thompson 1959, pp. 58–60) and Hereford (Shoesmith 1968, pp. 348–53). In the second half of the twelfth century, however, the distribution pattern has changed, as for example that of the technically advanced cooking pots and bowls of the northeast, which stop short at the Humber but penetrate beyond the Scottish border and across the Pennines to Carlisle (Le Patourel 1962–4, figure 30). Kent, London, the midlands and the southwest all have their characteristic regional development. It would be irrelevant to expand on this regionalization, though it is the salient characteristic of pre-industrial pottery. It must be emphasized that there are three variables—fabric, shape and decoration (in which last is included the use or otherwise of glaze) and that the situation is made more complex by the fact that the development of each is largely independent of the other.

Finally there is the question of archaeological reporting, for the reports are documents, and from them generalizations must ultimately be made. Not only are there many important excavations not yet published, but there is wide diversity in the thoroughness of reporting. Some excavators have published only their 'best' finds; others the range of material but not its quantity; others again have failed to relate it to its precise context. Few have given all the necessary information for valid comparison between sites of different social type and different period. The situation is changing now, but it will be some time before the new methods give adequate evidence on which to base general conclusions.

Pottery as evidence for economic change

Given the foregoing limitations and qualifications, there is still a good deal to be learnt from the pottery record, provided always that precision of dating is not required. In the sphere of economic structure and change, surviving pot sherds give direct evidence of the nature and evolution of the pottery industry itself, and this has general significance in periods when little is known of other industry, since its nature may well be indicative of the general type of industrial structure. It must always be remembered however that potters tend to be at the lowest end of the industrial hierarchy.

In sub-Roman Britain, change in the nature, the scale of production and the distribution of pottery, as well as in the technical know-how of the potters, was nothing short of catastrophic. Such total change is difficult to understand. Taken at its face value it indicates disruption lower down the social scale than might be expected and stands in marked contrast to the contemporary situation in Gaul and to the unbroken pottery tradition at the time of the Danish or Norman settlements. Though potting had been in the hands of natives for at least two centuries, the break with Roman wheel-made pottery was complete, unless we are misinterpreting much of the late Roman material. In the east the Anglo-Saxons established their own tradition of coiled or hand-moulded pot. In the southwest, where there had never been much of a Roman presence, manufacture continued in the local tradition, though not, except perhaps in Cornwall, on any great scale (Fowler 1966, p. 36; Thomas 1954, p. 66). Elsewhere production seems to have ceased altogether.

Among the settlers a phase of domestic industry has been postulated for the migration period on the evidence of cremation urns and ancillary vessels from inhumations. This concept has been modified as study has indicated products of various individual potters even among the funerary vessels. There is now a growing body of pot from settlement sites whose composition and nature, though not yet completely studied, already suggest a closer relationship between funerary and household pot than had been suspected. If the urns should prove to be an occasional *ad hoc* product of an industry geared to domestic production, it would be unnecessary to postulate a preliminary period of back-yard potting. Such evidence as we have of industrial activity, the traces at Sutton Courtney (Leeds 1948, p. 83), the kiln at Cassington (Arthur and Jope 1962–3, pp. 1–14), and the antler stamps at West Stow (West 1969a, pp. 11–13; 1969b, pp. 175–81), seem to tip the scale rather towards specialized production from the first. However this may be, the change from Roman industrial production is complete and stands in contrast to the continuity found in northwest Europe.

Such scraps of evidence that we have suggest that industry was located within the settlements and was on a small scale until near the middle of the seventh century when more intensive production, combined with the use of a primitive form of potter's wheel, is found in the town of Ipswich (West 1963, pp. 233–303). How far change was general it is difficult to say, for in later times, when more evidence is available, there seems little correlation between the numbers of potters at work and the stage of technology reached and we have no means of knowing the ratio of the number of excavated kilns of early date to the original number working. By the end of the eleventh century excavation has indicated production on a considerable scale, with the new fast wheel confined for the most part to towns in southern and eastern England. Throughout the middle ages the quantity of waste material associated with a given kiln, as well as the number of kilns in any one settlement, varied greatly. There were hamlets where almost everyone was engaged in the craft; there were potters working singly or in groups in towns and in villages and others in wood or waste land clearings. Sometimes the evidence suggests seasonal work, sometimes continuous production (Le Patourel 1968). Often the industry continued in the same place for as long as two centuries. Towards the end of the period there are signs of concentration of industry in villages in the neighbourhood of large town markets, as with the Surrey potters of Cheam, Limpsfield or Kingston for London. The evidence is still too sporadic to do more than make the generalization that there is a continuous, but uneven, increase in the amount of pottery made. This is particularly clear in the later thirteenth century, for many excavated kilns produce pottery of no earlier date. The nature of archaeological reporting and the number of excavated kilns still unpublished allow of no quantitative assessment of the increase. By calling in other forms of evidence we can say that rudimentary organization existed as early as the eleventh century (Le Patourel 1968, pp. 103–8), but that, contrary to the continental situation, potters seldom, if ever, achieved guild status. After the mid-twelfth century the pot itself gives evidence of only two major phases of change—a proliferation of highly decorated and glazed jugs during the thirteenth century and signs of increased specialization early in the fifteenth century, some potters concentrating on coarse pot for kitchen use, especially in the north, others making standardized jugs for the town market, and others again, at the very end of the period, concentrating on the production of such specialized pots as Cistercian ware, which required new firing methods involving the use of protective saggers (Mayes and Pirie 1966, p. 261).

There is rather more to be learnt from a study of distribution patterns. Internal trade is governed by the high cost of transport in relation to the price of the article; transport could cost as much as 25 per cent or more in some cases (Le Patourel 1968, p. 120). In the thirteenth century coarse pot travelled little more than a radius of twenty miles from its place of origin—perhaps a day's carting. Contemporary decorated pot went considerably further (Jope 1963, p. 341), which could be taken to indicate either distribution by middlemen or the existence of permanent stores in the market towns, for both of which there is written evidence. This marks a considerable advance from the pagan Saxon period when decorated urns of the Illington/Lackford type have much the same distribution radius as that of medieval coarse pot (Myres 1969, p. 135). To the general pattern of sale in the immediate neighbourhood, Stamford ware, flourishing between the late ninth and the twelfth centuries, is an interesting exception. It is a specially fine pottery and the first in the country to be glazed. Its superior quality must have interested middlemen in the industry, for it is an occasional excavation find in most parts of England.

Distribution by sea was another matter. There is considerable evidence for trade along the east coast from the middle Saxon period onwards, an activity which has left few traces apart from pottery (Hurst 1957, pp. 29–42). Dunning has shown that imports from France followed the pattern of the medieval wine trade (Dunning 1968, pp. 51–4), with fine jugs imported from the Rouen area in the thirteenth century overlapping with jugs from the Saintonge that continued to arrive well into the fourteenth century. Such association of pottery with trade in a more valuable commodity raises the possibility that there may have been similar connections in earlier and less well-documented periods. E ware from western France found in Cornwall and countries bordering the Irish Sea (figure 6.2) would then be the tangible remainder of trade in less durable but more expensive commodities. Alternatively, since the west produced no good pottery of its own at this early date, E ware may itself have been regarded as a luxury article and well worth its cost of transport. Either explanation would also fit the Rhineland pots excavated in the Low Countries and from Baltic sites from the ninth century onwards (Altena 1969, pp. 129–33), though later in the middle ages the Rhineland exported its pots in complete shiploads (information from W. Janssen) especially to Scandinavia, whose own industry developed late.

Although no quantitive assessment can be made, it is clear that English imports throughout the period came principally from France and secondarily from the Low Countries, with occasional imports from more distant places. On occasion English pots are also found on the other side of the

Figure 6.2 Distribution of E ware round the Irish Sea. (*By kind permission of Professor C. Thomas.*)

Channel (Dunning 1968), but the interesting question of cross-Channel influences that this raises cannot be pursued here.

As evidence of a rising standard of living pottery has only a limited value since, as we have shown, it is difficult to assess its ratio to other materials in use. Two small indications, both indirect, may illustrate its partial abandonment in favour of the more expensive metal pots. In the fifth and sixth centuries there are pottery copies of lugged metal cooking pots (Thompson 1956, pp. 192–9). After this there is a gap in such copying, for what reason it is impossible to say at present. But from the late thirteenth century onwards there is a proliferation of such imitation. Jugs following precisely the lines of metal ewers are not infrequent (Rackham 1973, figure 65); Dunning has published copies of church cruets in pot (Dunning 1969, pp. 226–7); there are lobed cups, aquamaniles and cooking pots with sharp everted rims and angular handles, all with metal prototypes, testifying to the wide dissemination of the originals (figure 6.3). This seems to suggest a rising standard of living, with the poorer population copying the style of their betters, albeit in what was considered an inferior material. During the same period cooking pots tend to die out in the south and they are virtually unknown in the fifteenth century, replaced presumably by metal. In the north their numbers remain constant even on manor house sites—perhaps an indication of differing degrees of prosperity.

Pottery as evidence of social change

Within the later centuries of Roman rule there are changes in decoration and fabric that illuminate relationships between the various social groupings. Myres, using cemetery material, demonstrated the use of Romano-Saxon pottery in the late fourth century and there is evidence of similar forms in use as early as the second century. This was a conventional factory-made pottery with decoration modified to suit the taste of the Germanic settlers (Myres 1956, pp. 16–39). Its importance lies in the fact that there is little other evidence for settled family groups at such a time.

While such pottery demonstrates the presence of settled barbarians within the province, there are other groups illustrating changing relationships between predominantly Romanized groups and the comparatively untouched native settlements. One of a number of such developments is the hybridization of traditional iron age calcite-gritted fabric with elements of Roman factory-made pot. Huntcliffe ware, for example, a type of pot made late in the second century and throughout the third century, is found with the body moulded by hand but with Roman shapes and with the rims wheel-thrown in the Roman manner. Cunliffe at Portchester has found coarse pot imitating Roman wares from the third century onwards (Cunliffe 1970, pp. 67–85). These are examples of a sub-culture present to a greater or lesser degree in most parts of the country. They are a phenomenon quite distinct from the revival of Celtic fashions of decoration on sophisticated pottery like Castor ware or Celtic influence on fibulae and other artifacts, a fusion of Roman and native tradition at a much higher level.

Writing on pagan Saxon pottery, Myres has made two observations. First, that decoration in some cases has a magico-religious significance—such stamps as the swastika symbol of Thor, the rune symbolizing the god Tiw and the serpent appearing with some frequency on cremation urns, in its capacity as guardian (Myres 1969, pp. 137–40). Middle Saxon Ipswich potters adopted many of the decorations current in the pagan period but completely dropped the symbolic stamps, corroboration, if such were needed, of their correct interpretation. Such ritual use of decoration is not unknown in other periods. Wenham has brought to my notice three pots with applied slip in the shape of anvils, hammers and pincers, symbols of Vulcan. Much later there are medieval jugs with bold crosses applied below the lip. They were made at a number of excavated kilns, including those at Brandsby, Yorkshire and Toynton, Lincolnshire. Some found their way to religious houses like Fountains Abbey or the Templar site at Etton; others were probably regarded as protective symbols in a domestic context. Dunning has suggested a similar function for a group of fifteenth-century midland jugs with lettering on the handles, associating them particularly with protection against witchcraft (Dunning 1967, pp. 233–41). The general idea is constant; the deities change.

Myres also pointed out that there can have been no antagonism between groups in the pagan period practising cremation and those who buried their dead, for the Girton potter made both cremation urns and ancillary vessels for inhumations, using the same stamps for both (Myres 1969, p. 123). The general adoption of Christianity led to complete abandonment of funerary pottery in this country,

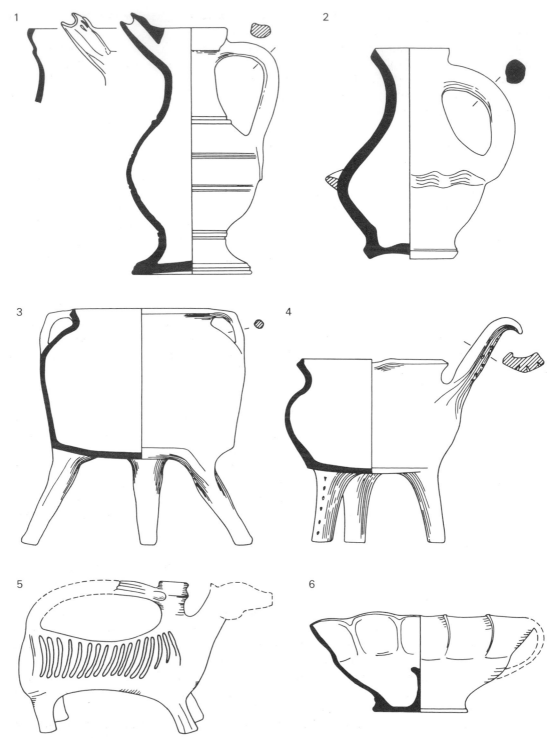

Figure 6.3   Medieval clay pots with metal prototypes.
1   Jug from Whitefriars Street, London (*published by courtesy of the London Museum*).
2   Church cruet, Upper Ettington, Warwickshire.
3   Pipkin from a kiln at Rye.
4   Cooking pot from Jewry Wall site, Leicester.
5   Zoomorphic aquamanile, Petergate excavations, York.
6   Lobed cup, Kirkstall Abbey excavations.
Scale ½ except no. 3 which is ¼ (*drawings of numbers 1–4 kindly supplied by G. C. Dunning*).

though not in Merovingian Gaul. Across the Channel, pots were in intermittent use as accessories to burials as late as the fourteenth century (Delmaire 1969, pp. 350–52).

It has already been shown that potters copied vessels in more expensive fabrics. This is evidence of a general downward spread of ideas through the various social strata. On a slightly different note, copying of exotic pottery is part of the same phenomenon. The process probably begins in the larger towns since there are imitations, for example, of Rouen jugs in thirteenth-century London and of the plainer type of Saintonge jug in York. But the process spread quickly to the country potters. At Cowick kiln, for example, there was part of a French lobed cup found along with the local imitation. There is no evidence to show the time-lag before such derived wares became incorporated into the local tradition. It is one of the means whereby decorative ideas in circulation among other craftsmen were diffused among the potters, who represented the lowest ranks in the craft hierarchy, and thence into the peasant home. It seems that the process was often complex, involving masons, tilers and metal-workers who incorporated gradually, sometimes through a number of intervening agencies, diverse strands such as the heraldic and armorial symbolism of the knightly class, the composite animals of the medieval bestiary and religious symbolism into a cadre of traditional and often functional ornament. The important point is that such decoration enriched the environment even of the peasant, for there are few excavated longhouses that have not produced one or more highly decorated jugs.

Pottery is intimately connected with the process of cooking and serving food and drink. We have discussed in other connections the difficulty of assessing the quantity of pot in relation to other materials in general use. There are however one or two significant changes in excavated material. Saxo-Norman cooking pots are small, modelled ultimately on the Roman *olla*. Their medieval successors, making their first appearance early in the eleventh century, though spreading only slowly to common use, are much larger. This looks like a change in cooking or feeding habits. By contrast the change from spouted pitchers of middle-Saxon and Saxo-Norman date to the lipped jugs of later years has more the appearance of a change in fashion. Jugs with a bung-hole an inch or so above the basal angle, which begin to appear in different parts of the country late in the thirteenth century, seem to indicate a drink with a sediment. It is tempting to suggest a change in methods of home-brewing, but this would be mere speculation. The disappearance of large storage jars, common from the ninth to the early thirteenth centuries, may represent the substitution of one type of container for another in a different material, since the necessity they served must surely have continued. As far as plates and cups were concerned change did not occur until the post-medieval period. Earlier they were normally in wood, or for the more wealthy, in base or precious metal, though towards the beginning of the fifteenth century there are small, lipless jugs that may have been in use for drinking, on the analogy of the sixteenth-century Rhenish pots that figure so largely in the paintings of Breughel.

There are other additions to the ceramic material which penetrated little below the seignorial class. We have seen purchase of pots for filling the bath at Methley. Large jugs that may well have served a similar function are relatively common finds in the later middle ages on manor house sites. Aqua-maniles (figure 6.3, number 6), tangible evidence of washing habits that figure in books of etiquette of the fifteenth century, are relatively unusual, while pottery urinals seem to spread from monastic communities into more general use only slightly earlier. The one domestic appliance that is found, and then in no great numbers, in association with peasant households, is the curfew or firecover. In England these are found occasionally from pre-Conquest times onwards, but they never achieved the popularity over here that they enjoyed on the continent, particularly in northern France and in the Low Countries, where they are excavated in quantity.

A change likely to reflect rising living standards, especially in the towns and among the land-holding class, is the increase in building accessories made by potters from the late thirteenth century onwards. These include glazed and often decorated ridge tiles, probably to cap thatch as well as tiled roofs, chimney pots, louvres and even drain pipes. There is little evidence that such improvements percolated through to the peasantry, though they are found on occasion in town excavations as well as those of manor houses or religious houses.

It ought to be possible, from ceramic evidence, to show the extent to which pottery differs, if at all, between monastic and secular establishments and between seignorial and peasant households. In Stamford, Mahany has observed a difference in quality between pottery from the castle and that from houses in the town, but in general material has not been presented in such a way as to make possible valid generalizations of this sort, though changes in recent reporting should soon modify the position.

A final point, postponed because it fits neatly into the problem neither of economic nor of social change, though it partakes of both, is the use of pottery scatter to locate the changing sites of early settlements. This type of field work was used successfully to locate Chalton in Hampshire, while in Norfolk, Wade-Martins has shown the value of a systematic approach on these lines. Such field work together with recent developments in methods of handling large groups of ceramic material will do much in the future to increase the evidential value of early pottery.

7

The Distinction between Land and Moveable Wealth in Anglo-Saxon England

T. M. Charles-Edwards

That the Anglo-Saxons made a distinction between land and moveable wealth is easy to prove: *fēoh* and *sceatt* stand for moveable wealth, or particular kinds of moveable wealth, whereas *land* has much the same range of meaning as in modern English. It is more difficult to answer the question as to what function this distinction had, in terms both of their view of their own society and also of social behaviour.

There are two stages in the answer which I shall propose. The first is to show the function of exchange in Anglo-Saxon society. Most of the evidence bears upon moveable wealth since exchange of moveables appears to have been the usual type of exchange, whereas exchange of land only occurred in a restricted range of relationships. The second stage is to show what marked off the relationships in which land changed hands from those in which only moveables were exchanged. At this point the early history of the charter, especially the evidence of Bede's letter to Egbert, becomes crucial. I shall concentrate on the early period, the seventh and eighth centuries, for early evidence provides the key to the problem.

The primary function of exchange of wealth, both land and moveables, was to maintain *frēondscipe*, 'friendship', 'alliance'.[1] The economic value of exchange was subordinate to this primary function. Because exchange of wealth maintained *frēondscipe* it was caught up in a sharply articulated system of values inherited from the pagan past. This system of values is explicit in Old English heroic poetry, but implicit in certain passages of Bede. The evidence, therefore, suggests that these values were part of the current social morality of early Anglo-Saxon England.

The basis of this system of values was a strong version of the principle of reciprocity. The honourable man was required to maintain and continue any exchange in which he participated, whether this exchange was in itself good or evil. Thus he was expected to answer injury with injury, benefit with benefit. These exchanges could not honourably be ended within the lifetime of the participants, but an exchange of injuries could, with difficulty, be converted into an exchange of benefits. The conversion was accomplished by different forms of compensation for injury followed by the initiation of an exchange of benefits. By contrast, it was not honourable to convert an exchange of benefits into an exchange of injuries.

These moral concepts were applicable to all active relationships: it was not thought possible that any active relationship could be merely neutral in value, and it was dishonourable to mix benefit and injury in one relationship. Consistency in love and hatred alike was the mark of the honourable man. Through these principles all relationships were assigned to two categories, those of *frēondscipe* and *fēondscipe* (*fǣhðu*), or friendship and hostility. Any man with whom one had dealings was either *frēond* or *fēond* (*gefā*).

Exchange of wealth, being an exchange of benefits, maintained *frēondscipe* and was subject to the principles of reciprocity and consistency. An example of the combination of exchange of wealth and

---

[1] I shall discuss the notions of *frēondscipe* and *fēondscipe* and their relationship to the Anglo-Saxon concept of freedom in an article to appear in *Past and Present*. The references to law-codes, which are all in Liebermann 1903–16, I, are given in conventional form.

other benefits into one process is provided by the ceremonies of betrothal and marriage. As far as can be seen, marriage, in the early Anglo-Saxon period, implied exchange of moveables but not of land. The marriage itself, as distinct from the betrothal, is called the *gyft*, the gift of the woman by her family to the bridegroom (Ine c. 31). This gift is a return for the gifts which he has given to the family, in particular to the man who, before the marriage, had *mund*, authority and the duty of protection, over her (Ine c. 31; Æthelberht c. 77). These gifts are described as *scæt* and *fēoh*, and therefore consist of moveables. They have been promised at the betrothal, for a woman is said to be *in scæt bewyddod*, in other words pledges have been given to guarantee the moveables which the bridegroom will give (Æthelberht c. 83). In exchange for this promise the man who has the *mund* over her is obliged to protect her virginity until the *gyft* since, if he is to give an unmarried girl, he should promise to give her as a virgin (it seems that the virginity of the bride may be covered by the term *unfacne*; Æthelbert, c. 77).

The exchange between her family and the man is the most obvious in the laws, but it is not the only exchange. At the *beweddung*, the betrothal, the bridegroom declares what he will give her if she 'choose his will', that is consent to his proposal of marriage. This is known only from a later Anglo-Saxon text (*Wifmannes Beweddung* c. 3), but it can be paralleled in the early Germanic lawcode which is most detailed on marriage, the Lombard *Edictus Rothari*, and may thus continue earlier practice.[2] If the parallel is correct then this gift is distinct from yet another present from the bridegroom to the bride given on the morning after the consummation of the marriage. This, the *morgengifu*, is a counter-gift for the bride's gift of her virginity (Liebermann 1903–16, II, part ii, s.v. *Morgengabe*). Again, whenever the early laws refer to the nature of these gifts they refer to moveables.

In the later text to which I have just referred, a short tract on betrothal dated by Liebermann to *c.* 970–*c.* 1060, there is one possible reference to a gift of land. The text speaks first of the prospective bridegroom's declaration of what he will give the girl as her portion if she should survive him. It goes on to say that if the betrothal proceedings have gone well then she is entitled to half, or if she has borne a child to him, the whole; but the two MSS differ on the word which follows *healfes*, 'of half' (*Wifmannes Beweddung* c. 4). One MS implies that the woman will be entitled to a half of his cattle, the other MS that she will be entitled to a half of his inheritance. The two words are *orfe* (cattle) and *yrfe* (inheritance). The disagreement is easily explicable on the following lines: *orfe* (cattle) represents the old law, now out of date as other evidence shows; *yrfe* (inheritance) is probably an up-dating since the *y* is written on an erasure, so that the MS may well have had *orfe* originally. *Yrfe* can refer to both land and moveables, but unless qualified by some such word as *cwic* (alive), or defined by the context, it seems to refer to land and to the moveable goods which went with the land. The reading *yrfe* implies, therefore, that a bridegroom could promise to leave land to his bride. Marriage was a process of gifts of moveables in the early Anglo-Saxon period, but might include gifts, or promises of gifts, of land in the late Anglo-Saxon period.

The relationship between lord and vassal included all types of exchange of benefits—gifts of services, of moveable wealth and of land. It was the internal relationship among these exchanges which defined the relative positions and functions of lord and vassal. This can best be shown by an account of evidence which suggests the existence of a typical career for the seventh- and early eighth-century English nobleman. This career-pattern is dictated by the linking together of marriage, a grant of land and retirement from full-time service at court at the age of twenty-five or thereabouts. Bede's *Historia Abbatum* begins with an account of Benedict Biscop's early life and conversion to the religious life (Plummer 1896, I, pp. 364–5). This took place when he was about twenty-five; previously he had been Oswiu's thegn. His conversion implied the renunciation of a gift of land from Oswiu, the renunciation of any gift he might receive as a member of Oswiu's *comitatus* and the renunciation of marriage and

---

[2] The *meta* or *metfio*; see the references on pp. 224 and 225 of *Leges Langobardorum*, 643–866, edited by F. Beyerle, 2nd edition (Witzenhausen, 1962).

home. Guthlac, according to his biographer Felix, was a member of the Mercian royal family, and was able to lead his own *comitatus* until, at the age of twenty-five, he renounced the riches of this world and its glory to become a *famulus Christi* (Colgrave 1956, caps. I–II (descent), XVI (leads *comitatus*), XVIII–XIX (renunciation)). This implied the renunciation of family, home and of his *comites*.

On the face of it, it looks as though the mid-twenties may have been a period in which a nobleman was likely to change his form of life in such a way as to make this age one for decision between a secular and a religious life. The ordinary nobleman has been a thegn, and a man of royal blood may have been the leader of a *comitatus*, but both must decide whether to marry and settle down upon an estate or to pursue a religious vocation.

The same pattern may perhaps be implied elsewhere. It appears that noblemen might attach themselves to the service of a foreign king as thegns, *ministri*.[3] Such mobility seems more likely when the nobleman was still unattached to land or wife. The *comites*, who appear in the lives of St Cuthbert as the chief men in villages or small areas, with halls, lands and local influence, can hardly have been in a position to seek fame in other kingdoms. In the poetry, Beowulf, the Geat, acquires fame in the service of Hrothgar, king of the Danes, while still a young man. When he returns home he gives presents which he has received from Hrothgar to his own king, Hygelac, whereupon Hygelac gives him an heirloom and a great estate of seven thousand hides (Beowulf, ll. 2152–99). His reputation is now established; he is a veteran warrior, and if he had married he would doubtless have done so at this point. This pattern might extend to poets: Widsith is portrayed as winning reputation and gifts abroad, and then returning to his own king to give presents and receive land in the same way as Beowulf (Widsith, ll. 88–98).

There is a distinction in *Beowulf* between the *geoguð* and the *duguð*. Sometimes these words are used as abstract nouns, *geoguð* as modern English 'youth' ('youth' is derived from *geoguð*), and *duguð* for tried military experience; but they are also used as collective nouns for particular groups within the *comitatus*, *geoguð* for the young retainers, *duguð* for the veterans (Whitelock 1951, pp. 89–91). In Bede's Latin there are possible equivalents. He says that the sons of Aethelfrith—Eanfrith, Oswald and Oswiu—went into their enforced exile during Edwin's reign *cum magna nobilium iuuentute* (*Hist. Eccl.*, III, c. 1). *Iuuentus* is best explained as a Latin equivalent for *geoguð*. In his letter to Egbert, in the passage denouncing the bogus monasteries, he argues that so many such establishments have been set up that there is not enough land for 'the sons of noblemen or veteran soldiers' to receive estates (Plummer 1896, p. 415). These sons are, therefore, unable to marry at home, and often compelled to leave Northumbria to look for land and home elsewhere. The *filii nobilium aut emeritorum militum* are probably to be identified with the *iuuentus* or *geoguð* without, as yet, wife or land, and thus potentially mobile (Whitelock 1951, p. 89). It may be that *emeriti milites* is Bede's word for the *duguð*, the group of veterans within the *comitatus*.[4]

If these suggestions are correct then it is possible to compare Bede on Benedict Biscop's conversion

[3] Bede, *Historia Ecclesiastica*, III, c. 14 (edited by Plummer, pp. 155–6): p. 155, Oswine is impressive in appearance, cultivated in manners and generous; p. 156, hence even the noblest come *ad eius ministerium de cunctis prope prouinciis*.

[4] The aristocratic status of the *miles* is clear in Book iv, c. xx/xxii of the *Historia Ecclesiastica* (edited by Plummer, p. 250) where *miles* appears to mean member of a *comitatus*, and *militia* (p. 249) to mean the *comitatus* itself. Similarly, Oswald's *milites* baptized among the Irish in *HE* iii, c. 3 belong to the *magna nobilium iuuentus* of *HE* iii, c. 1. It is as a member of the *comitatus* that Imma might bear the feud. Cf. *comitibus ac militibus*, Book iii, c. 21 (edited by Plummer, p. 170). This does not imply that Bede assumed that only *milites* in this sense ever fought. Imma, pretending not to be a *miles*, claimed to be (1) a *rusticus*, (2) a *pauper*, (3) *uxoreo uinculo conligatus*, and to have come (4) *propter uictum militibus adferendum in expeditionem*. Eric John's arguments in *Orbis Britanniae* (Leicester, 1966), pp. 136–7, depend upon the idea that Bede assumed that (4) followed automatically from (1), and followed without any need to take into consideration (2) and (3). For this there is no evidence. Bede sometimes seems to suggest a distinction between *milites* and *auxiliarii*: in *HE* iii, c. 14 Oswine has a large and distinguished *comitatus*, but Oswiu more *auxiliarii* and thus a more powerful army; in *HE* iii, c. 24 both Penda's *milites* and his *auxilarii* are killed, *perditis militibus siue auxiliariis*. *Auxiliarii* may consist of the *comitatus* of allied kings and *duces*, but may also have consisted of *ceorlas* and even mercenaries (cf. Beowulf, ll. 2493–6).

to the religious life, Felix on Guthlac's conversion and *Beowulf* and *Widsith* on their respective heroes' landed endowment with the more detailed material in Bede's letter to Egbert. From such a comparison, there emerges a picture of change in the eighth century, not merely the extension of the use of the charter, but the undermining of an old career-pattern. One of Bede's assumptions in the letter to Egbert is that, at least for the majority, a royal grant of land is necessary in order to be able to get married. If the *filii nobilium aut emeritorum militum* are aged about twenty-five, they may well have living fathers. Inheritance of hall and land normally only occurred on the death of the father, and yet it seems that possession of hall and land was a prerequisite for marriage. Furthermore, the royal grant was an occasion for the king to honour achievement as a *magoþegn* (young thegn), one of the *geoguð*. The grant which Benedict Biscop was to receive from Oswiu was to have been of 'land appropriate to his rank'. He came of a noble kindred, but this was not necessarily enough since nobility had to be sustained through deeds deserving prestige and honour (Beowulf, ll. 2183–9). Inherited status lost much of its value if not matched by status acquired through service of kings or, for a prince like Guthlac, leadership of a *comitatus*.[5] If inherited nobility is sustained by acquired reputation, then royal generosity will both reward fame and match nobility. Though Bede is primarily thinking of inherited rank when he says that the *possessio terrae* given by Oswiu to Benedict Biscop was *suo gradui competens*, this does not exclude the possibility that such grants might be merited.

If the royal grant came at the turning-point in a nobleman's career, rewarding fame, sustaining rank, permitting marriage, making him a landed *comes*, and so translating him from *geoguð* to *duguð*, then it is necessary to ask what the king received in exchange for his grant. His gift, like any other, looked for a return. As the pivot of the beneficiary's career, it required a particularly generous return.

The principal point about such gifts of land is that they were not answered by a gift of land but by a gift of service. The gift of land is made once for all: there is no repetition of the gift. The grant is probably not hereditary, but it is lifelong unless the recipient fails in his duty to serve his lord.[6] On the other hand, the gift of service is open-ended and indefinite: the vassal can never claim that his services have now answered the gift of land and that no further service is due. The contrast between the completed gift of land and the incomplete gift of service is the basis of the superiority of lord over vassal. The vassal is always in debt to his lord.

The transformation of such grants of land into heritable estates undermined both the landed wealth of the Northumbrian kings in the eighth century and the internal balance of the exchange between lord and vassal. This is not to say that land was not inherited before the transformation of bookland from land held *ecclesiastico (monastico) iure* and thus *haereditario iure* to land held by secular nobles but still by hereditary right. The use of the charter in favour, first of founders of bogus monasteries and then of openly secular nobles certainly transferred land from royal ownership to that of the nobility; but there is no evidence to show that all land held by the nobility had previously been held only during the tenant's lifetime or for a number of lives. On the contrary, the assumption made by Bede is that sons will divide the inheritance of their father between them, though the eldest son will receive something over and above what the other sons obtain—probably the paternal home.[7] The natural

---

[5] Colgrave, 1956, c. xvi, shows that Guthlac was *lofgeorn*, 'eager for fame', stimulated by the heroic traditions embodied in poetry.

[6] To this extent I agree with Eric John's argument in his *Land Tenure in Early England* (Leicester, 1960), pp. 44–5.

[7] Bede, *Historia Abbatum*, c. 11 (edited by Plummer, pp. 375–6). *Partienda hereditas* is equivalent to OE *yrfe (ierfe)*: cf. *Maxims I*, ll. 79–80, *yrfe gedæled deades monnes*. I cannot accept Eric John's explanation of Felix's *Life of Guthlac*, c. xxvi (edited by Colgrave, p. 90) in *Land Tenure*, p. 62. The *supradictus locus* which is the *paternae hereditatis habitaculum* is Crowland, i.e. the island and not specifically the hermitage which he only builds in the next chapter. Only the latter could be equated with a homestead. I therefore cannot accept Eric John's thesis that before the extension of bookland only moveables and the homestead could be inherited and so be described as *yrfe* or *hereditas*. For the paternal home see Ine c. 38 (edited by Liebermann, pp. 104–6). *Frumstol*, however, is not necessarily restricted to house as opposed to land: the *ethelstol* of *Genesis A*, l. 1129, becomes the *yrfe* of l. 1144, the *eðel* of l. 1159, *land and yrfe* l. 1167, *land*, ll. 1180, 1196, *yrfe*, l. 1218, etc.

interpretation of the evidence seems to be that the typical noble acquired land at two different moments in his career and from two different sources. He acquired land by grant from the king, perhaps in his mid-twenties, and this land was not hereditary. He acquired land by inheritance from his father, or occasionally from a more distant kinsman, and he would expect to leave this land to his sons.[8]

If this is correct, then it is worth asking the further question whether inheritance of land, like the receipt of a royal grant of land, was seen as part of an exchange. It is certainly true that *frēond* may refer to a kinsman, but was inheritance part of an exchange expressing and sustaining *frēondscipe* between kinsmen? The question is a difficult one for, to show that such inheritance was subject to the same rules as gifts, it would be necessary to pick out counter-benefits given by the heir because he was the heir, and not just because he was the son or other close relative of the previous owner of the land. For example, it would be necessary to show that it was the principle of reciprocity that required the son to submit to the authority of his father; or that it was the same principle which, in the pagan period, required the son to be generous with grave-goods for his father or, in the Christian period, to confirm and maintain his ancestors' gifts to churches in return for prayers for the salvation of their souls. I do not think that it is possible to find evidence that it was the principle of reciprocity in exchange which dictated such acts of piety. On the contrary, it looks as though a different principle is relevant, that of the continuity of a family's interests. Beowulf sails to help Hrothgar partly to achieve personal fame, but also to repay Hrothgar for the latter's goodness to Beowulf's father, Ecgtheow in healing a feud on his behalf (Beowulf, ll. 456–72). Similarly, Beowulf inherited the feud of previous kings of the Geats against the Swedish kings, just as seventh-century Bernician kings inherited the family's feuds against the Deiran and Mercian royal kindreds. It is nowhere suggested that a man must maintain his father's friendships and feuds because he has received an inheritance from his father; rather, the friendships and feuds appear to be part of the inheritance. Inheritance of land, therefore, appears to be quite distinct from the receipt of a grant of land. Father and son are too close for their relationship to be seen as one of exchange. This is not true of husband and wife. Marriage is an alliance of kindreds; it does not fuse them.

It is, therefore, wrong to compare inheritance with exchange of moveables, for inheritance belongs to a different category. What can be compared is the grant of land. The only type of grant so far discussed is the gift of land by a king to a nobleman for the latter's lifetime; but land was granted to peasants as well as to nobles and by nobles as well as by the king.

The most instructive early evidence on the nature and implication of grants of land to peasants is provided by chapter 67 of Ine's laws. It is not entirely easy to interpret. It states the following rule: if a man agrees to accept a yardland or more at a fixed rent and ploughs it, then, if the lord requests both rent and work from him, he need not comply with the request unless the lord gives him his dwelling; he does, however, lose the land. On the face of it, this rule is about the conditions which obtain before a lord can compel a tenant to do work for his land as well as pay rent. If the tenant has received both land and home from the lord, he has no option but to accede to his lord's wish to demand work as well as rent. It is not just that he must comply with the demand or lose the land—that is true in any case—but he has not even the option of leaving land and home. For if he had the option of leaving land and home then his case would be precisely the same as that of the man who has received only land: accept new conditions or give up whatever has been given.

There is another possible interpretation. One of the difficulties in interpreting Ine 67 is the phrase *gif he him nan botl ne selð* ('if he does not give him [the tenant] a dwelling'). The problem is to know whether the author of the rule understood the gift of the *botl*, the dwelling, to have occurred before the

---

[8] If one assumes either (*a*) that the royal grant of land is usually earlier than the acquisition of inherited land, or (*b*) that the two together were required to sustain inherited status and so permit a marriage which did not disparage the bridegroom, this will account for the marital difficulties of Bede's *filii nobilium aut emeritorum militum* in c. 11 of the *Letter to Egbert*.

lord raised the issue of work or only in exchange for the tenant's agreement to the new conditions. If it was only in exchange for the tenant's agreement, one might interpret the rule as implying that to secure new conditions requiring both work and rent the lord had to offer a home as well as the land. This offer could be refused though the tenant would then lose the land.

There are arguments for both interpretations. The verb *selð* is in the present indicative and this might be taken as implying that the gift of the dwelling would only take place when the tenant agreed to work as well as pay rent. But timeless present tenses are common in legal material so this proves nothing. A more interesting argument derives from the context in which the rule appears. Using the rubrics it is as follows:

> CVII (63) Be gesiðcundes monnes fære. 'Concerning a nobleman's journey'.
> CVIII (64) Be þon þe hæfð xx hida londes. 'Concerning the man who has 20 hides of land.
> CVIII (65) Be x hidum. 'Concerning 10 hides'.
> CX (66) Be iii hidum. 'Concerning 3 hides'.
> CXI (67) Be gyrde londes. 'Concerning a yardland'.
> CXII (68) Be gesiðcundes monnes dræfe of londe. 'Concerning the driving of a nobleman from his land'.

63–6 undoubtedly form a group: 63 states which people may be taken by a nobleman when he moves from an estate; 64–6 state what he must leave behind him in terms of a proportion of the estate left with its complement of men, animals and other equipment.[9] Thus the rubric for 63 is in fact the title of the group and not specifically of 63 itself, for unlike the rubrics of 64–6 it does not define the contents of its rule in relation to the other rules of the group. There is no corresponding group of rules attached to 68—only a single decree—but it appears that it is none the less parallel to 63: in the one it is a question of a nobleman's voluntary departure, in the other of his compulsory departure. But if 68 is linked to 63 through parallelism, and 64–6 are linked to 63 through subordination, then it looks as though 67 should also be linked to 63.

The rubrics suggest one connection: 64–6, all subordinate to 63, deal in turn with decreasing areas of land, twenty hides, ten hides, three hides. Then we have 67 for which the rubric is 'Concerning a virgate of land.' Despite this, the text shows that there is a break between 66 and 67. 64–6 all begin with the relative construction, 'He who . . ', a mark of subordination. 67, on the other hand, like 63 and 68, consists of a conditional clause, the commonest construction for independent rules in the early laws. Though the rubrics might suggest that 67 is merely one more particular sub-case continuing the series 64–6, an analysis of the syntax shows that this is not so.

A different line of approach is to compare the main preoccupations of the different rules. 63–6 are all concerned with a nobleman's voluntary departure from the land. 63 states who may go with him, 64–6 what must be left behind. 68 is concerned with a nobleman's involuntary departure (*Be . . . dræfe* as opposed to *Be . . . fære*). One might, therefore, expect 67 to be about voluntary departure from the land, but in this case the departure of a tenant of lower status rather than of a lord, and departure from a smaller unit of land (one yardland or more). This expectation is, I think, justifiable. 67 ends *7 þolie þara æcra*, (and let him forfeit the arable). This forfeiture is the consequence of a decision on the part of the tenant not to accept the new terms demanded by the lord, namely that he should perform labour-dues as well as pay rent. He thus departs through his own decision.

---

[9] For the distinction between demesne and tenanted land implied, see T. H. Aston, 'The Origins of the Manor in England', *Trans. Roy. Hist. Soc.* 5th series, VIII (1958), pp. 65 ff. In line 68 *botl* appears to refer to the demesne, just as later 'hall' may refer to the building or the demesne as a whole. There seem to be no good grounds for distinguishing between *seo seten* in 68 and *gesett land* in 64 and 65. The distinction between *sittan* and its causative *settan* disappears in the past participle. For *seo seten* derived from the past participle *seten*, cf. the cpds. *hondseten* and *landseten* (also feminine).

The next step is to analyse more closely that part of 67 which states the tenant's freedom. It goes as follows:

ne þearf he him onfon, gif he him nan botl ne selð, 7 þolie þara aecra.

he [the tenant] need not receive it [the land], if he [the lord] gives no dwelling to him, and let him forfeit the arable.

In the first clause *him* refers to the land which is to be 'raised to work and rent'. It is evident that the voluntary departure of the tenant presupposes that the lord has not given a dwelling to the tenant, for his freedom depends upon that condition. If the argument from the present indicative tense of *selð* is then pressed it only leads to a greater accentuation of the lord's power, for it would mean that the lord can compel the tenant to accept the land on the new conditions if he gives a dwelling to the tenant when he proposes the new conditions. It is a necessary corollary of this interpretation that the tenant is obliged to accept the dwelling. The argument for this position derives partly from the general context analysed above, and partly from the syntax. From 63–6 the lawgiver is interested in the nobleman's capacity to leave an estate and the limitations upon that capacity. In 67 he is interested in a peasant's capacity to leave his holding and the limitations upon that capacity. The peasant may leave the land, refusing the new conditions. The limitations upon this freedom are stated in the clause *gif he him nan botl ne selð* which may be translated 'provided that he [the lord] gives no dwelling to him'. The correctness of the translation of *gif* by 'provided that', rather than just 'if', depends upon the case for regarding the clause as a statement of a limitation upon the peasant's freedom. Given the position of the clause in the sentence, and given the context in which 67 appears, this case seems secure. Since the clause limits the peasant's freedom, it follows that if the offer of the dwelling is contemporaneous with the demand for new conditions, the dwelling cannot be refused. Otherwise the limitation would have no effect. The dwelling can only be refused if we assume that it would have been given as part of the original agreement, before the lord made the demand for new conditions of tenure.

If, however, one interprets *selð* as a timeless present tense of the type common in the laws, then one may attribute the gift of the dwelling to the original agreement (*geþingad* is clearly a timeless present indicative), and thus give the lord the ultimate power to compel acceptance of the land on the new terms only if the tenant originally accepted a dwelling, and give the tenant the ability to refuse and so depart provided that he had not previously accepted the dwelling. This interpretation would also allow the tenant the right to refuse the dwelling, though only by refusing to accept the original agreement. If one also makes a further plausible assumption that the whole question of new conditions of tenancy comes up at the end of some fixed period during which the tenancy has run without alteration of the terms, then we have made the strongest case possible for the liberty of the tenant. This case implies a radical distinction between a tenancy of land and home on the one hand and a tenancy of only land on the other. By living in a home provided by the lord the tenant renounces the right to depart from land or lord, and gives the lord the power to choose whether to demand only rent or both labour and rent. It is the acceptance of a home which lies at the root of villeinage, not the acceptance of land. It is not, of course, clear that this villeinage is of precisely the same type as the villeinage of the thirteenth century, for there is nothing to show that the children succeeded to the status of the father unless they too accepted both home and land from the lord. Nevertheless, it is probable that here lies the root of medieval English villeinage.

When considering the nature of early royal grants to the nobility I argued that the relationship between the completed gift of land and the incomplete counter-gift of service implied the subordination of grantee to grantor. The debt could never be said to be fully discharged for there was no standard by which the value of a nobleman's services could be compared with the value of the land which he had received. It is not clear that the same conclusion applies to grants of land to peasants, for rent could be compared in value to land. It is therefore possible that lords and peasants often agreed upon a tenancy of land to last for a fixed period which was less than a life. After a fixed period, the debt could be acknowledged to have been discharged. It is also entirely possible that noblemen as well as commoners accepted such tenancies.

The radical distinction between tenancies of land and tenancies of land and home implies that the gift of a home was of a different order of value from the gift of land, at least when the recipient was a peasant. The important of the *botl*, the dwelling, is perhaps in part a consequence of the nature of the *ceorl*'s status. The word *ceorl* means both 'husband' and 'commoner'. The word may be used with both meanings simultaneously present (Charles-Edwards 1972, p. 10). He is the head of a household and has *mund* over his house and the people within it. The association of house and family is a close one. It is therefore arguable that the lord's grant of a dwelling was different from a grant of land in that it affected the deepest roots of his social status. It may be that the *ceorl* was, at a very early period, the holder of a hide of land, the land of one family, and that his status depended upon the extent of his land, but none the less dependence on the lord for his home was a deeper dependence than that implied by the gift of land.

The home was probably not so important to the nobleman for two reasons. First, his status was not associated with the home in the same way. Secondly, though the grant of land enabled him to get married, and may therefore have included a hall, he had the prospect of succeeding to his paternal estates by inheritance. There is no such association of grants of land to peasants with a particular age as we find with grants to noblemen.

These conclusions about the nature of grants of land show the nature of the distinction between land and moveable wealth in early Anglo-Saxon England. Land was given to subordinate the recipient as well as to benefit him. Indeed the subordination occurred precisely because of the value of the grant. Grants of land to noblemen secured their lifelong service, attached them firmly to the king. Typically, so it seems, such grants permitted marriage, rewarded fame acquired as a member of the *geoguð*, and translated the recipient into the ranks of the *duguð*. Land granted to peasants may, at first sight paradoxically, not have subordinated them so effectively to their lords. Such grants might be for a relatively short period, and the debt created by the grant might be discharged by the rent. Grants of a home to peasants, however, were completely effective in subordinating them for life to their lords. The latter could demand rent alone or rent and labour as it suited them, and thus achieve a balanced and tolerably flexible workforce for their demesnes.

Gifts of moveable wealth had a much wider function than gifts of land. All types of friendship, whether between equals or unequals, were expressed and sustained by exchange of moveable wealth, just as they were expressed and sustained by exchange of services. Gifts of land also sustained friendship, but they were used for friendship between unequals. Moreover gifts of land operated only in one direction, in the sense that they were not answered by counter-gifts of land, but rather by services and renders of moveable wealth. Gifts of land operated only vertically and downwards, from lords to subordinates. In this they were not wholly unlike inheritance which similarly moved land in one direction only. Gifts of moveable wealth were again more flexible: they operated in all social directions. The distinction between the social functions of land and moveables in early Anglo-Saxon England consisted therefore in the limited use of gifts of land and their power of subordination.

8

Evidence for Settlement Study: Domesday Book

S. P. J. Harvey

This chapter has two parts. The first discusses the effect of the administrative bias of Domesday Book on its use for settlement study, and is indeed a warning of limitations in the use of Domesday data. The second part airs a suggestion that a class of Domesday information might afford one clue to the dynamics of settlement.

Domesday Book and settlement study

Administrative structures determine the places named in Domesday Book, as well as the number of settlements included under those place-names.

The surviving Domesday texts have long epitomized the several stages of collecting and sorting information which were necessary in order to complete the Domesday inquiry. But it has been argued only recently that embodied in the returns are documents of an earlier date, documents which were constructed before the Domesday inquiry for a more limited purpose. These earlier records provided the skeletal framework of the survey (Harvey 1971). I will come soon to the consequences for settlement study of the use of these other and earlier records in Domesday Book, but first to a brief outline of their nature and how they come to be there.

The government of late Anglo-Saxon England and early Anglo-Norman England used lists of lords, hundreds, place-names and liability in hides (Douglas 1944, pp. 80–81; Hoyt 1962, pp. 189–202; DB I, 299–302a). During the reign of William I devastations of land and the eventual recovery of some of it necessitated changes in the number of hides at which some counties and their constituent hundreds and settlements were rated. Northamptonshire is one county where we have clear evidence that such adjustments took place. So, in some counties, the lists of holdings and hides were updated, in some they were replaced, and in some they continued in use unchanged. Then, towards the close of William I's reign, the Domesday survey was set afoot. The method was to use the existing lists of estates, hundred and hides as a basic index of estates and, according to such lists, which varied in date, tenants-in-chief were required to furnish details on assets and values.

Several biases, which affect the use of Domesday Book as settlement evidence, follow from this procedure. First, and most obviously, the units of land-holding are included because of their tenurial and administrative significance, especially their significance in fiscal and hundredal organization, not because they have reached any particular size or economic importance. In some cases, in some whole counties—Huntingdonshire, Lincolnshire, Nottinghamshire, Derbyshire—the separate record of a place will not even reflect its significance at the time of Domesday Book, but rather twenty or more years earlier. In these cases the holdings and their assessments originate from King Edward's day. Other units, particularly manors which are heads of hundreds, and which have remained in royal hands, include many settlements which are physically and economically distinct. Bromsgrove in Worcestershire falls clearly into this category; its heading subsumes many different units up to fifteen miles away which are here named; elsewhere we are not so fortunate. So many eleventh-century settlements may be treated anonymously by Domesday Book with their vital statistics lumped together with their head of hundred. We have to expect this because of the character of the source.

Other biases of the evidence on settlements are the result of the administrative origins of Domesday Book. The survey attempts a country-wide uniformity and in some respects succeeds only too well, but it is dependent on regional administrative structures. Circuits of adjacent counties with common characteristics of notation have long been distinguished. Thus, at one and the same time, local distinctions within regions are blurred but comparisons between regions are made hazardous because either the classification and terminology of details differ, or the details themselves are very different.

A major example of how Domesday can slant its evidence on settlement population distribution in a regional way is volume II itself, the unabbreviated version for the eastern counties. Domesday evidence shows that these counties are the most populous in England. The freer tenures there permitted numerous autonomous small holders and they appear in volume II enumerated separately with their holdings and their geld liability. And so, one of the most plausible reasons advanced for the unabbreviated state of this volume is the complexity of the counties it covers. Details of the village of Coddenham in Suffolk, for example, are dealt with in no less than thirty-three entries; Bungay is described in more than a score of entries and sub-entries, and it is not unique. The sort of administrative structure which carefully reproduces these details derives from the society of the region itself, so that the interaction of the two is likely to over-sharpen the characteristic regional distinctions of East Anglia. Just because smallholders of land here had a direct and recorded responsibility for taxation (from $\frac{1}{2}d.$ upwards) they are more meticulously recorded than elsewhere—than, say, for the west, where lords of large manors seem to be the responsible units. We know from evidence from Burton abbey that the Domesday survey for Staffordshire can be cavalier about recording the rent-paying smallholders on some of the abbey's estates. Their presence at some places is only represented in the number of ploughlands (Walmsley 1968, pp. 73–80). As I would argue that the ploughland figure, the ambiguous *terra est x carrucis*, represents an attempt by the survey to provide a new fiscal rating, the omission becomes perfectly comprehensible, if most frustrating for the student of settlement. If the structure of Domesday Book is based on a platform of fiscal lists, it is more likely to include the small freeholder in the eastern regions where the vill and its freer population seems to be the fiscal entity, and to be less scrupulous about small freeholders in the west where the estate is the responsible unit and where the liability is contained within some other Domesday item.

Again, the boroughs of eastern England stand prominent as the largest, and we know of adequate reasons for this in the eleventh century and later. But we should remember, when drawing comparisons, that the Domesday version for the eastern counties is the unabbreviated volume II, and notice the enumeration therein of large numbers of 'poor men' and smallholders, classes of people well below the status and tax-paying ability of burgesses who are frequently the only town inhabitants recorded in the abbreviated Domesday volume I. In volume II, Norwich has 480 bordars who 'paid no customary dues on account of poverty', as well as 665 English burgesses. Ipswich had 100 'poor burgesses' as well as those that could pay their dues. At Dunwich, 178 'poor men' are recorded (DB II, 116b, 290a, 311b); York, unusually for volume I of Domesday Book, does include details of houses (DB I, 298a). On the other hand, several county towns of the western part of the country include only burgesses or burgages. Shrewsbury had possibly 151 tax-paying burgages in 1086 (Darby and Terrett, 1971, p. 153). Yet work on population and settlement size has unusually, and quite unwarrantedly, assumed that Domesday's 'burgesses' covered most urban heads of households. That Domesday is consistent with other sources in calling men of some substance or qualification 'burgess' is upheld by the high level of charges, of *firma*, that the Shrewsbury burgesses had to pay, which at £40 for the year before the survey would average out at over 5 shillings per head (DB I, 252a). Domesday's haphazard regard for the borough data is borne out further by the survival of a Domesday-like account of two boroughs of the west Midlands of within a decade or so of Domesday which shows 141 burgesses in Winchcombe, while Domesday records 29 burgesses; the survey shows 614 burgesses in Gloucester, while Domesday, only through the description of rural manors confesses to a mere 81 burgesses (incorrectly in Ellis 1833 II, pp. 446–7 and Darby and Terrett 1971, pp. 44–5), and a further 38 houses. This is not to impugn Domesday figures in general, for it was not the intention to survey the boroughs in the same way as the land, as the lack of any mention of boroughs in the terms of reference surviving in the Inquest of Ely shows; so it did not matter greatly if the borough information included was unsystematic. The different provenance of the boroughs is clear in the lay-out of Domesday Book; and the accounts of London, Winchester, and to all intents and purposes, Bristol, were never copied in. Again, this means that the contrast between the eastern part of the country and elsewhere is exaggerated.

In conclusion, we must be wary of comparing unlike Domesday figures for population sizes, and face the likelihood that settlements in the central and western part of the country were somewhat more numerous and more populous than a straight reading of Domesday figures will allow. Though the structure of Domesday Book reflects the bases of regional administration, this reflection may also sharpen, if not distort, the regional difference in the composition of the populations.

The bordars

This section concerns the Domesday personnel called 'bordars' (*bordarii*). They demand some attention from a student of Domesday Book if only because the name itself is almost a Domesday term in English history, unused before Domesday as far as I know, relatively little used afterwards, and eventually dropped. But within the great survey they are not a class which can be ignored.

The hypothesis which I should like to put forward is that the presence of bordars in large numbers is a mark of population and agricultural expansion; and that in many cases the presence of bordars is not just a symptom of expansion. They are its personnel: a class of people, perhaps formerly servile, who dwell in cottages on the edge of the existing village and its fields, who have taken in a few acres of land from the waste, common, or woodland, to form a smallholding.

To go briefly into the question of the name and its connotations, two main terms are used in Domesday Book for what appears to be basically the same class of person—'cottar' and 'bordar'. Cottar is the English term which can easily be brought up to date as 'cottager'. There is evidence in Domesday for the terms being used as parallel ones. Only in some counties are both used, for instance, Middlesex, where cottars tend to average less land than the bordars, less than three acres, whereas bordars there have commonly five, ten or fifteen acres (Lennard 1959, pp. 342–3). The distinction between the bordar and cottar class and that of the villeins would seem to be that the villeins have holdings which are recognized and integral parts of the vill and its arable land; the cottars and bordars are subordinate or peripheral to them. The two classes are caught accurately in Robert of Hereford's description of the Domesday inquiry which sought information on 'those dwelling in cottages', and 'those who have houses and holdings in the arable fields'.

What is the etymology of the word *bordarius*? One implication is well known: from *borde* (French, feminine) = hut, cabin, particularly a wooden hut, which makes 'bordar' a good parallel term for 'cottar'. (There is also a connotation taken up by one or two historians that the sense could be a wooden board, denoting a class of *famuli* which ate food provided by the lord, but this interpretation does not seem to fit well with the cottar alternative.) I would suggest that there is a second and indeed associate meaning with the French *borde* (feminine) = edge. These people have cottages on the margins of the village and its fields, often in the woods or waste and associated with a small assart.

Many dictionaries give the two words a totally separate history, but at the same time give them both an identical Teutonic ancestry in neuter plurals which turn eventually into French feminine singular. The two words are often given as

borda = a wooden cabin,
borda = the wooden planks of a ship,
        the edge of a ship,
        the edge.

Some technical dictionaries, however, say that they are cognate, and I cannot help but think that this is so. I would suggest that both connotations are often implied in the Domesday use of the term. One eighteenth-century dictionary, Trévaux, states that a *bordier* had lands *au bord des chemins*, which was certainly one of the few places a cottager of the modern period could branch out on his own. Vinogradoff has an interesting cross-reference which upholds the 'edge of cultivation' idea. In talking of the position of the bordar class, he refers to the European *Kötter* and to the *Brinksitzer* = the dweller on a grassy hill or grassy edge (Vinogradoff 1908, pp. 282, 457–60). The considerable study which has been made of the *Kötter* class in Germany is now easily accessible in A. Mayhew, *Rural Settlement and Farming in Germany*, and shows all the elements put forward here associated with the smallholder class. They are associated with population rise, with cottages, or with grants of land on common and waste. Even those who develop and prosper have proportionately less arable than the established husbandmen of the village. Sometimes the new class squatted on what they could find; sometimes they sold their labour or engaged in a handicraft (Mayhew 1973, pp. 19, 22, 123–9).

With the argument that *borde* has the connotation of edge of cultivation as well as cottage made of wood (and you will observe that the two are by no means mutually exclusive, and are indeed complementary), let us turn back to the evidence of Domesday Book. The Domesday 'bordar' seems to cover smallholders in several types of tenurial and economic situation. Of those in a rural context, two types are perhaps symptoms of past population and agricultural growth, and a third type is the likely and direct agent of expansion.

Some bordars represent the eleventh-century version of the twelfth-century *famuli* and work considerably on the lord's demesne. Clear examples of this function are the twenty-seven bordars who provided services for the central court of Evesham abbey, *servientes curiae*, but who also had four ploughs of their own, and the bordars of Tewkesbury who lived and presumably worked around the court, *circa aulam manebant* (DB I, 175b, 163a). This type will account for some of the bordars grouped with slaves, *servi*, on the demesne sector of a manor. Their presence is symptomatic of an organized demesne agriculture with a non-servile labour force who could also supply secondary services, like that of carpenter (as in the case of one cottar at Burton abbey a couple of decades later).

More numerous than the bordars attached to the demesne are those listed after the tenantry of an estate. Domesday Book sublty differentiates them from the villeins. The villeins 'have' or 'hold' their lands; the bordars are usually 'with' the villeins and seem sometimes to be appendent to them. At Brant Broughton in Lincolnshire, there are '26 villeins and 9 bordars, 15 sokemen and another 11 bordars'. Occasionally the villeins have bordars 'under them'. At Bury St Edmunds bordars were attached both to demesne officials and to other men: '13 reeves who supervised the lands' had '5 bordars under them', 118 men with 52 bordars 'under them', the 32 knights had 22 bordars 'under them' (DB I, 347b; DB II 372a). Such bordars I regard as either the work force of the villeins and freemen or their undersettlers or smaller undertenants which even the thirteenth-century manorial surveys tend to conceal by virtue of their concern with the virgate holdings. Like the thirteenth-century undersettlers, these bordars could be regarded as symptomatic of population expansion and intense cultivation.

A third role for the Domesday bordar is one of active expansion. It may be that this is the role from which the class derives its name and so should be regarded as primary. Two characteristics of Domesday bordars happily fit the thesis that they signify active expansion: one is that some appear in the west and southwest, paying a small, uneven amount of rent which looks neither old nor customary. They look in this role rather akin to the rent-paying and expansionist *hospites* who also feature in these counties. The second characteristic is that these bordars especially, and bordars generally as a class, are associated with forest, with grazing rights, but not with ploughs. In Cornwall, several of the smaller units which have no ploughs on them have no villeins either, just bordars. One solitary and prosperous-looking bordar at *Trevilla* (*Victoria County History, Cornwall* II, p. 99) has five acres of woodland and sixty acres of pasture. Du Cange's single reference to bordar land, *borderia terrae*, includes the information that they are *in foresta*. If we think back to the *famulus* bordar, the roles of swineherd, beekeeper, and even smith, which we know some of them held, are totally compatible with a dwelling in or at the edge of woodland. Lennard has even suggested that large round numbers of bordars may be the result of the lord's conscious policy of settlement and assart (Lennard 1951, p. 371).

The distribution of the heavily 'bordared' counties and the relatively lightly endowed counties upholds a thesis that the bordars indicate either fullish population levels or active expansion and woodland associations, or both. The proportion of county populations classed as bordars ranges between 15 per cent and 50 per cent, so there are marked variations. Nor is the major difference simply east/west or north/south as in much Domesday data. Those counties with a very high proportion of bordars, say over 40 per cent, are Hampshire, Berkshire, Dorset, Cornwall, Essex, Cambridgeshire and Worcestershire. To this 'high' category may be added those counties which number more bordars than villeins, Norfolk and Suffolk (with Cornwall, Worcestershire, Essex and Hampshire again of this number). In Hertfordshire, Wiltshire and Cambridgeshire, bordars and cottars together outnumber villeins. We know already from Little Domesday volume II, that East Anglia and Essex were the most heavily populated parts of England and there are many instances of their population rising over the Conquest period. Hampshire, Worcestershire and Cornwall are, of course, forest and pasture counties *par excellence*, though one would not rate them as wealthy, developed areas.

Of the counties with the low bordar count, particularly low are Lincolnshire, the North and East Riding of Yorkshire, Rutland and Huntingdon. Good reasons explain this situation in some cases. Large parts of Yorkshire had been devastated in the eleventh century. Thus opportunity was provided, and Domesday evidence suggests it was taken up, for men of the smaller and more fringe holdings to move to larger peasant holdings on more amenable soils (Bishop 1948). As for Lincolnshire, it was populated quite extensively with nearly 11,000 sokemen, many of whom, in size of holding at least, may parallel the bordar class elsewhere. However, an inexplicably low count of bordars in counties or localities may signify lack of expansion in settlement and cultivation in the decades preceding Domesday Book.

The ideas here need further working out both in relation to smaller geographical regions, and in relation to well-documented sites. Other Domesday measures should be taken into account for settlement studies; obviously the values in 1066 and 1086 may be indicators of expansion over the Conquest period. My aim here is merely to offer some food for thought for people who are particularly concerned with the distribution and dynamics of medieval settlements.

9

The Evidence of Place-Names I

Margaret Gelling

There are two main aspects to this subject: firstly, what deductions can be made about the racial composition of the population in an area where the place-names are in more than one language? Secondly, can a chronological sequence be observed in place-names in an area where they are mainly in the English language?

The appearance in a country of a number of people speaking a different language from the tongues already in use there does not always result in a major replacement of the stock of place-names. When place-names do appear in the new language, the number may be very small or very large. In England we had a late Conquest—that of the French-speaking Normans in 1066—which is so well documented that we can form a clear idea of the number of people involved, of the social status enjoyed by the newcomers, and of their relationship to the business of getting a living from the land. Our sources for English place-name study become abundant shortly after this, and we have rich contemporary material enabling us to identify new French place-names and to study the effects of French speech on long-established English place-names. My first suggestion is that we should use the effects of the Norman Conquest as a control in attempts to estimate from place-name evidence the nature of earlier conquests/ invasions/infiltrations, for which we do not have comparable historical documentation. Where there is abundant place-name material available for study it should be possible to estimate whether earlier population movements were comparable to the Norman Conquest or were of a totally different nature.

The first point to be noted is that French place-names are rare in England, the total in most counties being about half a dozen. It is an event to find a French settlement-name in the Domesday survey, though there are a few, such as Bray (Berkshire) and Kirmond (Lincolnshire). Most of our French place-names are recorded at a later date than 1086, and a high proportion of them are of the stereotyped kind represented by Bewley, Beaufort, Beaudesert, Beaumont, Beauchief, Beauvoir, Beamish, and the contrasting Malpas. French field-names, though not unknown, are probably the rarest type of field-name. Though they did not establish a large number of new place-names, the French-speaking newcomers did have a widespread influence on the forms of English names, many of which they found difficult to pronounce. To give a few examples, it was French pronunciation which caused *Knock* to become Cannock, *Snotingham* to become Nottingham and *Dunholm* to become Durham, and which produced such pairs as Salop/Shrewsbury and Sarum/Salisbury. Also, the Normans' feudal relationship to some English estates is commemorated by the affixing of their family-names to English or Norse place-names, such as Stoke Poges and Ashby de la Zouch.

We know of three conquests of all or part of the British Isles before 1066 (leaving aside the prehistoric population movements for which there is only archaeological evidence). These are the Roman conquest in the mid-first century AD, the coming of the Anglo-Saxons after the Roman period, and the various Norse settlements—Danish in the east, Norwegian in the northwest—in the period 865–950. These are only partly historical, and we are dependent on place-names and archaeology for an evaluation of their nature.

As regards the place-name evidence, the effect of the Roman conquest was not dissimilar to that of the Norman Conquest, in that only a small number of new place-names appears to have been coined in the language of the invaders. A fair number of place-names are recorded from Roman Britain, the total probably being between 350 and 400. Some of these are obscure (as *Alauna, Cunetio, Venta*); but a high proportion of them can be confidently ascribed to the language known as British, which is the ancestor of modern Welsh (a few instances are *Abone* (river), *Camboduno* (fort by the river-bend), *Condate* (confluence), *Letocetum* (grey wood), *Mediolano* (central plain)). British was the language spoken by the people of most of Britain at the time of the Roman conquest. The new rulers of the province spoke Latin, and the interesting point is that among the place-names recorded from Roman Britain there are very few in Latin, perhaps fewer than twenty-five certain examples. Only a tiny handful of Latin names have survived until today—Aust Gloucestershire (not recorded in Romano-British sources, but almost certainly Latin), Catterick (Cumberland), Speen (Berkshire), the second element of Lincoln. The sources from which we derive knowledge of the place-names in use in Roman Britain might be expected to exaggerate, rather than diminish, the proportion of Latin to British, and the scarcity of Latin names is a significant factor, which may be compared with the small number of names coined in the Norman French tongue after 1066. The evidence from Roman Britain, like that from Norman England, suggests that when a new language is spoken mainly by the governing class it does not cause a transformation of the place-names; the old stock of names, which is in the language of the people who cultivate the land, continues to be used, and is subject to drastic alteration only if the new rulers have difficulty with the pronunciation.

One of the few certainties about the coming of the English to Britain is that it resulted in a wholesale transformation of place-names from British to Old English in that part of the country which became England. (It resulted eventually in the new language being universally spoken, but this article is only concerned with the place-name evidence.) We cannot know how many names which appear from their earliest recorded spellings to be Old English are in fact renderings of earlier Celtic toponyms. York can be seen as a warning against ignoring this possibility. The British name of the town was *Eburācon* (the yew grove), which had developed to *Evorōg* when it became familiar to Germanic mercenaries in the Roman army. It was eventually replaced by *Eoforwīc*, which could be translated 'boar farm' if it were Old English, and if we had not known the British name from classical sources we might have accepted *Eoforwīc* as a newly coined Old English name. On the other hand, we know of many Celtic names which were not treated in this fashion but were faithfully adopted by the English (as Dover, Wendover, Malvern, the first part of Lichfield), so there is a great deal of evidence to show that substitution of a Germanic name bearing a general resemblance to the sound of the Celtic one was not a general procedure. It does not seem likely that many English names could have arisen in that way, as most of them make better sense than would be expected from such a process. But even if more Old English names than have been allowed for are in fact translations or adaptations of British names, the Anglicization of the place-name stock, whether by adaptation or new coinage, is in striking contrast to the earlier failure of Latin and the later failure of Norman French to have a similar effect. French speakers did alter the forms of Old English names, but not so as to make them meaningful in French, only to make them pronounceable. From this, two points seem to emerge. One is that there must have been a considerable number of English-speaking settlers; the other is that many of the people speaking the new language were peasant farmers. Attempts to represent the Anglo-Saxons as a small aristocracy break down in the face of the place-name evidence.

The same criteria may be applied to the Scandinavian invasions and settlements in various parts of Britain in the ninth to eleventh centuries. If an area has a dense layer of Norse place-names, and if some of these are field-names, then it is necessary to conclude that in that area there were a lot of Norse-speaking settlers who were wresting a living from the land with their own hands. An attempt has been made by the present writer (Gelling 1970; 1971) to demonstrate that the place-names

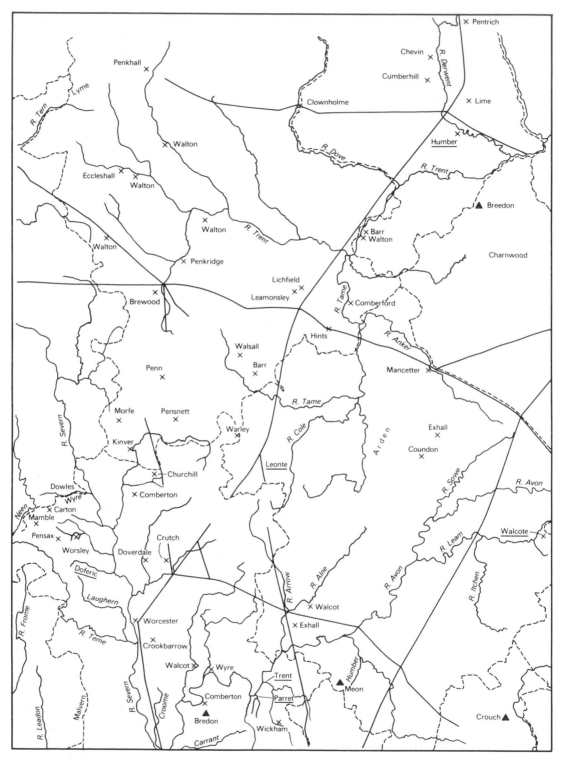

Figure 9.1 Map of the Birmingham region, showing place-names which may indicate the presence of Welsh-speaking people after the English settlement.

recorded in the Isle of Man in the twelfth to fourteenth centuries are so predominantly Norse that it is probable that the island was wholly Norse-speaking for a time. A similar case (Oftedal 1962) has been presented for the Isle of Lewis, though there it has to be based on surviving place-names rather than on those in early records. There is no doubt about the overwhelmingly Norse nature of the place-names of Orkney. The importance of Norse field-names in medieval records from parts of England subject to Norwegian and Danish settlement has been emphasized by F. T. Wainwright (Wainwright 1945; 1945–6) and recently by K. Cameron (Cameron 1973).

If, therefore, we consider the Anglicization of the place-name stock in this country as part of a sequence of evidence which extends from the Roman to the Norman conquests, we may suggest that there is a consistent relationship between the degree of transformation of the place-names and the numbers and social status of the people speaking a new language. To bring about a change of language in most of the place-names, the number of the newcomers must be relatively high and the social status of the majority of them relatively low.

This insistence that only a large number of Anglo-Saxon peasant settlers could have caused the Anglicization of our place-names (and only a large number of Norse-speaking farmers could have produced a similar effect in Man, Lewis, Orkney and parts of eastern England) does not lessen the interest and importance of those pre-English place-names which did survive in England, and this is the next topic to be considered. The identification of Celtic (and pre-Celtic) place-names is one of the most important tasks of English place-name studies, but it is also one of the most difficult. The scholars to whom the work of the English Place-Name Society is entrusted are necessarily specialists in Old English and Old Norse, the languages of the vast majority of our place-names, and this means that they are not well-equipped to identify or interpret Celtic names.

The bible of this field of study is K. H. Jackson's *Language and History in Early Britain* (Jackson 1953). This book sets out all the available evidence for the exact form which British words and names would have had at the supposed period of the Anglo-Saxon settlement, and shows how the sounds of the British language were accommodated in Old English. No one would claim that this is an easy book to use; but in fact even a person untrained in the Celtic languages can, with patience and determination, learn from it what he needs to know in order to avoid gross error in the identification of British place-names which were passed on to English speakers. To take one example: claims have recently been made that the place called *Badon* which was the site of the battle of *Mons Badonicus*, fought c. 500, may be identified with Bath. L. Alcock (1971, pp. 70–71) bases this identification on the fact that -*d*- in *Badon* would have been pronounced -*th*- c. 500; but on p. 558 of *Language and History* Jackson demonstrates, in a paragraph which is not difficult for the non-specialist to understand, that this lenited *d* of the British language was represented by *d* in Old English, so the pseudo-phonological basis of Alcock's argument is invalidated. Scholars wishing to engage in the study of pre-English place-names must look up each consonant and vowel of the name they are discussing in Jackson's book and ascertain whether the sound-development they wish to postulate is in accordance with the evidence set out there; they will find that the book is not as difficult as it looks.

Language and History is not, of course, a comprehensive guide to the pre-English place-names of England. There are a great many names certainly or probably belonging in this category which are recorded too late to fall within the body of evidence examined there. Anyone wishing to assemble the material for studying Celtic survival in a region has to consult a number of reference books of very varying quality in this respect. Professor Jackson is now vetting the county surveys of the English Place-Name Society while they are in preparation, so that recent and forthcoming surveys should be sound in their lists of names likely to be of pre-English origin. The pre-war county surveys, on the other hand, are very unreliable in this respect, and E. Ekwall's *Oxford Dictionary of English Place-Names* must be used with great caution. In spite of these difficulties and dangers, it is highly desirable that attempts should be made to identify pre-English names in all areas, and to draw maps which make it possible to study their distribution and their relationship to other types of place-name and to archaeological remains from the Roman and early Anglo-Saxon periods. Jackson provided only one distribution map, showing rivers which have British names. This class of evidence is much more common in the west than in the east, and Jackson divided the country from east to west into areas I–IV, most of England falling into areas I and II, where the survival of such river-names is very much the exception.

The importance of our stock of pre-English place-names is such that it merits more detailed mapping than this. One of A. H. Smith's maps (Smith 1956a) shows a great deal of relevant material in addition to the British river-names. This is one of the most interesting place-name distribution maps to have been printed, but the scale is so tiny and the printing so poor that the student is liable to give up in despair after trying to decide which place-names are represented by the symbols. In this field my suggestion is that students wishing to examine the significance of these names in any area should compile relatively large-scale maps on which the names considered to be relevant should be written in full. If such maps are to be published, they should be accompanied by a list of the names stated by some reference books to be Celtic which it has been decided not to include on the map, and reasons should be given for each omission. The map included here (figure 19.1), which is of a region with Birmingham at its centre, has been published (Gelling 1974c) with a detailed commentary on the names shown in the Warwickshire section, which occupies most of the southeast quarter. It would take up too much space to reproduce that discussion here, or to discuss the evidence presented on the map for Worcestershire, south Staffordshire and parts of Shropshire, Derbyshire and Leicestershire. Two general points, however, may be made about the distribution pattern.

First, it is not a simple matter of the material increasing from east to west. The names show a tendency to cluster, and there are some marked anomalies in the general broad pattern. The part of Shropshire shown on the west central portion of this map is blank, apart from the name Neen. If the map were continued to the west, it would be clear that Shropshire, apart from its western fringe, does not contain as many of these names as might have been expected, and as has been loosely assumed by previous authorities. Cannock and Lizard in Staffordshire have been assigned to a Celtic origin in reference books, but the grounds for this proved, on investigation, to be unsound, and these names have been omitted from the map. They were probably assumed to be Celtic because they were in an area where Celtic names were expected, and similarly some names in east Shropshire, such as Ercall and Ewdness, have been assumed to be Celtic though they are more easily explained as English. After these adjustments, the distribution pattern shows clusters of Celtic names and of English names referring to Celtic-speaking people in some areas, such as southeast and northwest Worcestershire, and blank areas which, besides occurring where they were expected, as in Warwickshire, are also to be found on the western side of the map, in Shropshire.

Elsewhere in England it is possible to point to anomalies in the distribution of the types of place-name which suggest Anglo-Saxon cognisance of pre-English institutions and people of Celtic stock. There is a cluster of such names southwest of London—Penge, which is a wholly Celtic name; Caterham, which probably has a Celtic first element; Croydon, which refers to a plant of Roman introduction by a name adopted from Latin; Addiscombe, which has a Latin loan-word as second element; Wickham, which may have been coined before the end of the Roman period; Walworth, Wallington and Walton, which probably refer to Welsh-speaking people; and Chertsey, the western outlier of the group, which has a Celtic personal name as first element. This tendency to cluster, and to be present in some areas where they would not be expected and absent from others where they would have seemed appropriate, are characteristics of these names which have not been sufficiently stressed. Such local anomalies may be of considerable interest to the regional historian, though they do not, of course, invalidate the broader distribution pattern brought out by Jackson's map of river-names. It can be seen from the list of names southwest of London that I am suggesting that the same kind of historical significance may be attached to some names containing loan-words from Latin as belongs to those which contain Celtic words or personal names. The evidence relating to place-names from Old English *wīchām* and those containing *camp* has been set out in Gelling 1967 and 1976. Croydon is discussed in Gelling, Nicolaisen and Richards, *The Names of Towns and Cities in Britain* (1970). For the names in *eccles* which are shown on figure 9.1, see Cameron 1968.

My second general point about detailed distribution maps of the type represented by figure 19.1 is that the categories of names represented there may sometimes show an interesting correlation with the Romano-British archaeology of the area. In particular, in an area where surviving pre-English names are very rare, special significance may sometimes be claimed for an isolated specimen, especially if it is the name of a comparatively insignificant stream surviving in an area where otherwise only some of the major rivers keep their ancient names. If it is accepted that the first element of Coundon (Warwickshire) is the Celtic river-name *Cunetiu*, then this survival may be connected with the exploitation of the adjacent part of Warwickshire by Romano-British industry (Gelling 1974c, p. 62). In Oxfordshire it has been suggested that the survival into Anglo-Saxon times of the pre-English name *yccen* for a small stream north of Witney is part of the complex evidence for late Roman and post-Roman activity at the Shakenoak villa-site (Gelling 1972). The evidence of Celtic place-names and of English names containing Latin loan-words in Berkshire has been examined in detail in Gelling 1976 (pp. 801–7), and has been considered to show a definite correlation with Romano-British archaeological remains.

The second main aspect of my subject is the chronology of the great mass of place-names in the English language, many of which, on purely linguistic grounds, could have been coined at any time from the first coming of the Anglo-Saxons to the years following the Norman Conquest. In the last decade important new work has been published on several aspects of this subject. About 1960 a number of place-name specialists began to feel dissatisfied with the assumptions of the preceding generation of toponymists about the nature of the 'earliest' English place-names. These were considered to be:

1 Names in which the suffixes *-ingas* and *-ingahām* were added to a man's name, giving place-names like Reading, Hastings, Gillingham, Wokingham. These compounds, which mean 'the followers of Rēad (or Hæsta)' and 'the homestead of the followers of Gylla (or Wocca)' were supposed to represent, in the case of the *-ingas*-names, the first land-takings of bands of immigrant Anglo-Saxons and, in the case of the *-ingahām* names, the immediate second stage of the settlement. This hypothesis, first questioned in print in Gelling 1962, was examined in detail in Dodgson 1966, and has now been abandoned by the specialists, though it is proving difficult to dislodge from the beliefs of interested general readers (Gelling 1974a).

2 Names which refer to the sites of pagan religious worship or to Germanic gods. This category has been re-examined (Gelling 1961 and 1973), and found to need fairly drastic pruning. It is now suggested that the distribution pattern indicates a date of coinage near the end of the pagan period, and that places with this type of name are those where the pagan religion lingered longest, rather than those where it was earliest or most strongly established.

3 Names containing personal names or words which there is evidence for considering 'archaic', i.e. only current in the Old English language during the earliest years of the Anglo-Saxon presence in this country. For instance, the use of a small number of archaic words was considered in the introduction to *The Place-Names of Cambridgeshire* (English Place-Name Society XIX, p. xviii) to compensate for the scarcity of *-ingas*, *-ingahām* names in the county, and some surprisingly concrete assertions were made on the basis of supposed lines of place-names containing related archaic personal names: in *The Place-Names of Buckinghamshire* (English Place-Name Society II, pp. xiv–xv) it was suggested that the occurrence of *Hygerēd* in Harlington Middlesex and *Hycga*

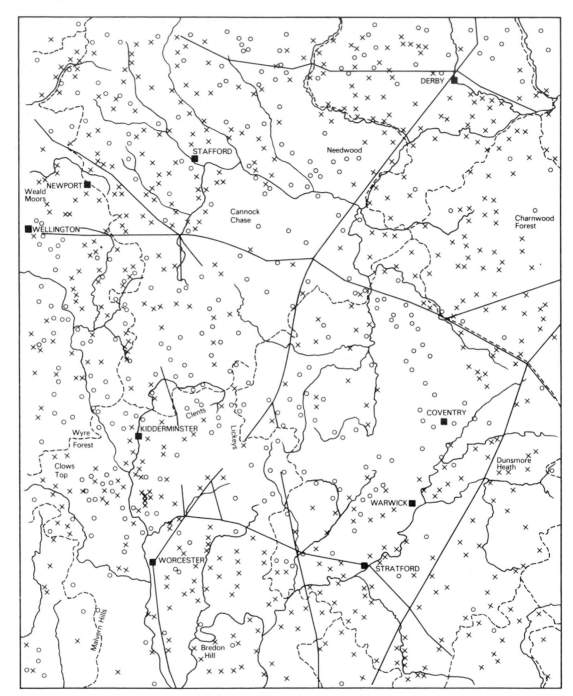

Figure 9.2 Place-names in *tūn* and *lēah* in the Birmingham region. X = *tūn*, O = *lēah*.

in Hitcham, Hedgerley and Hughenden in south Buckinghamshire showed that there was an original connection between the two regions, and that 'the southern slopes of the Chilterns were colonized from the early settlements on the Thames bank, of which Hitcham, OE *Hycgan ham*, is one.' As regards the argument from 'archaic' words, allowance should probably be made for the use of a more conservative vocabulary in the countryside than in the centres from which our written records come. Every county of which a detailed place-name survey is made produces additions to the known vocabulary of Old English, and it would be useful to have a fresh survey of this aspect of place-name studies; but it is doubtful whether such rare words need indicate a very early date for the place-names in which they occur. As regards the argument from personal names, this is only valid if the personal names are assumed to be those of very early settlers, so that Hygerēd and Hycga are the founding fathers of the villages of Harlington and Hitcham, or at least the Saxon leaders who took them from the British. The difficult problem of the significance of the personal names which are the first elements of a great number of English compound place-names is discussed in detail in Gelling 1976 (pp. 822–9). It is suggested there that the possibility of all or most of such personal names being those of manorial overlords, that is king's thegns or their dependent womenfolk (some of whom can be shown to have lived as late as the tenth and eleventh centuries), is sufficiently strong to render it unwise to use the personal names as evidence for the first coming of English-speaking people to a region.

Most of the names which fall into the three categories listed above are relatively early. The pagan names were probably coined between AD 600 and AD 700; Dodgson 1966 (p. 19) suggests that 'the -*ingas* place-name seems to be the result of a social development contemporary with a colonizing process later than, but soon after, the immigration-settlement that is recorded in the early pagan burials'; and a king's thegn with an archaic personal name is more likely to be an estate owner of the sixth or seventh century than of the later Anglo-Saxon period. But there is no reason to believe that any of the place-names in these categories are the best guides to the process by which English-speaking settlers first made their homes in an area.

Apart from the failure to stand up to detailed examination of these assumptions about the 'earliest' English place-names, there was a fault in the attitude which picked out the exceptional names for this sort of attention. The main characteristic of the English place-names in this country is their abundance and, if sound historical conclusions are to be drawn from them, some of these conclusions should be based on patterns discernible in the mass of material. Such patterns have not always been systematically looked for. The reference in the introduction to *The Place-Names of Nottinghamshire* (Gover, Mawer and Stenton 1940, XVII, p. xiv) to 'the neutral character of the local place-names', and my own statement in the introduction to *The Place-Names of Oxfordshire* (Gelling 1953–4, XXIII, p. xxii) that 'the great majority of Oxfordshire place-names . . . are not in any way remarkable', show the blinkered approach which prevailed till quite recently.

In an attempt to discern significant patterns in the general mass of place-name material the main tool must be distribution maps. The subject of place-name distribution maps is under discussion at the moment. The maps supplied with part two of *The Place-Names of Berkshire* (Gelling 1973–6) break some new ground, but it is probable that future surveys will improve on these. Perhaps the most important innovation attempted for Berkshire is the mapping of all settlement-names of topographical meaning. It has become customary to recognize two broad categories of settlement-names: the habitative, which contain a word for a settlement such as *hām*, *tūn*, *wīc*, *stoc*, *worð*, *cot*, and the topographical, which describe the site of the settlement but contain no word for a building. There has been a general assumption that the habitative are likely to be 'earlier' than the topographical type, and the latter have not been systematically mapped or their distribution studied in relation to the general pattern of settlement. Some topographical place-name elements, such as *feld* and *lēah*, have been mapped as evidence for woodland, and others, *scēat* and *ceart* in Surrey, for example, were mapped because of their peculiarly limited distribution; but some of the more important topographical terms which occur as the final element in settlement-names, such as *ford*, *ēg*, *dūn*, were not shown on distribution maps, nor were settlement-names derived from rivers. This has been a serious omission, as it is clear that at any rate in some areas settlement-names of topographical meaning have a better claim to be the primary English place-names than those which contain a word for a farm or village; this is especially so with names transferred to a settlement from a river. It has been possible in Berkshire (Gelling 1976) to point to some topographical terms which are used in English names for land-units which were long-established when the change to the English language occurred, and to others, particularly *lēah*, *feld* and *hyrst*, which refer to settlements in assarts made during the Anglo-Saxon period.

Methods of perceiving significant patterns in the general mass of place-name material have not yet been perfected, and one of my main aims in the present article is to suggest that there is much scope for experiment with distribution maps, and that this work is suitable for students who have not had the philological training required for the work of place-name etymology. Figures 9.2 and 9.3 are experimental maps, and are presented here more as suggestions for possible methods than for their significance for the history of the Birmingham region.

The map in figure 9.2 is based on the idea that if two contrasting types of place-name element predominate heavily over all others in a given area, it may be useful to plot these two elements on the same map, to study their distribution in relation to each other, and to see if there are parts of the area in which, in spite of their general predominance, neither is represented. This map has been discussed in two articles (Gelling 1974b, 1974c), and only a very brief summary of those can be offered here. The map shows that there is a very high degree of separation between the two elements, and that clusters of names in *lēah* (as opposed to occasional isolated specimens) have a close correlation with areas known to have been forested in the early middle ages, such as Arden, Needwood, Wyre and Feckenham. Similar conditions may be presumed in the Black Country and in the Ironbridge region of Shropshire, which are also marked on this map by clusters of names in -ley. The other element, *tūn*, is hardly used at all in forest areas, with the single exception of an area of Worcestershire, northwest of Worcester.

The second point to emerge from figure 19.2 is that not all parts of the region shown are characterized by one or other of these two place-name types. Leaving aside regions which are still not settled (such as Cannock Chase, Wyre Forest, Dunsmore Heath), the areas which are blank on this map can be divided into two main categories, those of very early and those of very late English settlement. There is one area where English-named estates are known to have been flourishing at a relatively early date, and several where settlement is known to have been very late, in one case after the Norman Conquest.

The area which is largely blank on this map but where English-named estates were flourishing at the time of the earliest records (see the Worcestershire section of Finberg 1961) is that of the lower Avon, from Evesham to the junction with the Severn at Tewkesbury. The major place-names in this area are mainly topographical, including several in *hamm* (here 'land in a river-bend'), Pershore (the most northerly example in England of *ōra*, 'river-bank'), several names in *ford*, and some 'one-off' names like Ripple and Lench. The probability is that these names were coined before the fashion for using *tūn* for settlements in open country had become prevalent.

The most obvious of several areas which are virtually blank on this map and in which some of the settlement is known to have been as late as the early Norman period is the one which stretches from the south to the east of Birmingham (Birmingham is the central point on the map); this is bounded by the river Blythe on its northern and western edge, and extends from Tanworth through Balsall and Meriden to Whitacre. The parish-names of this belt are, from south to north, Tanworth, Packwood, Knowle, Balsall, Berkswell, Meriden, Packington (a rather isolated *tūn* name which can be seen on the eastern bank of the Blythe in figure 9.2), Maxstoke, Shustoke, Whitacre. More than half of these are topographical names, and since topographical names predominate also in the lower Avon region, it may be that this is a characteristic both of areas of very early English penetration, and of those where settlement is exceptionally late. Between these two extremes lies a long period in which the prevailing fashion was for names in -ton and -ley. Detailed study of topographical settlement-names in areas of both early and late settlement might show a marked difference in vocabulary between the two. Certainly there is very little overlap between the elements used in major place-names in the Vale of Evesham and those used in the southern part of the Forest of Arden, these being the two regions discussed above.

Figure 9.3 is another experiment, this time in the extension of the methods recently developed for estimating the chronology of settlement-names in the Danelaw. The pioneer work of K. Cameron in this field (Cameron 1965; 1970; 1971), now supported by that of Gillian Fellows Jensen (Fellows Jensen 1972), is of fundamental importance, not only for the history of Danish settlement in eastern England but also, by implication, for the study of place-name chronology elsewhere. Figure 9.3, like figures 9.1 and 9.2, has been discussed in detail elsewhere (Gelling 1974c), and only a brief summary of the conclusions drawn from it can be attempted here. The method of study is that of relating types of settlement-name to the drift geology of the area in which they occur. Figure 9.3 is based on Ordnance Survey geological map sheet 169; ideally the study requires more detailed maps, but the OS map was judged adequate for the purpose of this experiment. The area shown includes part of the Danelaw boundary, which ran for a brief period along Watling Street. The crossing of Watling Street and the Fosse Way, some ten miles northeast of Coventry, is near the centre of figure 9.3, and there is a substantial overlap between this and the eastern edge of figure 9.2.

It has been established that in areas such as this, where there is a great deal of clay, with slightly raised patches of sand and gravel and belts of alluvium along the streams, the preferred sites for villages will be on the islands of sand and gravel rather than on the clay. It is probably safe to say that most of the villages on figure 9.3 are sited so as to avoid the clay. There is a similar avoidance of the larger areas of sand and gravel, probably because the soil in the central parts of these is poor, but the medium-sized sand and gravel patches are very heavily settled and several of the very small ones have a settlement also.

An attempt to establish some general relationships between types of settlement-name and sites of villages led to the following conclusions. First, most of the wholly or partly Scandinavian names (underlined on the map) have either 'second-best' sites like those of Wibtoft and Bittesby, at the very edge of the sand and gravel patch in which the English-named villages of Claybrook Magna and Parva are situated, or they are out on the boulder clay like Primethorpe and Ashby. The exceptions are Kirby and Copston. Kirby (or Kirkby) is a relatively common name in areas subject to Danish or Norwegian settlement; it means 'church village', and in a number of instances in the Danelaw, as here in Warwickshire, it differs from the general run of Scandinavian place-names in referring to a settlement as well-sited as the English-named villages. Probably the name is a replacement of an English one. Copston is an example of the so-called Grimston hybrids, in which English *tūn* is combined with a Danish personal name, and it has been observed by Cameron and Fellows Jensen that (with the exception of most examples of Grimston) these names belong to villages with 'good' sites, indistinguishable from those with wholly English names. Probably many of the Danes referred to in these hybrid place-names had a temporary manorial overlordship of a long-established land unit, and the place-names arose in the same way as some of the 'x's *tun*' names outside the Danelaw (Gelling 1976, pp. 822–9).

Among the English place-names on figure 9.3, the one which has the most demonstrable claim to be early is Higham, one of the place-names in *hām* discussed by B. Cox in an important recent article (Cox 1973). Otherwise, the 'good' sites are occupied in roughly equal proportions by villages with habitative names in *tūn* (Burton, Bulkington, Ryton, Shilton, Stretton) or *worth* (Frolesworth), and by

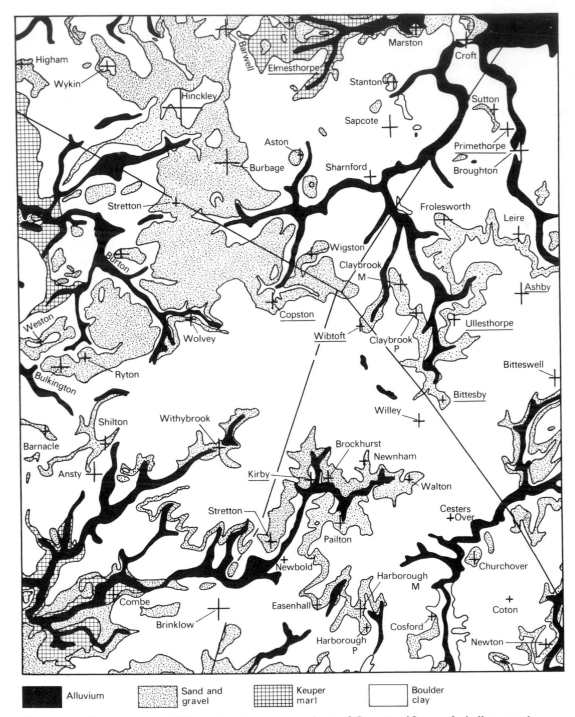

Figure 9.3 Place-names and drift geology in an area northeast of Coventry. Names of wholly or partly Scandinavian origin are underlined.

villages with topographical names, such as Brockhurst, Burbage, Claybrook, Combe, Easenhall, Harborough. Both types of settlement-name are well-represented among settlements which were apparently able to make an early choice of sites on sand and gravel spreads. In most instances, this choice would be made long before the coming of the Anglo-Saxons, and most of the English names for these settlements will be replacements of earlier Celtic names. The Danish names on the map, however, apart from Kirby and Copston, seem more likely to be ninth or tenth century coinages for new settlements on less desirable sites, not so likely to have been inhabited from prehistoric times.

Perhaps the most interesting point to be brought out by figure 9.3 is that there are distinct categories of English place-names which belong to settlements situated on very small patches of sand and gravel or out on the boulder clay, in situations comparable to those of the typical Danish-named villages. These include some of the 'geographically related' *tūn*-names, in particular Aston, probably named from its relationship to Burbage, and Sutton, in the northeastern corner of the map, which is south of Croft. They also include the three names which have *nīwe* (new) as first element—Newnham Paddox, Newbold and Newton, all in the southeastern corner. Coton 'at the cottages' lies out on the boulder-clay in the same area. It seems possible that these settlements represent a later stage of colonization than that which produced Claybrook Parva and Harborough Parva, though these are presumably in some sense secondary to Claybrook and Harborough Magna. If these findings were confirmed by further studies of this kind, the conclusion might be that some of our 'geographically related' names in *tūn* and some names in *nīwe* arise from a process of settlement expansion of comparable date to that of the Danish colonization of areas to the east.

10

The Evidence of Place-Names II*

V. E. Watts

Historical information to be deduced when the place-names of an area are in two or more languages

I should like to distinguish two kinds of name: (*a*) pre-English appellatives adopted by the newcomers with or without the addition of an English suffix, such as Breedon Lei (PrW ***bre3** 'hill' and OE **dūn** 'a hill'), Avon Wa (PrW ***aßon** 'a river'), and (*b*) names wholly in English but referring to the presence of people of a different race, for example, Walcot Wo (OE **Walacot** 'cottage of the Welsh').

Names of this kind, (*a*), mainly hill and river names, are important evidence of the contact between Welsh- and English-speaking peoples, though, as Wainwright (1962, pp. 60–62) pointed out, they do not in themselves provide proof of the survival of a British population (any more than the complete absence of such names provides proof of their extermination or that the contact was but brief and superficial).[1]

More important, perhaps, is the possibility that names passed from one linguistic community to another may offer valuable clues about the date at which such contact was made, and incidentally about the possible survival of Welsh-speaking enclaves. When one language comes into contact with another and borrows words and names from it, it is possible in principle, if there is independent evidence for the absolute chronology of the sound changes which occur in each, to date the borrowings with some exactitude. This is what J. Dodgson attempted in his paper on *The English Arrival in Cheshire* (Dodgson 1968a), based on the chronology proposed in Jackson 1953, and it works quite well. So far as I can see only two instances on the map of Celtic names in the Birmingham area require a date before *c.* 550, the rivers Severn and Sowe. The first is a great river whose name was probably known to the English long before they reached this area, while the second is of quite doubtful etymology (Jackson 1953, pp. 520, 519, 372). As you move to the west the date gets later, so that names like Dowles, *Doferic* and Leadon, all on the Hereford or Shropshire borders, were probably borrowed in the early to mid-seventh century (*ibid.*, pp. 438, 677, 672). In the northeast of England the Du Deerness and Nb Devil's Water (DIUERNESS, DIUELES on figure 10.1) require a similar dating which fits well the late occupation of Northumbria and the remote location of the Deerness in the then thickly-wooded Pennine upland region of Durham (*ibid.*, pp. 680, 438).

Anyone who has attempted to use Jackson 1953 for such a purpose will know how difficult it is for a

* Abbreviations used:

Brit:	British	OE:	Old English	PrW:	primitive Welsh
Du:	Durham (County)	OED:	Oxford English Dictionary	W:	Welsh
Lei:	Leicestershire	pers. n.:	personal name	Wa:	Warwickshire
Nb:	Northumberland	p.n.:	place name		

This chapter originally appeared as 'Comment on "The Evidence of Place-Names" by Margaret Gelling'.

[1] Tautologous names of the type 'hill-hill' seem to show indifference to or incompetence in the Welsh language.

non-Celtic specialist to assess the evidence. There are certainly difficulties. Again in the northeast in Nb, some four miles south of Bamburgh there is a small stream called the Long Nanny, *Nauny* 1245, apparently derived from PrW **nant* 'a glen' with an *-i* plural or collective suffix (Ekwall 1928, 298; Jackson 1953, pp. 351–3). It thus contrasts with the Du Derwent, Alwent, Nb Du Pont, in having assimilated *-nn-* from original *-nt-*, a sound change dated on W evidence to *c.* 800 (Jackson 1953, pp. 505–6). Furthermore it must have been borrowed into English after the English sound change known as i-mutation. Philologists have differed over the dating of this sound change, and most would not now go further than to say that it was an insular change which took place sometime before *c.* 700.[2]

At any rate, comparable examples of PrW names borrowed after English i-mutation all came from the far west—Devon, Somerset, Shropshire and Hereford—that is to say, from areas of settlement much later than the Northumberland coast where Ida landed in 547. Indeed, the English names of this area, Bamburgh itself, Beadnell and Ellingham [elɪndʒəm] (see below), are archaic in character. Even if we were to stretch the Welsh evidence and push the change *-nt-* to *nn-* back to *c.* 700 (Jackson 1953, p. 505) and even if we allowed for the early restriction of the Anglian coastal settlement chronicled by Nennius (Stenton 1971, p. 76), it is hard to believe that after the battles of *Degsastan*[3] in 603 and Chester in *c.* 613 the men of Bernicia did not know the name of a stream so near their capital.

The difficulties led Jackson (1953, p. 612) to call the assumption of a late enclave of Welsh speakers as 'hazardous but not impossible'.

It is worth noting, however, that just inland we find a group of names in the hills which may be British—Ros Castle (a hill-fort overlooking Chillingham), Rosebrough and Cateran Hill. Early forms for these names have not been collected, but the possibility that PrW **ros* 'a moor' and (less probably) **cadeir* 'a chair' in some topographical sense underlie these names must be left open.[4] It has also been suggested that among the hill-forts in this area, which are notoriously difficult to date, there may exist post-Roman defensive works (Pevsner 1957, p. 15).

Finally, if there was a Welsh-speaking population here in the eighth century it would account for the semantic change in **nant** apparently required by this instance. The late sense, 'a brook', is here topographically more appropriate than 'glen' (Nicolaisen 1957, p. 217 and n. 8).

Lichfield is another problem. Bede's forms of the name *Lyccid-Licidfelth* have been taken by Förster to show the results of a sound change (PrW ę>ui) the earliest Welsh evidence for which is dated *c.* 820 though the change itself is ascribed to *c.* 675 (Förster 1942, p. 587; Jackson 1953, pp. 333–4). According to this view Lichfield would be a name taken over in the later seventh century, contemporary with Chad's appointment to the Mercian bishopric in 669, in an area otherwise settled up to a century earlier: indeed on the Worcester/Hereford border the river name Neen still shows no sign of the ę>ui sound change. In spite of objections to the likelihood that a bishop appointed to evangelize the Mercians should choose as his base a remote spot in a thickly wooded area and still in British occupation—as a disciple of Aidan Chad was trained in the Irish tradition and might well, like his brother, prefer a site '*in montibus arduis ac remotis*' (Colgrave and Mynors 1969, p. 286) as a source of spiritual renewal—this does seem to fit well the data of Gelling's distribution map of the elements **tūn** and **lēah**. Lichfield lies in a district where there are no **tūn**'s and few **lēah**'s—precisely the kind of district which she suggested was settled either earlier or considerably later than the mass of

---

[2] Cf. Smith 1964–5, IV, p. 35 note 4; Luick suggested a sixth-century date, *Historische Grammatik der englischen Sprache* §201; Girvan the seventh century, *Angelsaksisch Handboek* §85; and Förster the eighth century, *Anglia*, 59, 1935, p. 295.

[3] A hybrid name with a Brit pers. n. which *does* exhibit the effects of English i-mutation if Förster's derivation is accepted (Jackson 1953, p. 612). On phonological grounds the identification of this and of Gaimar's form *Dexestane c.* 1140 (13) with Dawston in Liddesdale is improbable.

[4] Ros Castle is *Ross Castle* in 1799 (*A History of Northumberland*, XIV, Newcastle, 1935, opp. p. 303 where the variant spellings *Ras* and *Raws* are also recorded); Rosebrough is *Rosebery c.* 1620 (*ibid.*, I, Newcastle, 1893, opp. p. 256. The editor of vol. II suggested that Rosebrough preserves in a corrupt form the name *Osberwik*, *Oseburghwik*, the original name of Newstead, but this is not accepted in Mawer 1920, p. 168.)

settlements. It would appear possible, therefore, that this was just such a district occupied later than the main Anglo-Saxon settlement.[5]

Names of the second kind, (*b*), seem to require a different kind of assessment. All names arise from the need to identify and distinguish one place from another, and therefore refer to distinguishing features of topography, ownership or settlement within a certain area of local or more than local significance, depending upon the importance of the place in question. What appears to have been the distinguishing feature of the genuine Walcot names is that they refer to places where a group or family of distinctively Welsh origin were living—or used to live—or had come back.[6] Probably they were the only purely Welsh villages, and it seems that elsewhere the Welsh that remained or returned soon intermarried and adopted English speech habits (see above p. 122).

At all events, they cannot by themselves be taken as evidence of the extensive survival of a Welsh-*speaking* population: they may be a late type of formation. Conversely the famous Pensax must be seen as a name given by Welsh-speaking people to mark an isolated English intrusion precisely at the point where names of the first kind, (*a*), show that the English penetration was latest.

Thus the place-name evidence reveals where larger Welsh-speaking enclaves or isolated Welsh-speaking villages persisted. The failure of Welsh names to survive elsewhere—like the absence of early Celtic loan-words in the English language in general—most probably testifies to absorption and to the adoption of English-speaking habits, to Anglo-Saxon indifference and contempt rather than to slaughter and destruction.

The possibility of relating British names to archaeological evidence looks promising in various areas, and especially in Durham. The concentration of Celtic river names and the hill name *cönōg* seem to be related to the Roman forts at Ebchester (*Vindomora*), Lanchester (*Longovicum*), Chester-le-Street (*Concangium*), Binchester (*Vinovium*), Piercebridge (*Magis*), South Shields (*Arbeia*), Corbridge (*Corstopitum*) and Washing Well (discovered by aerial photography in 1970: see *Archaeologia Æliana*[4] 49, 1971, pp. 120, 129). Unfortunately, however, there are phonological and morphological objections against relating the two most promising candidates, Binchester and Chester-le-Street (*Kuncacester c.* 700), to their Romano-British names (Watts 1970, p. 252).

Chester can be related to the element *cönōg* seen in Consett and Cong burn, a tributary of the Wear at Chester-le-Street, and may have been renamed from the stream. The apparent lack of continuity in this name would certainly fit the evidence of the anonymous *Life of St Cuthbert* (*c.* 700) which relates how St Cuthbert, caught in a storm near Chester-le-Street, could only find a deserted shieling in which to shelter (Colgrave 1940, p. 70), a story which seems to imply no permanent inhabitation of the town and its neighbourhood in the mid-seventh century, a tradition repeated by later writers.

On the other hand our approach may, perhaps, be too rigid. If the processes of folk etymology could at a later date transform words like *mousseron* into *mushroom* or *caucé* into *causeway* there is less difficulty in supposing that in some areas, at any rate, Anglian settlers indifferent to linguistic niceties contented themselves with simply borrowing the first syllable of foreign names or substituting a familiar

---

[5] The alternative theory, that the Bedan spellings indicate a sound substitution by the English of *ī* for PrW *ę̄* involves difficulties of a different kind since the Anglian dialect of OE possessed its own *ę̄*-sound. It seems preferable to assume, therefore, that the spellings with *i/y* were attempts to render a sound already partly or fully diphthongized, i.e. the *i*-spellings could be regarded as an attempt to reflect the intermediate stage *ę̄ⁱ* reached in the sixth century, and the *y*-spellings the final stage. But we do not know which of the spellings is in fact original or whether they may have been alternatives from the first. The two earliest MSS, the Moore MS and the Leningrad MS, have *Lyccidfelth*, *Lyccitfeldensi* and *Licidfelth*, *Liccitfeldensi* respectively, and later MSS all have *Lic(c)id-* or *Liccit-* spellings.

However, whatever reservations there may be about Förster's view, it is clear that the treatment of PrW *ę̄* in Lichfield is different from and very likely later than the treatment of the same vowel in the river name Neen. For full discussion see Förster 1942, pp. 587 ff. and Jackson 1953, pp. 332–5.

[6] As is well known, only names whose early forms with medial *-a-* or *-e-* prove that they derive from an original gen. pl. **Wala** are in question here: cf. the reference in Jackson 1953, p. 228.

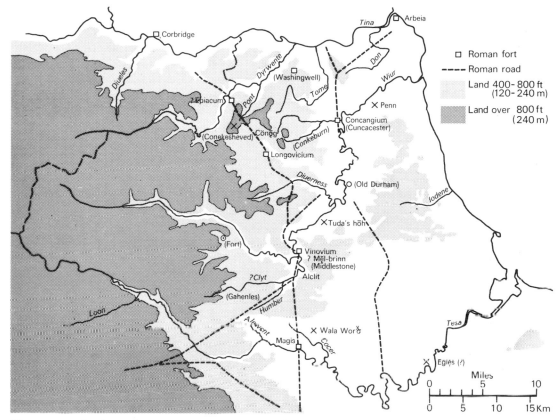

Figure 10.1 Durham place-names reflecting pre-English settlement.

for an unfamiliar element regardless of sense. Place-names do, in fact, frequently exhibit the processes of folk etymology, and *Alclit* itself subsequently remodelled as *Auklint* (with Danish **klint** 'cliff') and *Auckland* (with English **land**) is a good example.

In any case, one is reminded of W. G. Hoskins's argument that discontinuity in a name does not necessarily imply discontinuity in a settlement, citing the good examples of Wigston Lei, 'Viking's **tūn**', where the existence of a pagan Anglo-Saxon cemetery shows that the site was occupied (and presumably given a name now lost) long before the arrival of the Danish chieftain Viking, and of *Norðweorðig* later renamed Derby (Hoskins 1970, p. 72).

But we seem to have three kinds of continuity to consider—continuity of site, continuity of occupation and continuity of name. A break in the third is quite compatible with the first, but careful investigation of individual instances is needed before one can happily say it is compatible with the second. At the back of it all the question why the Anglo-Saxons were so inventive in their settlement naming, but so uninventive in their hill and river naming, still seems to await a fully satisfactory solution.[7]

On the subject of Scandinavian names it might be worth noting that in Du the situation seems to be slightly different from elsewhere. There are no names of the type Danby or Normanby[8] and

[7] N.B. Some of the entries on the map of Celtic names have sometimes been regarded as English names, e.g. Arden, Coundon—it is noteworthy that both lie close to an *English* r.n. Blythe, see Gover, Mawer, Stenton, Houghton 1936 and Ekwall 1960 s.nn.; the Eccles-names, Ekwall 1960; Warley and Worsley, Ekwall 1936.

[8] Except perhaps an isolated example of **Íri** + **tūn** in upper Weardale, but early forms are lacking for this instance.

the clearest indication of Scandinavian settlement seems to me to be the English names adopted by the settlers and given Scandinavian pronunciations, such as Gainford with [g] instead of [j].[9]

Although the Danes wintered on the Tyne in 874, they do not seem to have settled much in Du. Those that did seem to have penetrated from north Yorkshire and the modern form Coniscliffe (*Ciningesclif* 778 now [kʌnsklɪf]) seems to show that their linguistic affiliation was Danish since in this name the Danish word has replaced the English word for king. The main area of Scandinavianized names is marked on the map and, if this is right, the Grimston hybrids are much less significant in Durham. They occur mostly in the coastal strip, and I prefer to associate them with the tenth-century Norse–Irish kingdom of York; it is recorded that king Rægnald shared the coastal estates of Durham between two of his followers in 923. But these lands were back in English hands by 934 and the thinness of Norse settlement in this area is confirmed by the anglicized pronunciation from an early date of at least one of these hybrids—Sheraton (*Scurufatun c.* 1050, *Scurueton c.* 1200, 1385, *Surue-* 1183–13, *S(c)huru(e)-* 1183–1382).

It is rightly pointed out that the use of Norse names in the minor names of bounds proves the use of the invading language right down through to the bottom strata of society in the Isle of Man. Herein lies the importance of the study of field-names emphasized nearly thirty years ago by Wainwright in

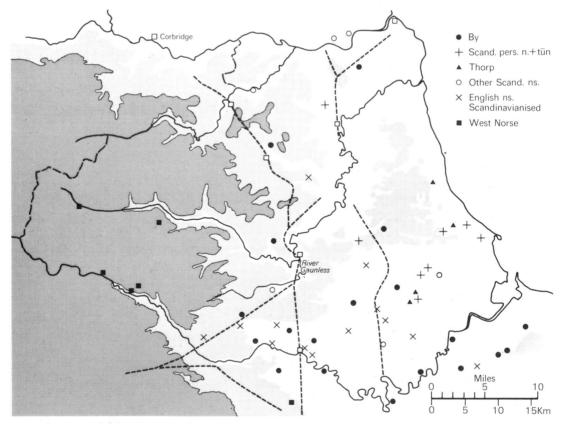

Figure 10.2 Scandinavian place-names in Durham.

---

[9] Even this criterion needs application with some caution. By the same token the occurrence in Du of Anglo-Norman pronunciations which have become accepted (e.g. Durham itself, Darlington, Whorlton, Lintz, Jarrow—see Watts 1970, pp. 262–3) along with a noticeable concentration of other Anglo-Norman names could be taken to suggest a considerable French-speaking population in the county in the twelfth century.

two fine papers on the Scandinavian settlements in Lancashire (Wainwright 1945, 1945–6). Here again, however, a certain delicacy in handling the evidence is required in England, since allowance must be made for the adoption into native speech of Scandinavian loan-words, and their subsequent spread beyond their original area. If such common words as 'husband', 'sky', 'skin', 'root' and 'anger' are Scandinavian loans, we must be wary in the deductions to be made from the occurrence in minor names of terms like *carr*, *crook*, *holm* and *intack* which also had some currency in English literary use in the middle ages.

The relative chronology of place-names in an area where the names are mostly in one language

As an attempt to identify earlier and later strata within the place-nomenclature in one language, comparison of the settlement names with the drift geology of the settlement sites seems a promising technique and could be particularly valuable in separating earlier and later names with an element like **tūn** which was productive throughout the Anglo-Saxon period and beyond. To some extent we can sort out earlier from later names by looking at the relative importance of settlements, and we can further assume that places of the type *Newton* and *Morton* are mostly later secondary settlements. In Du this appears to be confirmed by the fact that there are no **tūn** names of this kind on the best sites, and that three-quarters of them are on poor sites on boulder clay or areas of thin drift. Other elements which appear mainly on poorer sites in Du are **worð, by, feld, æcer** and **lēah**. **tūn** names are roughly equally divided as between good and poor geological sites, but most of the Grimston hybrids are on poorer sites, which seems to bear out my earlier suggestion about these names in Du.

What is illuminating is the discovery that the distribution as between good and poor sites of English non-habitation elements other than **lēah**—names in **dūn, burna, clif, ford**, etc.—appears to be very similar to that of the **tūn** names. In other words, provided we are right in assuming that the earliest English settlements were established on the best geological sites, the suggestions of Dodgson and Gelling that the non-habitation names deserve scrutiny for evidence of early settlement are dramatically justified. In particular a number of such names seem to fill in good areas in Du where **tūn** names are otherwise surprisingly absent, as in the Wear lowlands between the river and the east Durham plateau where we find Cocken (*Cokene* 1138, 'Cocca's stream' **ēa**), Hetton (*Heppedun* 1180–96, 'bramble hill' **hēopa, dūn**), South Pittington (*Pittinduna* c. 1123, 'Pitta's hill' **dūn**), and Shincliffe ('haunted bank' **scinn, clif**), while along with Shincliffe, Sedgefield (**feld**) and Staindrop (**hop**), likewise on good sites, are also on the early road system. Further infill on the map is obtained by adding the very few names recorded for Du in eighth-century sources which are, with only one exception, noticeably non-habitation names—Coniscliffe (*Ciningesclif* 778), Donmouth or Jarrow (*Donæmuþe* 757–8, *Ingyruum* c. 730), Elvet (*æt Ælfet ee* 762), Finchale (?*æt Pincan heale* 788, cf. Ekwall 1962, p. 21), Gateshead (*Ad Caprae Caput* c. 730), Hartlepool (*Heruteu* c. 730), Sockburn (*æt Soccabyrig* 780) and Wearmouth (*ad Uiuraemuda* c. 730).

What is rather alarming, on the other hand, is to find a number of what have been assumed to be early settlements in apparently the worst sites, for example, Billingham and Stockton, both in the middle of the boulder clay according to the one-inch Ordnance Survey drift geology map. Other sources, however (e.g. *Victoria County History, Durham*, III, pp. 195, 348), without contradicting this, comment on the present or past agricultural richness of these townships. The *Northern England Handbook* of *The British Regional Geology* draws attention to the many varieties of boulder clay in the area—'extremely stiff, or very sandy; almost stoneless, or so stony as to constitute a gravel with a clayey matrix' 3rd edition, p. 64).

I suspect that the evidence of the one-inch drift maps may need a good deal of refinement. (Unfortunately in any case it is impossible to produce a complete map for Durham since the one-inch and

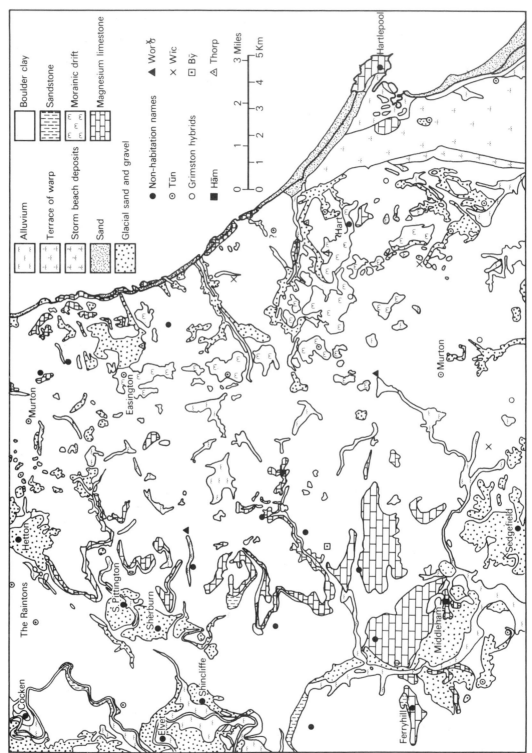

Figure 10.3   Drift geology of place-names in east Durham (derived from Ordnance Survey 1″ Drift Geology Sheet 27).

six-inch cover is incomplete.) It would be interesting to hear a geographer's comment on the quality of the drift evidence for the kind of exercise place-name scholars have been conducting. How thin is the drift that is marked on these maps? What kind of detail important for our purposes is omitted? How delicate ought our geological information ideally to be?

Thus one would like to know why, on the drift map of the Coventry area, Ullesthorpe and Ashby are planted on clay when there are apparently better sites unoccupied close by. And why there is such an empty area of sand and gravel between Burbage and Wolvey, and Wolvey and Ryton. Is sand and gravel always superior to clay? A. Steensberg suggested soil fertility rather than its geological constituency as the crucial factor—but how do we measure that?

What in any case are the factors which govern settlement sites? Soil quality must frequently have been a decisive factor, but the order of priorities need not have been constant as between fertility, drainage, water supply, climate, defence and availability of land already cleared and cultivated. It is noteworthy how many Du sites occupy prominent hill-tops crowned with ancient churches. The towers of Easington, Hart, Billingham and Merrington are widely conspicuous. Merrington, at an elevation of 650 feet, stands in the teeth of the prevailing wind and the drift cover is very thin; other factors than amenity or soil quality would seem to have prevailed in the choice of this site, and the suggestion that it was originally a British hill-site merits consideration.[10]

I have already mentioned the **tūn** and **lēah** distribution map, and I would like to add something about their distribution in Du. It shows three clearly-demarcated areas from east to west, a **tūn** area, a **lēah** area, and an area in which neither occur in the Pennine uplands and moors—and also on the coastal plateau. There are no gaps like the Lichfield gap, other than where the nature names already mentioned occur. The other point is this: in Weardale **lēah** twice occurs with French elements, **forestier** in Frosterley (*Frosterley* 1183) and the personal-name Roger in Rogerley (*Rogerloia* 1183), so that we must reckon with the occurrence of post-Conquest names with this element. Indeed, some of the Du **lēah** names must be associated with a deliberate policy of expansion into the waste reactivated in the twelfth century and documented in extant episcopal charters (Scammel 1956, p. 209).

With the **tūn** names also there are post-Conquest examples. In Du a small estate in Hart was granted by Robert Brus·II to his cupbearer Niel some time before 1194, after whom it is now called Nelson (*Nelestun* 12 cent), just as in Dorset Cruxton is named after one John Crox (D.B. *Froma*, 1178 *Fromma Johannis Croc*), Ranston (*Iwerne* in DB—a Brit r.n.) after a post-Conquest Randulf, and Waterston (*Pidere* for *Pidele* in DB) after a Walter mentioned in 1212. In these post-Conquest examples of names meaning 'so and so's estate' we seem to have a parallel to the other practice of appending manorial additions like Newton Hansard, Dalton Piercy, Hurworth Bryan, Witton Gilbert, Wharram Percy. It is usually argued that such additions arise from the need to distinguish two names of the same kind, Witton Gilbert from Witton-le-Wear, Newton Hansard from Longnewton, Wharram Percy from Wharram le Street, etc. In the case of names of the Nelson type we need to ask, therefore, what kind of distinction was intended. I am inclined to think that particularly in the case of minor settlements—single farmsteads—such names are likely to be new settlements due to expansion or estate division rather than new names for old settlements—if the old settlement had a distinctive name there would be no obvious reason for renaming it, unless the change of ownership was

---

[10] There are, in fact, three Merringtons along the ridge of the hill recorded in the thirteenth and fourteenth centuries as East, Mid and West Merrington, now Kirk Merrington, Middlestone (**midlest-tūn**) and Westerton (***wester-tūn**). Ekwall 1960 following Mawer 1920 attempts to link the name Middlestone with a 1366 form *Melderstayn, Malderstayn* in the *Halmota Prioratus Dunelmensis* (a text which consistently otherwise refers to Middlestone as *Mid Merrington*), and hesitantly suggests a derivation from Welsh *Moelfre* 'bare hill' as in Mellor Db (PrW ***melbrinn**). If correct this derivation would greatly strengthen the case for continuity, but unfortunately other explanations are possible if not preferable, e.g. pers. n. Maldred and OE *stān* 'stone'. The name Middlestone itself is first recorded, in 1584, but it is possible that there is a reference to it in 1367 in the *Halmota Prioratus Dunelmensis* in the form *Midelton*, in which case it would further be possible to identify it with the otherwise lost *Middeltun* of c. 1030–40 (Hinde, J. H. ed. 1867) which is known to have been near Bishop Auckland.

regarded as particularly noteworthy or important.[11] After all, what is striking about our place-name evidence is how conservative nomenclature is after the earliest Anglo-Saxon period. For a time, no doubt, compound names of the type 'so and so's **tūn**' had the status of grammatical phrase in which the personal-name element was in more or less free variation with other personal names distinctive for the place in question, much as at later periods local farm names of the type Smith's Farm some-times varied with changes of tenancy. At some early point, however, under circumstances which would be interesting though for the most part too elusive to determine, they must have lost this status and become fossilized conventions, as, for example, the OE tripartite prepositional phrase **æt þære lēage** ('at the clearing') lost grammatical status and became fossilized as the conventional unitary name Thurleigh. In the case of Bibury, therefore, one could well argue that what is striking is not that an unnamed estate or part of an estate was granted to Leppa and bears the name of his daughter, but that the name has then remained unchanged for 1200 years.

Nevertheless, there will certainly be cases where names change with changes of ownership or tenure which were for some reason considered noteworthy and important. Rainton, a village—or rather a pair of villages—northeast of Durham is known to have received its name from one Rægenwald, the son of one of the companions of St Cuthbert's body during its wanderings beginning in 875, yet Rainton lies in an area which was among those earliest settled in Du, and may well, therefore, have replaced an

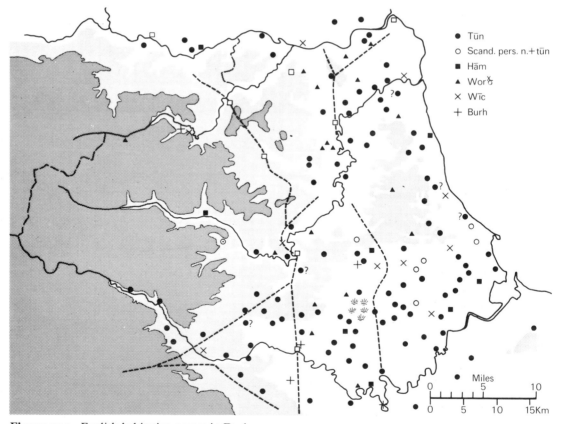

Figure 10.4 English habitation names in Durham.

[11] It is unlikely that in most cases we shall ever be able to recover the information to decide between the two possibilities, new site or new ownership. Allowance should also doubtlessly be made for simple human pride in ownership.

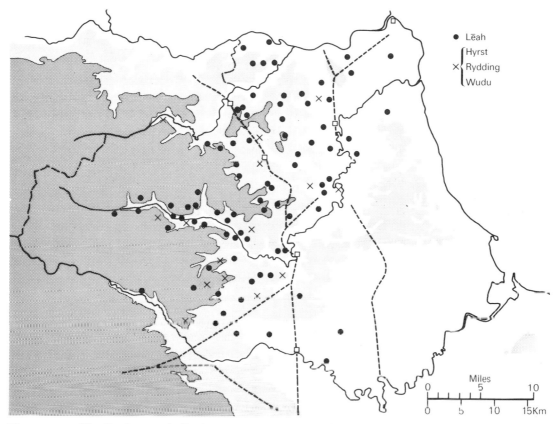

Figure 10.5 Woodland names in Durham.

earlier name. Certainly in Weardale a parcel of land called *Ebberleia* (perhaps 'Eadbeorht's clearing') was given *c.* 1160 to found a religious cell, and was thenceforth known as *Landa Dei*, now *Landieu* ('God's clearing').

An interesting group of names which seem to show estate division and change of ownership or tenure comes from Dorset. On or near the river Piddle occur Piddletrenthide, Piddlehinton, Little Piddle, Muston, Waterston already mentioned, Puddletown, Athelhampton, Tolpuddle, Affpuddle, Bryants Puddle, Turners Puddle, *Bardolfeston* and *Lovard* (both lost). Piddle itself, an apophonic variant of *puddle*, is an English word meaning 'swampy ground' (OED s.v. *puddle*, Smith 1956 s.v. ***pidele**) and seems to have replaced a Brit. r.n. Trent, though it is also just possible that this could be a back-formation from the -*trent*- of Trenthide, 'thirty hides'.[12] Domesday Book distinguishes only Puddletown (*Pitretone*), *Litelpidele* and *Affapidele* from the others which are all referred to as *Pidele* or *Pidere*.[13]

[12] The main piece of evidence in support of the antiquity of this name is Florence of Worcester's form *Terente*, Ekwall 1928, p. 416. However, since the presentation of this paper I have learnt from the editor of the forthcoming P.N. Society's volumes for Dorset, Mr. A. D. Mills, to whom I am much indebted for his comments, that he doubts the genuineness of the r.n. Trent and thinks that Florence may have confused the Piddle with the genuine Tarrant a few miles to the north. He makes the very interesting alternative suggestion that the original Brit name of the Piddle was Car(e)y, cf. Ekwall 1928, pp. 70–1, and points to two local farm names, Carey *Kerre*, *Keire* 1220, *Carry* 1318, and Keysworth *Kaerswurth* 1227, *Karesworthe*, *Keresworth* 1309, perhaps 'enclosure belonging to Carey' or 'enclosure by the r. Carey'.

[13] Piddletrenthide was (*at*) *Vppidelen*, *uppidele* 966(15). Ekwall 1960 and Fägersten 1933 wrongly assign these forms to Puddletown (*ex inf.* A. D. Mills).

Piddlehinton was held by the *hīwan* or monks (gen. pl. *hīgna*) of Marmoutier in the 1080s, Muston (*Pudelemusters* 1339) by the Musters family in the thirteenth century, Athelhampton (*Pidele Athelamston* 1285) by an unknown Æþelhelm, Tolpuddle by Tole, widow of Edward the Confessor's *huscarl* Orc, who gave it to Abbotsbury abbey *c.* 1050, Affpuddle by one Aelfriðus (Æffa for short) who gave it to Cerne Abbey in 987 (Kemble 1839–48, no. 656), Bryants Puddle (*Prestepidela* in the twelfth and thirteenth centuries, being held in 1086 by one Godric *presbiter* and later by the prior of Christchurch, Hampshire) by a fourteenth-century Brian de Turbervill, Turners Puddle by Walter Tonitrus or Tonere in 1084, and *Bardolfeston* by Bardulph de Chiselburneford *c.* 1165. *Lovard* (*Pudele Loveford* 1285) was probably 'Lufa's ford'. Here, and elsewhere in Dorset, is rich material for manorial history from the tenth century, and it is clear that few of these tenants and sub-tenants can have been the first occupiers of these estates. Studies in change and variant forms of name to supplement Ekwall 1962 would, therefore, be of great interest, and it would also be interesting to see whether there are any general factors which differentiate **tūn** names compounded with a personal name and **tūn** names compounded with names of natural features like **dæl**, **denu**, **hyll**, **stān**, as well as with crop names.

As a postscript may be added three grammatical criteria for early names. Northern names are frequently preserved with the dative plural inflexional ending: Hulam in Du, *Holum c.* 1030–40, 'at the hollows, burrows'. This ending was preserved in Old Northumbrian until the tenth century, but by the end of the OE period had fallen out of use. All such names must, therefore, be Anglo-Saxon, though it is not possible to distinguish between early and late examples, except perhaps in the case of folk names like Jarrow and Ripon, *Inhrypum c.* 730 '(the monastery) among the Hrype'. Most of the Du examples are noticeably names of minor settlements.[14]

According to Dodgson names in **-ing** which preserve or whose spelling shows that they once possessed an assibilated pronunciation [ɪndʒ] are derived from forms with a locative case ending in **-i** which became obsolete by about the middle of the seventh century. The Nb Ellingham mentioned above would be one of these (Dodgson 1967a, 1967b, 1968a, 1968b).

Names like Beadnell (*Bedenhala* 1177), Bamburgh (*Bebbanburh* 547) and Pittington (*Pittinduna c.* 1123) are formed from a personal-name with the gen. sg. ending **-an** (later reduced to **-en**, **-in**). But the Northumbrian dialect of OE lost the final **-n** of this ending at a very early date, certainly before 700. Any name, therefore, which preserves **-n** within the Northumbrian dialect area must have been coined in the first hundred or so years of the Bernician kingdom.[15]

[14] Bolam, Cleatlam, Coatham Mundeville, Coatham Stob, Cowpen Bewley, Escomb, Headlam, The Leam, Leamside, Newsham-on-Tees, Newsham (Winston), Polam (Darlington), Shelom (Merrington), Streatlam, Summerhouse (*Sumerhusum* 1200), Wingate (*æt winde gatum* 1071–80), Woodham.

[15] Sockburn Du (*Soccabyrig* 780) and *Degsastan c.* 730 may show the result of this loss, or may be uninflected genitival compounds. Another early example in Du is Cocken (*Cokene* 1138), 'Cocca's stream'. Bamburgh is interesting in that although founded in 547 by Ida the place is actually named after queen Bebbe, wife of Æþelfrið who reigned 593–617.

11

Palaeobotanical Evidence

D. D. Bartley

Plant remains of various kinds have been found during archaeological investigations. Fruits, seeds, timbers, charcoals and, more recently, pollen grains have been studied and it is the latter which will be considered in this paper. Under conditions of waterlogging and/or acidity, pollen grains are highly resistant to decay and many types are easily identifiable under the microscope. From the ecologist's point of view the best sites for pollen analysis are lakes and peat bogs where there is a gradual build up of mineral or organic sediments. Each layer of the sediment will contain pollen from vegetation growing on and near the site at the time of formation of the layer. A pollen diagram therefore presents a continuous record of the changes in the pollen flora throughout the formation of the sediment. In mineral soils, however, there is movement of pollen and other materials downwards and it is only if an impervious layer is formed that this process will be arrested. Consequently, pollen diagrams from mineral soils are very difficult to interpret and do not yield the same sort of information that can be derived from diagrams from a peat bog or lake.

The changing pollen curves of a pollen diagram must be interpreted in terms of changes in vegetation and of changing proportions of various species. There are many difficulties involved, including such problems as differential pollen production and mode of pollen transport so that pollen of hazel will tend to be overrepresented in comparison with lime pollen. Much work is now being done on the relationship between fossil and modern pollen assemblages. Another major problem is to determine from where the pollen at a site is derived. There are three sources which must be represented in varying degrees:

1   from plants growing on the site,
2   from the slopes surrounding the site (within a few kilometres),
3   from the region (up to hundreds of kilometres).

Source 1 is fairly easily separated from 2 and 3, but 2 and 3 are not easily separated. Tauber (1965) has shown that in a forested area pollen follows three paths—(1) through the trunk space, (2) just above the canopy and (3) high up in the atmosphere. Thus in a small bog, about 100 metres across and surrounded by forest, some 80 per cent of the pollen will come from the trunk space and will have travelled only a few hundred metres. In a large bog a sample from the edge will be largely trunk space pollen but at the centre of the bog (1,000 metres from the edge) 70 per cent of the pollen will be from above the canopy, 50 per cent of low density pollen will be from within 10–11 kilometres of the bog and 50 per cent from beyond. In other words, in forested areas small bogs yield pollen diagrams which reflect very local changes while large bogs reflect regional changes.

Judith Turner has exploited the work of Tauber in an attempt to get some indication of the extent and location of forest clearances (Turner 1970). Figure 11.1, freely adapted from Turner, shows three sites (A, B and C) on a large peat bog. Figure 11.1a shows the behaviour of the grass and tree pollen curves through a particular clearance. At B, near the centre of the bog, there is no rise in grass nor fall

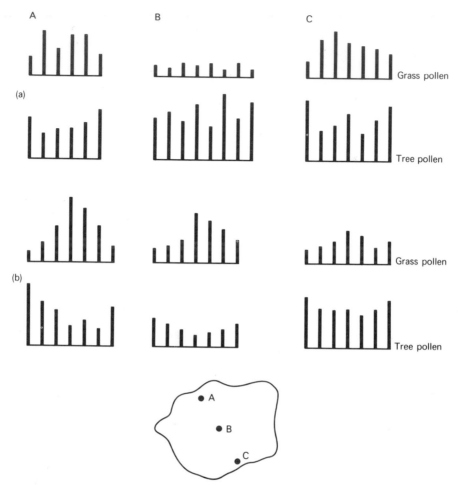

Figure 11.1 Changing values of grass and tree pollen at three sites on a large peat bog. 1(*a*) an early clearance, 1(*b*) a later clearance (*very freely adapted from Turner 1970*).

in tree pollen, suggesting that there was little regional clearance. At A and C there is a considerable rise in grass pollen and a corresponding fall in trees, suggesting local clearance around the bog. Figure 11.1b shows a later clearance where there is a rise in grass pollen at B and the level of tree pollen is much lower than in the previous case, thus suggesting considerable regional forest clearance. The high grass values at A also suggest local clearance near that side of the bog, but there appears to have been little clearance in the area next to site C.

These are two examples of modern trends in pollen analysis but most information of archaeological interest still comes from single pollen diagrams and two such diagrams from very different areas will now be considered. The first site is Flint Hill on Rishworth Moor near Ripponden in the Yorkshire Pennines. It lies at a height of 410 metres OD and is covered by about two metres of peat. Flint Hill has yielded many artifacts from the mesolithic, neolithic and bronze age but only one presumed iron age find, a Kimmeridge shale bracelet (figure 11.2). Pollen changes near the base of the pollen diagram and stratigraphic column (figures 11.3 and 11.4) record the changes from grassland with, perhaps, some trees, to *Sphagnum* and cotton-grass (*Eriophorum*) moor at 180 centimetres and later, heather (*Calluna*) moor at 150 centimetres, with woodlands remaining on the lower slopes. The fall in values of elm (*Ulmus*) pollen at 180 centimetres probably represents the 'elm decline' which is widespread throughout

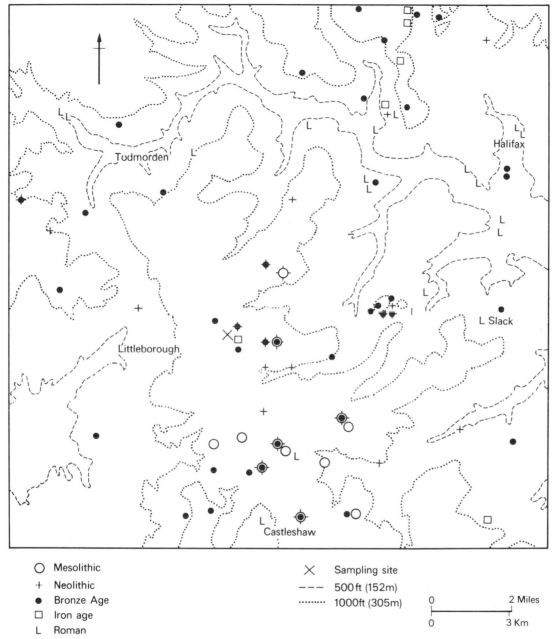

Figure 11.2 Map to show the distribution of archaeological finds in the region around Rishworth Moor (*based on the Ordnance Survey records for archaeology*).

Britain and is generally thought to have been brought about by a combination of human interference and soil deterioration. It is dated at about 3300 to 3000 BC and at Rishworth has a radiocarbon date of 3540 BC (5490 ± 140 BP–GaK-2822). Iversen (1949) showed that the appearance of pollen of plantain (*Plantago lanceolata*), sorrel (*Rumex acetosella*) and mugwort (*Artemisia*) and spores of bracken (*Pteridium*), combined with certain other changes in the pollen curves, indicates clearance of the forest

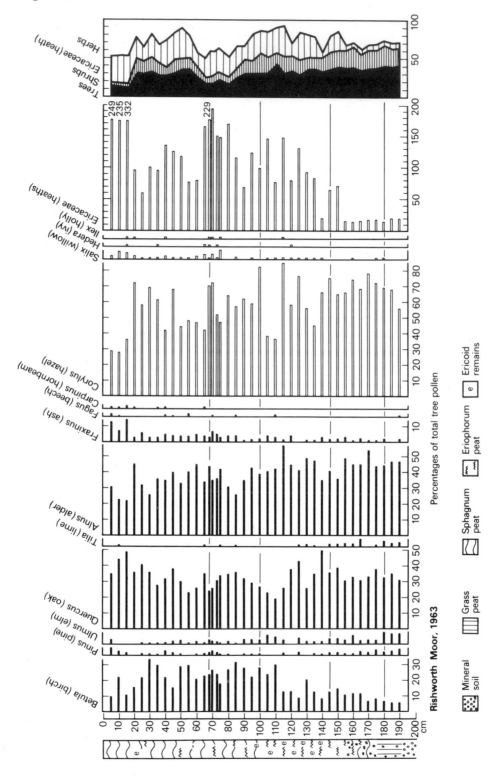

Figure 11.3   Pollen diagram from Rishworth Moor. All values are expressed as percentages of total tree pollen.

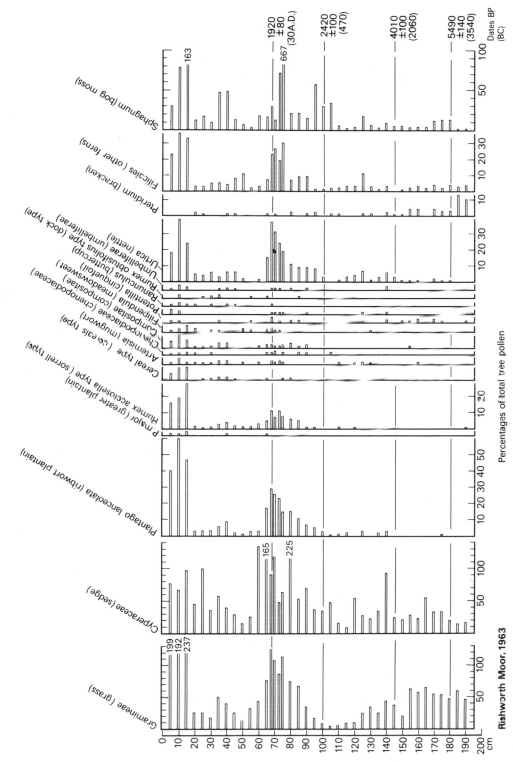

Figure 11.4　Continuation of the diagram in Figure 11.3.

and the establishment of pasturing. In the Rishworth diagram there is a single occurrence of plantain at the elm decline but very little change takes place in the trees—perhaps a very temporary neolithic clearance. From 140 centimetres plantain and bracken become more abundant and the curve for hazel (*Corylus*) fluctuates rather widely, suggesting patchy and temporary clearances of the forest between 2060 BC (4010 ± 100 BP–GaK-2823) and 470 BC (2420 ± 100 BP–GaK-2824). From 100 to 68 centimetres, plantain pollen increases greatly and is accompanied by increases in grasses and sedges, sorrel and some *Compositae*, *Chenopodiaceae* and cereals. Tree pollen falls from 30 per cent to 15 per cent of total pollen and herb pollen rises from 14 per cent to 40 per cent. All these changes culminate at 68 centimetres which has a radiocarbon date of AD 30 (1920 ± 80 BP–GaK-2825). There must therefore have been a spread of forest clearance and considerable agricultural activity. The latter, which was at first pastoral, seems later to have included some cereal growing. There follows a very steep decline in agricultural indicators suggesting that agriculture had fallen to a very low level by about AD 200 at the latest. The pattern of activity in a diagram from Featherbed Moss above Glossop in Derbyshire (Tallis and Switsur 1973) is very similar but there the iron age agriculture reaches a peak at about AD 200 and declines by about AD 400. There is a similar period of agricultural recovery at the top of the diagram (above 15 centimetres on the Rishworth diagram) and this is attributed to tenth-century Norse invaders. At Leash Fen in Derbyshire to the southwest of Sheffield (Hicks 1971) there is little evidence of a decline in agriculture and recovery of forest between the Roman and Norse periods.

Since most of the land in this area above 300 metres has been covered by blanket peat since about 3000 BC, the evidence for forest clearance must relate to the Pennine slopes below the peatlands and the human artifacts found in the peatlands can hardly be related to settlement within the area. The pollen curves suggest very limited forest clearance by neolithic people and only small amounts during the bronze age. Probably during these periods the people move around considerably and may have visited the uplands quite frequently, especially for summer grazing. This would account for the numerous artifacts attributable to these periods. During the iron age, however, the evidence suggests that there was very considerable and much more permanent clearance of the slopes accompanied by pastoral and some arable agriculture. Under these circumstances and possibly because of the marked deterioration in climate which led to a greatly increased wetness of the peatlands (as evidenced by the increase in *Sphagnum* in the peat) it is likely that iron age people were very infrequent visitors to the uplands and this would account for the very rare occurrence of artifacts. There is a marked lack of evidence for iron age settlements on the Pennine slopes, the major settlements being at such places as Almondbury and possibly Dewsbury. If this is so then, as Jones (1961b) suggests, the cleared areas of the Pennines are likely to have been used for summer grazing and cultivation. The rapid decline in agriculture from the beginning of the Roman period is difficult to explain. The site is only a few hundred metres from the Roman road over Blackstone Edge and one can perhaps speculate that after the abandonment of Almondbury by the Brigantes the Romans kept the native people away from this upland area. At the same time it must be admitted that any such drop in the lowland population would reduce pressure on these marginal uplands.

Pollen diagrams from the Durham lowlands are in marked contrast to those from the highland zone of Yorkshire, the major difference being in the much earlier intensive clearance of forest. In a diagram from Bishop Middleham near Ferryhill the first appearance of plantain pollen is at 3230 BC (5180 ± 110 BP–GaK-2071) with a continuous curve from 1710 BC (3660 ± 80 BP–GaK-2072) and reaching a maximum of 41 per cent of total pollen (600 per cent of total tree pollen) at about 1410 BC (3360 ± 80 BP–GaK-2073). After that time values of plantain pollen fall off somewhat but tree pollen values never rise above 10 per cent of total pollen, suggesting that there was little recovery of the forest after the bronze age clearance. About 800 metres from the farm of Thorpe Bulmer near Hart there is a kettle hole about 100 metres across. Figure 11.5 shows just a part of the pollen record from this site. The interest at this level is the curve for hemp (*Cannabis*) pollen which reaches values of 19 per cent

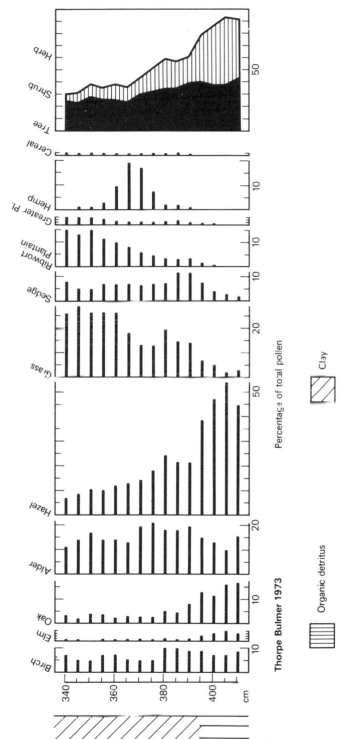

Figure 11.5 Part of a pollen diagram from near Thorpe Bulmer, County Durham. All values are expressed as percentages of total pollen.

of total pollen at 365 centimetres then falls and finally disappears at 345 centimetres. The explanation for these changes is that at about 114 BC (2064 ± 60 BP–SRR-404) there was considerable pasturing in the area with some cereal and hemp cultivation. By AD 220 (1730 ± 120 BP–GaK-3713) there must have been a field or fields of hemp on the slopes immediately surrounding the lake. Ploughing of these fields is the most reasonable explanation for the deposition of clay in the lake. After AD 220 there is a decline in values of hemp pollen and therefore presumably in hemp cultivation until it finally disappears at AD 1098 (852 ± 60 BP–SRR-405). The dip in the grass pollen curve which mirrors the rise in hemp pollen suggests that the intense cultivation of hemp was at the expense of existing grassland and that there was a return to grassland later, perhaps after the Roman period.

This situation is very different from that in Norfolk where Godwin (1967) shows that hemp was not extensively cultivated until Saxon times. Hicks (1971) found up to 2 per cent of hemp pollen at Leash Fen in layers dated to the Roman period and Birks (1965) showed a peak of *Cannabis-Humulus* (presumably hemp) pollen at Lindow Moss, Cheshire, again in deposits attributed to the Romano-British period. The present diagram is of interest therefore in showing that the pre-Roman iron age inhabitants of the Durham lowland cultivated hemp, at least in small amounts and there must have been continuous cultivation and settlement at or near Thorpe Bulmer from that time on. One might speculate that the ending of hemp cultivation was connected with the Norman devastation of the north. It is very interesting to note that at Steward Shield in Weardale Roberts, Turner and Ward (1973) find a period of clearance and agriculture between 110 BC and AD 1110, although they were hesitant to suggest continuous activity.

One last example concerns excavations at Sandal Castle, near Wakefield.[1] This is mentioned very briefly because it concerns the medieval period and it introduces the study of charcoals. Pollen analysis of soil from the ridge and furrow system on which the first castle was built in the early twelfth century

Table 11.1

Pollen analysis of two buried soils from the ridge and furrow system under Room V at Sandal Castle near Wakefield

Alnus (alder)	1·0	1·0
Quercus (oak)		1·0
Total tree pollen	1·0	2·0
Corylus (hazel)	1·0	4·0
Salix (willow)		1·0
Total shrub pollen	1·0	5·0
Calluna (ling)	1·0	2·0
Caryophyllaceae	3·0	2·0
Cereal	4·0	
cf. Convolvulus arvensis (bindweed)	3·0	
Cyperaceae (sedges)	21·0	11·0
Filipendula (meadowsweet)		2·0
Gramineae (grasses)	39·0	35·0
Plantago lanceolata (ribwort plantain)	2·0	
P. major (greater plantain)	1·0	1·0
Rosaceae	2·0	4·0
Senecio type (ragwort type)	18·0	23·0
Taraxacum type (dandelion type)	1·0	12·0
Umbelliferae	2·0	1·0
Total herb pollen	98·0	93·0

[1] The work on the charcoal from Sandal Castle was carried out by M. T. Smith and A. P. Hooper.

shows extremely low values of tree pollen with high values of weed species such as the ragwort type (*Senecio*) and also cereal pollen (table 11.1). This must mean that the castle was built in a completely cleared area with no forest for some distance, perhaps a kilometre or more. Large amounts of charcoal were found during the excavations at Sandal and the beautiful condition of the material suggests that it was purpose-made charcoal. The distribution of the various types is shown in figure 11.6. At about AD 1200 all the charcoal is oak (*Quercus*) though there was some holly (*Ilex*) from the wooden castle. After AD 1250 the variety of charcoals increases with hazel, rowan (*Sorbus aucuparia*), birch (*Betula*), etc. becoming abundant. This evidence might be interpreted as follows. When the castle was built, high forest, mainly of oak existed in the area (the discovery of large numbers of bones of forest animals supports this view) and provided the main source of material for the charcoal burners. As the forest was exploited for fuel and timber so it was opened up and secondary trees and shrubs such as hazel, birch and ash (*Fraxinus*) increased in abundance and were then used for charcoal. Maple (*Acer*) at the top of the diagram (AD 1500–1645), can not be distinguished as field maple (*Acer campestre*) which is native or as sycamore (*A. pseudoplatanus*) which is introduced, but it is interesting that sycamore was introduced into this country in the late sixteenth century and then spread very rapidly.

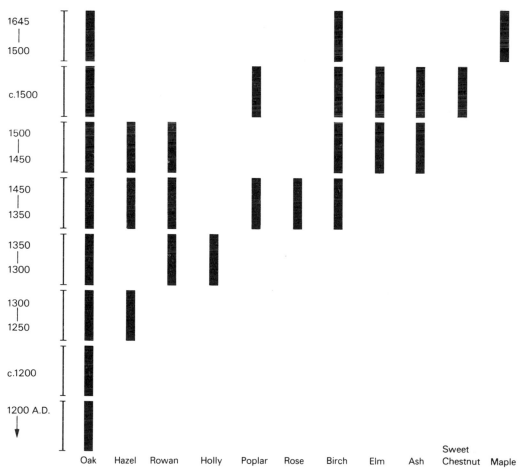

Figure 11.6 Diagram to show the distribution of the different charcoals recovered from successive levels in the barbican ditch at Sandal Castle, near Wakefield.

I hope that these few examples have shown how much useful information can be derived from pollen analysis and related studies. At the same time it must be emphasized that there are distinct limitations. In particular the old idea that pollen analysis can be used as a dating tool must in large part be abandoned since most of the changes in vegetation in Britain during the last five thousand years have been brought about by the activity of man and are not synchronous.

12

Some Settlement Patterns in the Central Region of the Warwickshire Avon

W. J. Ford

This paper comprises a summary of some aspects of a multi-disciplinary approach to settlement study over a limited area. The region of study comprised the drainage and catchment area formed by those tributaries of the Warwickshire Avon which flow into the river between Stoneleigh and Evesham. In addition to the central part of the Avon valley, it included the valleys of the rivers Alne and Arrow flowing from the north, and the Isbourne, Stour, Dene, Itchen and Leam on the south and east.

Anglo-Saxon colonization

The division of this region into two essentially contrasting parts, the Feldon, or open country of the south, and the forest lands of the Arden to the north, has been a pattern discernible since Roman times. Until the expansion of settlement in the thirteenth and fourteenth centuries, the Arden had remained mainly woodland interspersed by large tracts of heathy ground. From the available evidence, there is a marked contrast in the Roman period, between the paucity of finds in the Arden compared with the apparent proliferation in the valleys of the Feldon. It is also noticeable that what evidence there is for Roman industry is concentrated in the Arden, where timber for fuel would have been in plentiful supply (figure 12.1).

It can be argued that early Anglo-Saxon penetration of the region appears to have begun peaceably in the late Roman period, in all probability by mercenary settlers, and was initially confined to the Avon valley itself. Although no precise dating from the archaeological material is available, general trends in chronology and typology point to the foundation of the earliest and largest sites at Bidford, Stratford and Baginton, where Roman roads crossed the river. Roman settlement occurs near each site and their general situation accords with that of cremation cemeteries in eastern England, observed by J. N. L. Myres to be in 'obvious and direct relationship to Roman fortified towns and the principal communications between them'. From the evidence of grave goods, settlement elsewhere in the Avon valley appears to be of later foundation and contemporary with most of the sites in the valleys of the Stour, Dene and Itchen. It is arguable therefore that the cemeteries and their associated settlements at Bidford, Stratford and Baginton represented an Anglo-Saxon element, possibly part of a mercenary force which could have existed for some time in the midst of a native Romano-British society. The excavations at Stretton-on-Fosse in the Stour valley have provided the first archaeological evidence which can be directly related to a Romano-British presence in an Anglo-Saxon cemetery. This cemetery forms one of a series of burial grounds grouped near a Roman settlement, which give a total time-span ranging from the second to the sixth century AD. C14 dating has indicated a substantial period of overlap between the pagan Saxon cemetery and one of the adjacent Roman cemeteries.

It is noticeable that away from the Avon valley these Anglo-Saxon cemeteries contain relatively fewer burials, never more than sixty in number. In terms of settlement, this is unlikely to account for more than a single household in occupation at any one time, and suggests little more than perhaps an

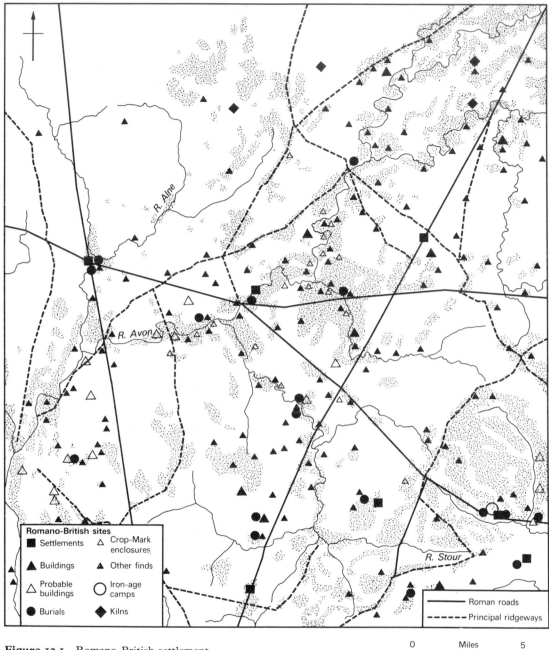

Figure 12.1   Romano-British settlement.

aristocratic element imposed upon existing native peasant settlement. The role of surviving native Romano-British people in a dominant Anglo-Saxon society has yet to be satisfactorily explained and, as there appears to be no real evidence for the presence of a peasant class in pagan cemeteries, it is perhaps they who formed the bulk of the peasantry.

The relationship of pagan Anglo-Saxon cemeteries to the known areas of woodland is virtually one of complete contrast. The burials are almost all based on the gravel terraces and superficial deposits in the Avon valley and its southern tributaries (figures 12.2 and 12.5).

As yet no confirmed evidence has emerged from the traditional Arden and, in consequence, it seems likely that movement into this area must have followed the settlement further south. Pagan place-names in the region have a wide-ranging distribution and it is remarkable that they appear only to have survived in areas of former woodland. Such names ought to be regarded as evidence of Anglo-Saxon settlement before the conversion to Christianity and it seems logical, therefore, to infer that the

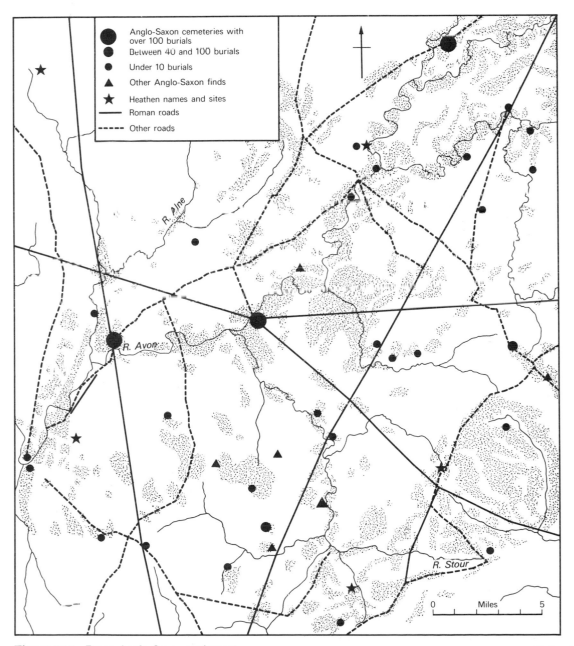

Figure 12.2 Pagan Anglo-Saxon settlement.

whole of the region was under Saxon influence in pagan times. The evidence as a whole suggests this may have been accomplished in three phases:

1   the foundation of the major Avon sites, possibly by Germanic mercenaries, from military considerations.
2   the establishment of sites in the Feldon, i.e. along the terraces of the river Avon and its southerly tributaries, during a period of co-existence with the native Romano-British element, where allocation not selection may have been the guiding factor.
3   a phase of occupation associated with the spread of heathen place-names into areas noticeably devoid of pagan burials, particularly north of the Avon in the woodlands and heathlands of the Arden.

Such a hypothesis would accord with the chronology of events in the Anglo-Saxon Chronicle. The battles fought by the West Saxons against the Britons at *Deorham* and *Fethanleage* in AD 577 and AD 584 respectively, may well have shattered native control over the area and enabled a re-organized kingdom known as the *Hwicce* to arise under Germanic leadership, thus allowing the influence of Anglo-Saxon settlers in the Avon region to infiltrate former non-occupied areas.

Political divisions and regional economies

The principality of the Hwicce

At the close of the eighth century, Mercia seems to have been divided, for purposes of civil adminis-tration, into five provinces, each with an *earldorman* at its head. In all probability these civil divisions coincided with the five dioceses of Lichfield, Hereford, Lindsey, Leicester and Worcester. The diocese of Worcester, as it was known in 1291, probably represents the original territory comprising the bishop-ric of the *Hwicce* created in AD 679–80 and therefore is probably approximate to the extent of that ancient kingdom. Documents of the seventh and eighth centuries mention a folk of this name and they occur in the tribal hidage as a people of 7,000 households, tributary to the Mercian kings (Smith 1964–5, IV. 34).

The border of this ancient kingdom appears to have run across the middle Avon, following the boundary of the diocese from Tanworth, by Warwick to Kineton and Whichford. There is some place-name evidence to support this and, while clearly it would be premature to attempt to define a boundary line too closely, its approximate course may be assumed. It is possible that the Tachbrook, a small stream entering the Avon south of Warwick, contains the Old English word *taecels* in the sense of boundary (Gover, Mawer, Stenton, Houghton 1936, pp. 258–9). Further south in Kineton, a charter reputedly dated AD 969 includes the reference *mercne mere*, meaning the boundary of the *Mierce* or Mercians, in its bounds, and in the neighbouring parish of Radway a field name Martinmow has been identified with *Merclemere* which occurs in AD 1265 (*ibid.*, p. 272; Birch 1885–93, no. 1234). The name *Hwicce* also occurs in Whichford and Wychwood, both of which must have been close to the border (Cameron 1961, p. 74). From Tanworth to Whichford place-name evidence suggests continuous woodlands and wastes along the frontier, which gave way to marsh land at the crossing of the Avon, and at the headwaters of the Stour and Evenlode. This entire belt of undeveloped land must have formed a natural no-mans-land between the kingdoms of Mercia and the *Hwicce*.

In the early days of their existence it is even possible that a closely defined boundary did not exist and a series of prominent features may have served to mark the bounds, in the manner of the earliest charters. In this respect it is significant that this frontier zone contains no less than ten earthworks of probable pre-Saxon date (figure 12.3). The underlying factor in the apparent contrast between those camps situated on watersheds and those located in valleys, particularly at river crossings, may well be a

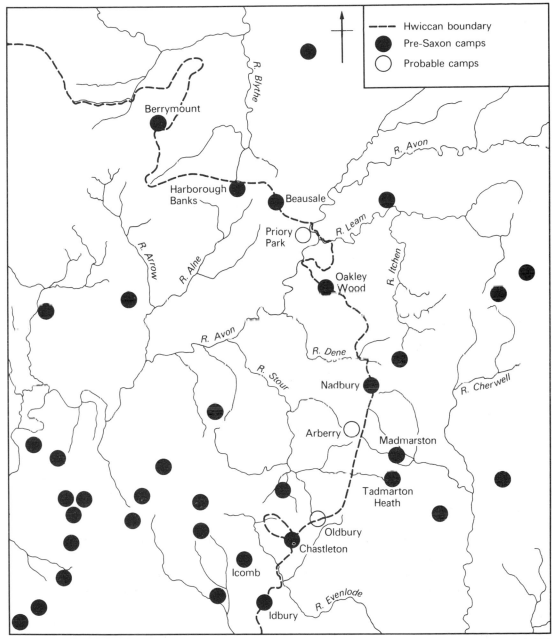

Figure 12.3 The boundary of the Hwicce.

Scale 1 : 250,000

difference in function, as many sites of the latter type are still foci of settlement. On the western side of the province the uplands of the Malvern hills and the great forest of Wyre, which divided it from the territory of the *Magonsaeten*, form a similar type of terrain, and it is possible that tracts of woodland and waste were the characteristic feature of the lands which generally formed the bounds of regions. The geography of the province of the *Hwicce* shows that it was based upon the lower basins of both the river Severn and its tributary the Avon. The boundaries in the main are formed by natural water-sheds between major river systems and are divisions which could have provided natural frontiers even before the Anglo-Saxon period. The *Andredsweald*, which is known to have extended from Hampshire to Kent, was literally the Weald of Andred (*Anderita* the Roman town, now Pevensey in Sussex). On its eastern part, it was common to Kent and Sussex as early as first records, and must in earliest times have formed not only a divide or no-mans-land between Saxon regions, but in all probability, the Romano-British subdivisions which proceeded them. Kent is derived from the territory of the *Cantii* while the fact that the weald was related to a Romano-British settlement suggests that it formed part of a region which was in existence in the late Roman period and recognizable by the Anglo-Saxons. *Dere* and *Bernicia*, the two Anglian kingdoms which amalgamated to form Northumbria, were both British district names and Lindsey seems formerly to have been the Roman *Lindis* (Cameron 1961, p. 55). Worcester, the Roman town of Wigoran, is probably derived from a tribal name, which same element also appears in the forest of Wyre, indicating another possible association between a pre-English settlement and a tract of woodland.

Common lands and colonization

The common use of woodland is attested all over southern England from a very early date and W. G. Hoskins has proposed from linked place-name evidence that the *Hwiccewudu*, for example, was the common woodland and pasture ground of the people known as *Hwicce* (Stamp and Hoskins 1963, pp. 5–13). By a process of limitation, the erstwhile open woodlands and pastures were gradually appropriated to regions, then particular individual settlements, and in the course of time, new habitation sites were established on these former common lands. If such a process has any basis in fact, and there is considerable supporting evidence, then the division of such woodland among smaller settlement units, if identifiable, should give an insight into the organization within a province or a region and might broadly indicate the extent of such political units.

In the middle Avon region there is evidence to show that a number of settlements held woodland at some distance from the parent community. Sir William Dugdale was the first to bring to notice an apparent connection between Tanworth in Arden and the Feldon village of Brailes which lay twenty-five miles to the southeast (Dugdale 1656, p. 774). In 1315 Tanworth was recorded as a hamlet of Brailes, and before AD 1202 Tanworth church was a dependent chapel of Brailes (*Victoria Country History, Warwicks* V, p. 174). Tanworth also lay in a detached portion of the Domesday hundred of Fexhole of which Brailes was a member, so that a pre-Conquest connection between the two settlements is a likely possibility. As Dugdale observed, the block of woodland attached to the manor of Brailes probably lay in Tanworth, with both places being assessed together. It is a factor of some significance, therefore, that the earliest documentary evidence for Tanworth only occurs during the period between AD 1150 and 1180. Similar connections can be established between such widely separated settlements as Packworth and Wasperton, Bushwood and Stratford-upon-Avon, Nuthurst and Shottery, Arley and Long Itchington, as well as Kingswood and Wellesbourne (Ford 1973, pp. 41–50).

The fragmented nature of many of the old hundreds frequently reveals a number of small isolated parts physically separated from the major blocks of settlement. Many of these isolated portions can be seen as the detached holdings of woodland, heath or pasture, in some cases even meadow land, belonging to settlements situated within the main hundred. An insight into these ancient patterns helps to disentangle the apparent disorder in the Domesday picture of Northamptonshire, where a number of manors situated in Wychwood in Oxfordshire are listed with that county's hundreds, and might well have originally formed detached holdings of woodland and pasture. Charter evidence shows even earlier links between such widely separated places as Bourton-on-the-Water and Daylesford, Beoley and Yardley, Bredon and Cutsdean, Dumbleton and Flyford, Hill Crome and Hill

Moor. It is possible to consider other connections between places held by the same lord or whose names disclose a common origin, particularly in areas where other settlement links are known to have existed. Such places as Sawbridge, Whitacres; Tredington, Tardebigge; Packington, Packwood, Packmores; Clapton, Clapley; Cornwell, *Cornewelelond*; Atherstone, Edstone; Charlecote and Chalcot Wood; Bloxham and *Bosco de Blocksham* (Stonesfield); Drayton and *Draytonsmore* (Kidlington); Banbury and Banbury Hill (Charlbury); and Bromwich and Bromwich Wood; each respectively in open country with some area of woodland or heath lying a distance away (Ford 1973, pp. 41–50).

Much of the firm evidence for detached settlement comes from documentary sources, some of which are traceable back to the eighth century. Their survival is the accident of history, and many former settlement relationships may have existed for which the evidence has not survived. The medieval picture is one which portrays the final disintegration of these distinctly regional ties as surviving detached territories became independent from their parent communities, at a time when forests and pastures were under pressure through increased land hunger. In Stoneleigh hundred, for example, there is no direct evidence for detached holdings of this type. The hundred, which is long and narrow, bestrides the Avon by which it is equally divided in area between Feldon and Arden. A number of parishes lying in the Arden are not recorded until the twelfth century and were probably assessed with other manors in Domesday, but the geography of the hundred suggests that some once formed detached woodland and pasture holdings of the Feldon settlements.

Domesday geographies

In the light of the foregoing evidence, it seems clear that a reappraisal of Domesday geographics might be required, if only on a local basis. In Warwickshire most of the woodland entries apparently located in the south of the county can be seen as holdings in the Arden, while in Oxfordshire the greater part of the woodland and pasture holdings of settlements in the Cherwell basin appear to have been located in the Wychwood forest. In Gloucestershire, the apparent paucity of Domesday entries for the forest of Dean, remarked upon by Darby, might also be explained by its assessment with manors elsewhere. As can be seen, the possessions of a manor did not necessarily lie within its physical boundaries, and meaningful local studies must take account of this.

The circumstances of transhumance are undoubtedly complex and it would be optimistic to think that at this stage they can be fully clarified, but at some date in the past it seems the vast belt of interspersed wooded and heathy lands in the north of the Avon region which included the forests of Feckenham and Arden formed an area in which intercommoning was practised by settlements of the open territories to the south. In earlier days these areas were presumably summer pastures, which would have acquired increased importance with the intensification of arable farming in the wake of a rising population.

Regional economies

W. G. Hoskins has defined a region as a 'territory, large or small in which conditions of soil, topography, climate and perhaps natural resources combine to produce distinctive characteristics of farming practice and rural economy in the widest sense, to mark it off clearly from its neighbouring territories' (Hoskins 1954a, p. 5). If so, then it is arguable that the manifestations of transhumance in the middle Avon provide an outstanding example of regional farming practices where the allotment of timber land, pasture and meadow on such a widespread basis could only have been possible in a well-ordered community. Close scrutiny reveals an emerging pattern where the evidence of transhumance is sufficiently distinctive as to suggest blocks of territory displaying such regional characteristics (figure 12.4).

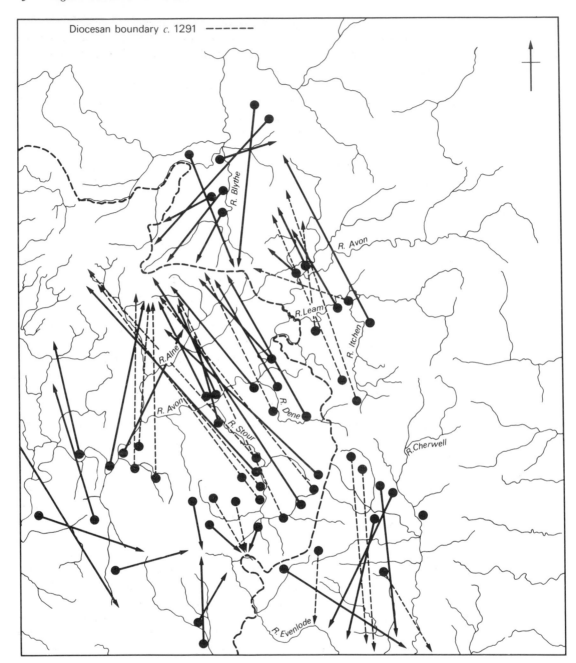

Figure 12.4 Linked settlement pattern.

Settlements in the valley of the river Avon from Evesham to Warwick and in the basins of the Dene and Stour in traditional Feldon country, were intercommoning in a block of woodland situated near the headwaters of the rivers Arrow and Alne. This forms a territory which can not only be marked off from surrounding areas because of these economic links, but is enclosed by natural boundaries. On the east and south, the water divide of the Severn and Thames catchment areas marks the limit of the district; the northern boundary is well defined by the watershed between the Trent and the northern tributary streams of the Avon, and the high ridge which runs from Tardebigge to Evesham marks the extent of the western side. There are no observable instances of estate grouping or transhumance which show any extra-territorial relationship and the whole district appears to have been bounded on all sides by land which was common to settlements contained within. Firmer evidence for the existence of such an early boundary occurs in a ninth-century charter of *Coftune* (Cofton Hacket) (Birch 1885–93, no. 455). From the text it seems clear that it lay on the boundary of a people known as the *Tomsetna*, on the watershed between the river Cole (one of the tributaries of the Tame) and the river Arrow. There seems little doubt therefore that this was a known political boundary at least in the middle Saxon period. A possible name for this district occurs in an eighth-century charter for Wootton Wawen, a settlement centrally placed in the territory, which states that Wootton Wawen was situated '*in regione quae antiquitus nominatur Stoppingas*' (Birch 1885–93, no. 158).

A second striking area of transhumance occurs in the basin of the upper Cherwell, a tributary of the Thames, where a large number of settlements in the valleys of this river and its tributaries were intercommoning southward to the forest of Wychwood. This is also an area with well-defined natural boundaries and it is fascinating to observe that settlements, closely situated on either side of the common divide with the middle Avon territory, are intercommoning in opposite directions to woodlands and waste fifty miles apart. If Sir Frank Stenton is correct in his suggestion that Charlbury in Oxfordshire is the place '*in regione quae vocatus Infeppingum*', where the first bishop of the Mercians died, then the *Feppingas* could be identified as the dwellers in the upper Cherwell basin and, therefore, the eastern neighbours of the *Stoppingas* (*Victoria County History*, Oxon 1; p. 378, n. 3). They could well have been the most southerly of the middle Anglian peoples, whose territories were thought to have extended as far south as the Thames valley, a possibility supported by M. Gelling's conclusions from her study of Oxfordshire place-names, that linguistically Oxfordshire was a border zone between Angles and Saxons (Gelling 1953–4, 1, p. xix).

North of the middle Avon, a third group of settlements in the valleys of the rivers Tame, Cole and Blythe were intercommoning southward to the forest of Arden. In this group the intercommoning is contained within the natural catchment and drainage area of the Tame, an area also suggestive of an early territorial unit, and from the evidence of the Cofton Hacket charter it can be established that the inhabitants were anciently known as the *Tomsetna*, the dwellers of the river Tame. The evidence as a whole tends to suggest that transhumance might well define economic and political areas, a possibility supported by the *leah* and *tun* distribution map of Margaret Gelling, which defines from toponymic evidence, similar regional settlement patterns.

A connection between a district name and a tract of woodland has already been observed in *Andredsweald* and further examples can be detected in the primitive divisions of the Kentish people. The names *Limenweara wold* and *Weowara weald* recorded in the early eighth century, show that the woodland described originally belonged to those areas which later appear as the lathes of Lyminge and Wye. These were areas peopled by folk-groups who, in accordance with ancient custom, divided the woodland and pasture between them (Stenton 1971, pp. 283–4). The evidence from the middle Avon region reveals a practice parallel to that in Kent and supports the argument that linked settlement patterns can indicate ancient regions.

The Saxon landscape

From the evidence of place-names, it is possible to produce a conjectural view of the landscape of the region as far back at least as the middle Saxon period, given sufficiently early forms. While it must be realized that such evidence has undoubted shortcomings, particularly because the necessary documents are not in existence for every parish, they are available in sufficient numbers in the region to give a reasonable distribution pattern without significant gaps. A high proportion of clearing and wood names, in any area, may justify a supposition of former woodland. Other place-names describe heath-land, fens and marsh as they may well have been found by the earliest Saxon settlers and probably represent the first names given by colonists in a new land (Dodgson 1966, p. 5).

A map of all place-name elements is shown in figure 12.5. It can be observed that the valleys of the river Avon and its southern tributaries appear to be devoid of any names which would indicate wood-land, which is almost entirely confined to areas of higher ground. It is also noticeable that the southern extent of the woodland belt which forms the traditional Arden appears to run along the northern limit of the Avon valley to meet the river near Warwick. The block of upland territory which comprises the northern extension of the Cotswolds as far as Meon Hill, also seems well wooded, and this woodland appears to have extended westward to meet the Avon at Evesham. Names implying woodland are also distributed in a great arc along the water divide between the Thames and Severn catchment areas, from Broadway through Moreton-in-Marsh to the Edge Hill escarpment and beyond. A tongue of woodland seems to have projected southwards along the ridge from Redditch to Evesham, and a second extended along the high ground between the rivers Dene and Itchen, from Barford to Burton Dassett while a smaller area appears to have existed in the minor hills at Loxley between the rivers Stour and Dene. These woodlands seem to have been interspersed by extensive tracts of open heath land, in fact the map clearly demonstrates that woodland and heath are almost inseparable. Parts of the Avon valley contained marshy tracts and almost the whole of the upper reaches of the river Stour seem to have formed a vast marshland, known as the *Hennemersche*, which extended into the valley of the river Evenlode, as Moreton, Compton, Sutton-under-Brailes, Barton and Chastleton are all described in documents of the twelfth and thirteenth centuries as lying in this area (Smith 1964–5, p. 251; Gover, Mawer, Stenton, Houghton 1936, pp. 298–300).

It can be seen that the area suggested as being co-terminous with the *regio* of the *Stoppingas* is entirely surrounded by heath, marsh and woodland and thus separated from neighbours by belts of marginal land. All the known examples of the element *feld* are found along the inner margin of these wooded areas and may indicate early settlement growth by clearing on the edge of the forest lands or reflect an existing contrast in the Romano-British landscape as observed by the first settlers. It is also noticeable that the element *worth* also seems to be confined to formerly wooded areas and their distri-bution tends to suggest a phase of settlement which cleared nearly all the land in the south of the region and which made considerable inroads into the Arden.

Early estate patterns

A high proportion of the Anglo-Saxon estates that are known from charters or inferred from other evidence, were composed of numerous sub-estates and their attendant settlements, seemingly from a very early date. Such evidence as we have, again largely the accident of history, suggests a tale of subsequent fragmentation. It can be shown that many seemingly independent villages of the twelfth and thirteenth centuries were originally components of such settlement groups and the later medieval period seems to have been a time of transformation in estate pattern through the break-up of a large number of pre-Conquest land-units and the creation of new estates, sometimes of a much more dis-persed nature. The extent of the earlier estates can be discovered by three different approaches: (*a*) grouping is sometimes indicated in manorial documents, the Domesday Survey and Anglo-Saxon charters; (*b*) ecclesiastical organization through mother church and chapel relationship can indicate estate grouping; (*c*) analysis of place-names can produce groupings which may have no other record. The three approaches are not only complementary, but act as a check upon each other, and the distri-bution of these estate patterns is illustrated in figure 12.6.

In north Oxfordshire, the ancient parish of Swalcliffe was known to contain the townships of Lea,

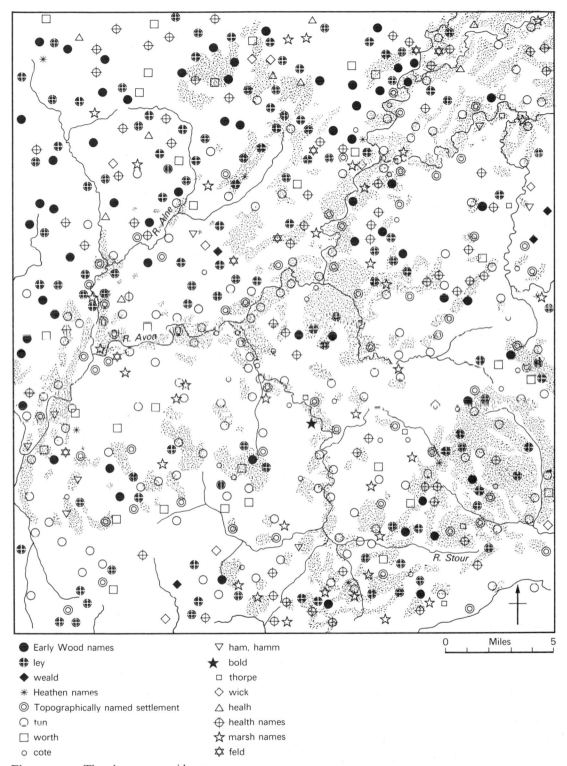

● Early Wood names	▽ ham, hamm
⊕ ley	★ bold
◆ weald	□ thorpe
✳ Heathen names	◇ wick
◎ Topographically named settlement	△ healh
◠ tun	⊕ health names
□ worth	✩ marsh names
○ cote	✪ feld

Figure 12.5 The place-name evidence.

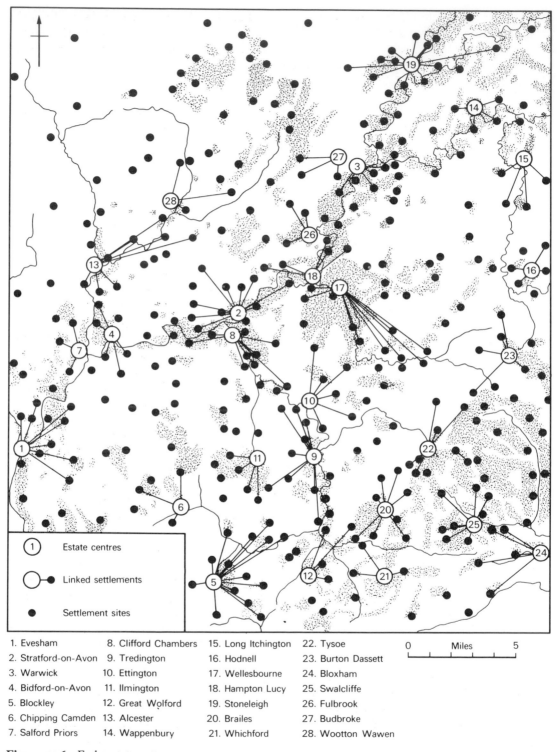

Figure 12.6 Early estate patterns.

1. Evesham	8. Clifford Chambers	15. Long Itchington	22. Tysoe
2. Stratford-on-Avon	9. Tredington	16. Hodnell	23. Burton Dassett
3. Warwick	10. Ettington	17. Wellesbourne	24. Bloxham
4. Bidford-on-Avon	11. Ilmington	18. Hampton Lucy	25. Swalcliffe
5. Blockley	12. Great Wolford	19. Stoneleigh	26. Fulbrook
6. Chipping Camden	13. Alcester	20. Brailes	27. Budbroke
7. Salford Priors	14. Wappenbury	21. Whichford	28. Wootton Wawen

Epwell, Shutford, Sibford Ferris, Sibford Gower and Burdrop, while Cropredy included Prestcote, Great and Little Bourton, Wardington, Mollington, Claydon, Coton, Williamscot and Clattercote. Further east, straddling what is now the Gloucestershire, Worcestershire and Warwickshire border, an estate centred on Blockley contained Stretton-on-Fosse, Moreton-in-Marsh, Northwick, Aston Magna, Draycott, Upton Wold, Dorn, Batsford, the three Ditchfords and Bourton-on-the-Hill (*Victoria County History, Oxon* x, pp. 160, 225; *Victoria County History, Worcs* III, pp. 267, 271). The primary and secondary relationships between the chief manor and its dependent members is reflected in the ecclesiastical organization with the mother church situated at Blockley and a series of chapelries sited in the hamlets. Toponymically the settlements of Northwick and Aston are of great importance; they are so named because of their geographical relationship to Blockley and this is typical of many settlement names in the region.

A similar settlement grouping occurred at Brailes, which lies near the southern boundary of Warwickshire near the foot of the Jurassic scarp. At the time of Domesday it was an estate of forty-six hides and appears to have included the manors of Over-Brailes, Chelmscote, Winderton and Cherrington, with the chief manor, presumably the administrative centre, located at Lower Brailes. The mother church lay at Lower Brailes and, with the exception of Over-Brailes, chapels were situated at each hamlet. The existence of two contra-posed settlements of Norton and Sutton in this group focuses the attention. Both these places seem to be named by reason of their situation in relation to Brailes, the centre of the estate. Norton (which is known only from a field-name in a terrier of AD 1616), as the name implies, lay to the north of the chief manor, and was apparently depopulated at an early date, while Sutton, or as it is now called Sutton under Brailes, is still a village lying on the southern slopes of Brailes Hill. It is reasonable to suppose that these two settlements were so called because of their original geographical positions in what was probably a single estate (Ford 1973, p. 21).

It would seem by contrasting the place-name evidence with manorial and ecclesiastical organization, that the mother–daughter church relationship evolved from an estate organization of sufficiently early date that it gave rise to the naming of settlements within it. This type of related settlement can contain not only the suffix *tun* but elements such as *cote, ham, thorp, wick* and *leah*, and they frequently occur on documents of the ninth, tenth and eleventh centuries. The earliest known reference to a place-name of this type in an Anglo-Saxon charter occurs at Aston near Stoke Priors in Worcestershire in AD 767 (Birch 1885–93, no. 202).

Other types of place-name also seem to be derived from the position of a settlement within an estate. Tadmarton, a parish in north Oxfordshire, contains the element *gemaere* and can be interpreted as meaning 'boundary farm' (Gelling 1953–4, II, p. 416). It lay on the western side of a group of settlements of which Bloxham was the centre (*Victoria County History, Oxon* IX, p. 2). Morrell in Warwickshire was one of the two manors which formed the parish of Moreton Morrell. It means literally 'boundary hill' and probably marked the northern limit of the royal estate of Wellesbourne (Gover, Mawer, Stenton, Houghton 1936, pp. 256–7). Halford, a small parish which lies in the Stour valley and seems to have been assessed with Ettington at the time of Domesday, contains the element *healh* meaning a 'corner' or 'nook of land'. This description fits its geographical situation as it occupies the southern corner of a group of settlements originally belonging to the greater manor of Ettington (*ibid.*, pp. 254–5).

In addition to geographically related names, others give an insight into possible early economic and husbandry practices which may well give some indication of estate policy and management. One of the member manors of Brailes was the hamlet of Winderton, a name which can be interpreted as the 'winter farm', or 'settlement used during winter months', and the hamlet is situated on a sheltered spur of dry sandy land under the ridge of Edgehill (*ibid.*, p. 278). The name mirrors a practice still carried out by local farmers as late as 1933, when in winter livestock was moved from the cold wet clays of the vale of Sutton Brook up to the drier areas on the Marlstone and Northampton sands.

There is also some indication of the existence of specialist farming practices resulting in settlements being named because of a particular aspect of husbandry. Concentration on the production of a certain type of crop seems to have led to such settlement names as Ryton, 'the rye farm', Whatcote, 'the place where wheat was cultivated', Barton, 'the barley farm'. Ryton-on-Dunsmore, for example, was part of the extensive royal manor of Stoneleigh, while Barton was originally part of the royal manor of Bidford-on-Avon (Hilton 1960).' The existence of fruit farms is suggested by the numerous Appletons and Pirtons, while other aspects of husbandry are indicated in Honington, 'honey-farm'; Cheswick, 'cheese-farm'; Hardwick, 'dairy-farm'; Shipton, 'sheep-farm'; functions likely to have been the most notable at the time they acquired their names. It is also possible that place-names containing the prefix *ceorl* and *walh*, as in Charlecote and Walton, when considered in an estate context, could be interpreted as places where the tenancy or lordship had been granted to a churl or a Briton. Acquisition of the prefix *walh* therefore could be comparatively late in date and need not necessarily indicate the presence of a Romano-British settlement site.

Specialization by farms or settlements is more likely to take place in a well-ordered, planned community. Concentration on the various aspects of husbandry, such as the growth of wheat, barley, fruit and vegetables or the raising of sheep, cattle, pigs and horses as well as inland fisheries, and milling, seems more acceptable when viewed as a contribution towards a balanced economy on a considerably broader basis than that of single settlements with a supposedly subsistence economy.

Taking the evidence as a whole, the grouping of settlements into estates, the geographical position of settlements within them, and their specific agricultural practices, have endowed the region with a substantial proportion of its place-names, and might well have been important factors in the spread of English toponymy. What is not clear, however, is the original number of settlements contained in any settlement group. So far we have been dealing with places which are well-attested in documents, and indisputedly habitation sites. Examples of field-names which suggest settlement sites, however, are widespread throughout the region and include names containing the elements *worth*, *thorp*, *cote* and sometimes even *tun*. The forms *Cleyhemsugworth*, AD 1246–7, in Farnborough; *Weresworth*, AD 1369, in Tanworth, and *Bosseworth*, AD 1479–80, in Warwick provide instances where a settlement origin would be acceptable (Stokes 1932, p. 651; Gover, Mawer, Houghton 1936, p. 378; Hilton 1952, p. 12). In the region, all told, twenty-three *worth*-names, ten *cote*-names, two *thorpes* and one *tun* have so far been recorded. Even allowing for a margin of interpretive error, this could represent a substantial proportion of settlement unrecognizable in the context of the known medieval settlement pattern.

In Brailes, a field called Norton lies to the northwest of the present village, and another called Ditchingworth is situated half a mile north of the church, both fields until recently being covered by substantial ridge and furrow. In 1970 Ditchingworth was levelled and ploughed, producing large quantities of late Romano-British material and subsequent trial excavation provided evidence of long lasting occupation, with coins ranging from the first to the early fifth centuries AD. Baldicote, in Tredington, provides a further example of a habitative field-name subsequently proven to be an occupation site. After ploughing, the field revealed substantial quantities of late Roman and sub-Roman pottery and in a small trial excavation carried out in 1971, in addition to Romano-British material, a few sherds of Saxon pottery were discovered in a shallow ditch with a single inhumation burial nearby (Records of Shipston-on-Stour Local Hist. Soc., Warwicks County Museum Records). It is significant that both sites were overlain by ridge and furrow suggesting that the settlements and their appendant lands, of which there is no trace, were ultimately absorbed into a larger unit. If the other habitative field names prove to be occupation sites, then the number of settlement units in the region in a post-Roman context will be considerably increased, posing the question whether such sites represent a pre-nucleation phase with their subsequent abandonment marking a movement towards nucleation.

Pagan settlement and estate development

The general distribution of estate development coincides remarkably with the area of pagan-Saxon cemeteries. How the transition took place has yet to be deduced, but a cardinal factor must have been the achievement of control of the region by the Anglo-Saxons. There appears to be no discernible pattern; in some instances cemeteries are located at estate centres; others are situated within constituent members of estates. Bidford and Stratford-upon-Avon, the sites of two of the larger burial groups, are the only cemeteries to be found in the whole of the estates of which they were the centre.

Baginton, the site of the third major cemetery, later emerges only as a member of the large royal manor of Stoneleigh, but no other pagan-Saxon burials have been found within the bounds of this extensive land unit. Other burial grounds located at estate centres include Burton Dassett, Long Itchington and Ettington, and in the two latter instances cemeteries are also located in the dependent hamlets of Bascote and Halford. Most other burial sites like those at Baginton are found in secondary settlement situations, Stretton-on-Fosse and Northwick, for example, were both hamlets of Blockley, while Kineton and Compton Verney were part of the extensive Wellesbourne estate.

By far the most consistent factor in estate relationship seems to be the presence of substantial Roman remains near their administrative centres. There are Roman settlements at Alcester, Stratford, Ettington, Swalcliffe while Mancetter, the Roman *Manduessedum*, appears to have been the centre of an estate including Oldbury, Atherstone and Hartshill, which contained a thriving Roman pottery industry (*Transactions of Birmingham and Midland Archaeological Society* 65 (1943-4), p. 165, 76 (1958), pp 1–9). This may reflect a more widespread relationship between important Roman settlements and administrative centres of Anglo-Saxon estates. From geographically related place-name evidence it is possible to see Wroxeter, the Roman *Virconium*, as the centre of an extensive estate; Winchester also exhibits elements suggesting an associated land unit much more extensive than the town, while the area around South Cadbury includes a number of geographically related settlement names which indicate the existence of a land-unit based upon South Cadbury itself, where occupation goes back beyond Roman times.

It is a matter for consideration whether estates apparently with the more important Roman sites near their centres were created in Saxon times, or whether they could possibly have developed from the lands or *territoria* which surrounded the Roman settlements. From a study of Anglo-Saxon charters, pagan-Saxon burials, linear earthworks and Roman roads in relation to parish and manorial bounds, Desmond Bonney has argued in favour of estates having had a continuous existence since Roman times, or earlier (Bonney 1972) and it is noticeable in some examples in the middle Avon region, notably the villages of Wappenbury, Bourton-on-the-Water and Swalcliffe, that the Roman settlements appear to be the successors of iron-age fortified sites.

The siting of settlements

Glacial sands and gravels and other permeable soils

The extreme importance of glacial sands and gravels in relation to the siting of settlement is a factor not wholly appreciated. The publication in 1962 of an aerial survey of ancient settlement sites in the valleys of the Avon and Severn first revealed the complexity of features on the gravel terraces flanking both rivers (Webster and Hobley 1964). This pioneer work, however, did not consider the relationship of present-day villages to these same tracts of land. The system of villages as we know it today is mainly a direct inheritance from medieval times and the land units, except for comparatively recent boundary changes, are basically the same, in fact many can be taken back to pre-Conquest times through Anglo-Saxon land charters.

It can be argued, therefore, that the siting of the greater part of medieval settlements in these river valleys is associated with the same gravel tracts (figure 12.6). The inadequacy of existing published drift maps has hitherto made any examination beyond the river valleys inadequate. Recent fieldwork, however, coupled with an extensive survey of field names has considerably increased the knowledge of the subsoils of the region and shows that, away from the major rivers, the affinity of settlement for sand and gravel areas follows the same pattern. Ettington, for example, a parish which extends from the river Stour to the river Dene, contained five ancient manors, where each settlement nucleus was sited beside a tract of permeable soil (figure 12.7).

The attraction of settlement to these specific areas of land was twofold. They provided the soils most suited to arable farming, being light textured, tractable and free draining and easily managed in all seasons, even with the lighter plough. The Land Utilization Survey of 1933 emphasizes the close connection between superficial deposits and land utilization, and clearly shows that soils derived from drift deposits were particularly intensively cultivated while the heavy, badly drained soils based on the clays tended to be avoided and left under grass (McPherson 1946, p. 725). These areas appear to have been the foci of settlement from which expansion took place on to more marginal lands in times of need and were usually the areas still under cultivation when arable farming retreated.

Water supply

The second but equally important factor in determining the selection of settlement sites was the need for water. An adequate water supply is essential if man, animals and crops are to survive. The majority of springs in the region emerge from the base of superficial deposits resting on the clay formation, so that good water supply and superior soils march hand in hand. Any town, village or even isolated dwelling resting on the Lias Clays or Keuper Marl would be badly off for water if dependent on supplies from these formations. The lands of the middle Lias and the Arden Sandstone were equally suited for primitive arable cultivation and provide further examples of the juxtaposition of better soils and good water supply. It is not surprising therefore that sites on the periphery of the glacial deposits, the hills of Arden Sandstone, and middle Lias, from which these abundant clear springs issued, were apparently chosen by early medieval settlers for the nuclei of their farms.

Evidence of early cultivated lands

There is some evidence to show that the lighter, more easily-worked soils were a factor of some significance in the establishment of early Anglo-Saxon settlement, in as much as arable cultivation appears at one time to have been limited to these tracts of land. Oldfield is a term which frequently occurs in field and minor names through the region and close scrutiny has shown that, where there is positive evidence of their location, they are invariably situated on the river terraces and superficial deposits. In Clifford Chambers, Oldfield is derived from an isolated tract of sands and gravels forming part of the second terrace which flanks the river Stour; (*Victoria County History, Gloucs* VI, p. 211) figure 12.8). Similarly, Stivichall, now part of the Coventry conurbation, possessed an Oldfield in AD 1275 which also lay on a tract of the second terrace of the river Avon (Shakespeare Birthplace Library, Stratford, Gregory Hood Coll., DR 10, fo. 604). Oldfield in Stareton was also similarly based on river gravels, while at Sibford Gower, Oldfield lay on the excellent red soils of the middle Lias (Stoneleigh Abbey Estate Maps; Gelling 1953–4, II, p. 406). It is feasible that the various Oldfields represent the early nuclei of arable lands of the forerunner of townships, and that population growth subsequently made territorial expansion on to less favourable land a necessity, a process that eventually absorbed the heaths, pastures and woodlands of many settlements, particularly in the Feldon.

Through the interpretation of the documentary and field-name evidence of Stretton-on-Fosse, it

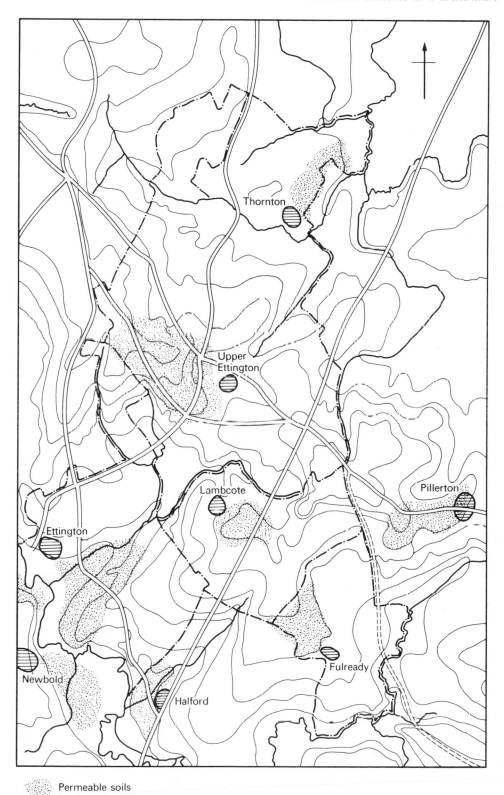

Permeable soils

Figure 12.7 Settlement and permeable soils, Ettington, Warwickshire.

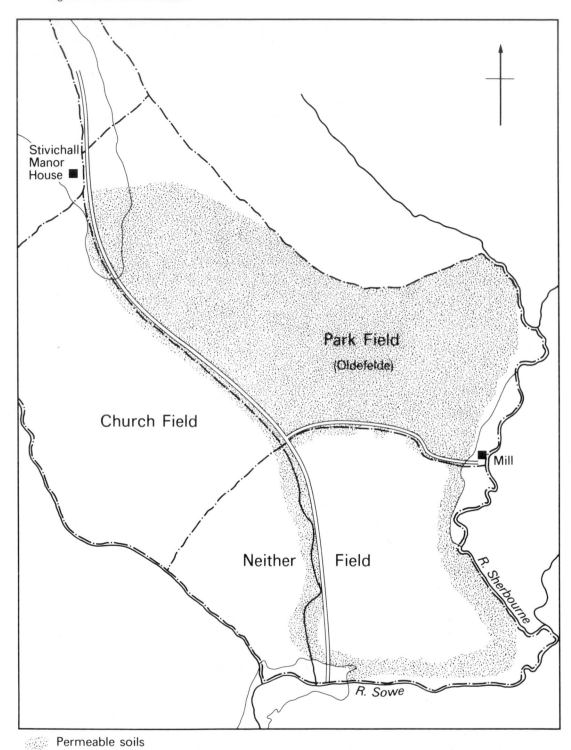

Permeable soils

Figure 12.8 Common fields and permeable soils, Stivichall, near Coventry.

can be shown that a sand and gravel-capped hill at one time seemed to constitute the only arable land of the village. It is significant therefore that a pagan Anglo-Saxon cemetery should lie on the periphery of this area. The Anglo-Saxon cemeteries at Napton-on-the-Hill, Long Itchington, Ebrington, Burton Dassett and Farnborough appear to be similarly situated, each lying on the margin of glacial spreads capping minor hills, while, on the river terraces, the cemeteries at Bidford-on-Avon, Alveston, Longbridge and Emscote all lie at the edge of gravel tracts. For cemeteries to be sited on the periphery of the gravels in all probability suggests that they were sited on the edge of cultivated fields (Ford 1973, pp. 99–101).

Not all burials however are similarly situated; the cemetery at Long Compton for example is located on the parish boundary. From evidence in Wessex, it had been suggested that these latter burials were deliberately placed and that some boundaries were in being at least as early as the pagan period. The relative chronology of the two types is a matter of some importance and could well be a crucial factor for the evolution of settlement in terms of Anglo-Saxon cemeteries.

The pattern of site distribution in both Anglo-Saxon and Romano-British times shows the same marked attraction to these glacial plots and it is likely that the lighter permeable soils to which they gave rise have formed the hub of many settlement units throughout these periods, although other sites may also have been established on less productive lands. Agricultural considerations are most likely to have ensured continuity of occupation on or near these richer farming areas, possibly since the first appearance of sedentary farmers in the region. This occupation, however, need not be envisaged as the continuous use of the same habitation sites, creating a vertical stratigraphy with each period represented in an imaginary section, but rather a palimpsest of features giving rise to a horizontal stratigraphy possibly over a wide area. In such an assemblage, settlement sites of different periods may coincide, be in juxtaposition, or be at a distance apart, moving in an amoeba-like fashion around a central core of more permeable soils. On the other hand, if land, in a particular period, perhaps as part of agricultural re-organization, was farmed from elsewhere, evidence of habitation in that period would be absent. An abandoned site, therefore, should not be taken as evidence of decline or cessation of farming in that area (Ford 1973, pp. 146–7).

Arable fields

Fields or arable plots have been necessary in one form or another since the development of settled agriculture. The divisions of the open field system of cultivation have often been described and the region provides some of the more outstanding examples of surviving ridge and furrow, particularly in the Feldon. This phenomenon is frequently represented as a legacy of medieval farming. By contrast, the Arden contained a large number of single farmsteads in enclosed fields, although patterns suggestive of open field cultivation have been found in areas close to villages and hamlets. The relationship between the two types of field formation constitutes a major problem in relative chronology.

Joan Thirsk has emphasized the principal difference between the communal farming practices of the woodland or pastoral areas on the one hand and on the arable areas on the other. She argues that, in lands such as the Feldon, the common fields system reached a more mature stage of development. In pastoral areas, like the Arden, arable crops were grown for subsistence only, so the arable fields did not have to be cropped with the utmost economy nor did the stubble need to be economically grazed. There was no reason therefore for rigorous control of cultivation of ploughlands (Thirsk 1964).

In the Feldon, with a large and growing population, land needed to be intensively cultivated and grazed and this would be particularly so if any settlement ceased to have access to its traditional pasture and woodland in the Arden. Where settlements were deprived of these facilities, perhaps by the achievement of independence of their secondary settlements in the Arden, then a more rigorous order of cultivation would be required in the erstwhile parent community. As it would appear that breaking of

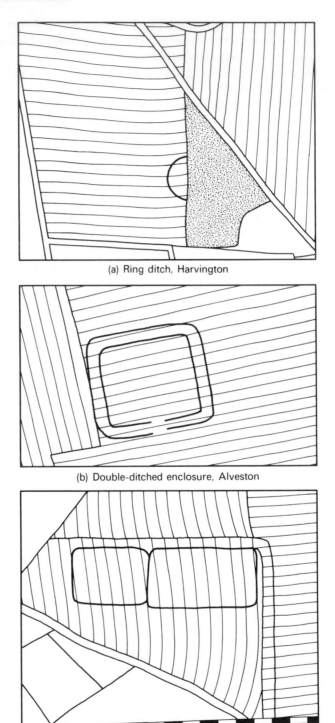

(a) Ring ditch, Harvington

(b) Double-ditched enclosure, Alveston

(c) Conjoined enclosure, Cropredy

Figure 12.9   Strip cultivation and pre-medieval features.

traditional links between Feldon communities and their Arden holdings began prior to the Conquest, then conditions would exist in the Feldon for the introduction of common field agriculture at that time. Furthermore, as the movement towards separation seems to have been gradual, lasting until the thirteenth century, then the introduction of more ordered systems of cultivation in Feldon settlements need not necessarily have been a uniform process.

There is some evidence available particularly in the centre and south of the middle Avon region which suggests that medieval surveyors, in setting out furlongs, were aware of, and used pre-existing landmarks and land divisions. Many of these alignments, which were legacies of the Roman and earlier periods, also appear to have influenced the orientation of ploughstrips. Examples where enclosures of Romano-British type have determined the layout of furlongs occur at Alveston, Hunscote, Cropredy, Hampton Lucy and Crewe Farm, Kenilworth, while at King's Newnham, Church Lawford, Long-bridge, Harvington and Burton Hastings, the relationship between ring ditches, barrow sites and headlands of furlongs is such that continuity of some prehistoric field boundaries into the medieval period must be given serious consideration (Ford 1973, pp. 108–14) (figure 12.9). It reflects the relationship between barrows and Celtic fields in Wessex where many burial mounds are sited at the corners of fields or along the scarps which divide them. If it is known that medieval field re-organization included some pre-existing boundaries while excluding others and, if some minor Roman and pre-historic land divisions have survived in the geography of present-day parishes, then survival of major boundaries is also feasible.

Bibliography

ADDYMAN, P. V. and LEIGH, D. 1973: The Anglo-Saxon village at Chalton, Hampshire: second interim report. *Medieval Archaeology* XVII, 1–25.

ADDYMAN, P. V. and WHITWELL, J. B. 1970: Some Middle Saxon pottery types in Lincolnshire. *Antiquaries Journal* I, 96–102.

AGERSKOW, M. 1958: *The Reclamation of Waste in the Forest of Knaresborough: A Study of Settlement and Enclosure.* MA thesis, Dept of Geography, University of Leeds.

ALCOCK, L. 1971: *Arthur's Britain.* London.

ALTENA, H. H. VAN REGTEREN 1969: Red-painted and glazed pottery in western Europe from the eighth to the twelfth century: the Netherlands. *Medieval Archaeology* XIII, 129–32.

ANDERSON, O. S. 1936: *The English Hundred-Names* III. Lund.

ANDREWS, D. D. and MILNE, G. eds 1979: *Domestic Settlement I: Areas 10 and 6. Vol. I of Wharram: A Study of Settlement on the Yorkshire Wolds,* ed. J. G. Hurst, Society of Medieval Archaeology Monographs no. 8.

ARTHUR, B. V. and JOPE, E. M. 1962–3: Early Saxon pottery kilns at Purwell Farm, Cassington, Oxfordshire. *Medieval Archaeology* VI–VII, 1–14.

ASTON, T. H. 1958: The origins of the manor in England. *Transactions of the Royal Historical Society,* 5th series, VIII, 59–83.

BAKER, A. R. H. and BUTLIN, R. A. eds 1973: *Studies of Field Systems in the British Isles.* Cambridge.

BARLOW, F. 1963: *The English Church 1000–1066.*

BARROW, G. W. S. 1973: Pre-feudal Scotland: shires and thanes. *The Kingdom of the Scots.* London, 7–68.

1975: The pattern of lordship and feudal settlement in Cumbria. *Journal of Medieval History* I, 117–38.

BARTLEY, D.D., CHAMBERS, C. and HART-JONES, B. 1976: The vegetational history of parts of south and east Durham. *New Phytologist* LXXVII, 437–68.

BERESFORD, M. 1967: *New Towns of the Middle Ages.* London.

BERESFORD, M. and HURST, J. G. eds 1971: *Deserted Medieval Villages.* London.

BINCHY, D. A. 1970: *Celtic and Anglo-Saxon Kingship.* Oxford.

BIRCH, W. de G. 1885–93: *Cartularium Saxonicum.* 3 vols, London.

BIRKS, H. J. B. 1965: Pollen analytical investigations at Holcroft Moss, Lancashire, and Lindow Moss, Cheshire. *Journal of Ecology* LIII, 299–314.

BISHOP, T. A. M. 1948: The Norman settlement in Yorkshire. *Studies in Medieval History Presented to F. M. Powicke,* ed. R. W. Hunt, W. A. Pantin and R. W. Southern. Oxford, 1–14.

BONNEY, D. J. 1966: Pagan Saxon burials and boundaries in Wiltshire. *Wiltshire Archaeological and Natural History Magazine* LXI, 25–30.

1972: Early boundaries in Wessex. *Archaeology and the Landscape: Essays for L. V. Grinsell*, ed. P. J. Fowler. London, 168–86.

BOWEN, H. C. and FOWLER, P. J. eds 1978: *Early Land Allotment*. British Archaeological Reports XLVIII.

BRANDON, P. F. 1969: Medieval clearances in the East Sussex Weald. *Transactions of the Institute of British Geographers* XLVIII, 135–53.

1974: *The Sussex Landscape*. London.

BROTHWELL, D. 1972: British palaeodemography and earlier British populations. *World Archaeology* IV, 75–87.

BRUCE-MITFORD, R. L. S. 1972: *The Sutton Hoo Ship Burial*. London.

BRYANT, G. F. and STEANE, J. M. 1969: The pottery: excavations at the deserted medieval settlement at Lyveden. *Northampton Museums and Art Gallery Journal* V, 19–33.

BURSTOW, G. P. and HOLLEYMAN, G. A. 1964: Excavations at Ranscombe Camp, 1959–60. *Sussex Archaeological Collections* LII, 55–67.

CAM, H. M. 1944: *Liberties and Communities in Medieval England*. Cambridge, 64–105.

CAMERON, K. 1961: *English Place-Names*. London.

1965: *Scandinavian Settlement in the Territory of the Five Boroughs: The Place-Name Evidence.* Inaugural lecture, University of Nottingham.

1968: Eccles in English place-names. *Christianity in Britain 300–700*, ed. M. W. Barley and R. P. C. Hanson. Leicester, 87–92.

1970: Scandinavian settlement in the territory of the five boroughs: the place-name evidence. Part II, place-names in Thorp. *Medieval Scandinavia* III, 35–49.

1971: Scandinavian settlement in the territory of the five boroughs: the place-name evidence. Part III, the Grimston hybrids. *England Before the Conquest: Studies in Primary Sources Presented to Dorothy Whitelock*, ed. P. Clemoes and Kathleen Hughes. Cambridge, 147–63.

1973: Early field-names in an English-named Lincolnshire village. *Otium et Negotium: Studies in Onomatology and Library Science Presented to Olof von Feilitzen*, ed. F. Sandgren. Stockholm, 38–43.

CHARLES-EDWARDS, T. M. 1971: Some Celtic kinship terms. *Bulletin of the Board of Celtic Studies* XXIV 105–22.

1972: Kinship, status and the origins of the hide. *Past and Present* LII, 3–33.

CHARLESTON, R. J. 1965: *Roman Pottery*. London.

COLGRAVE, B. ed. 1927: *The Life of Bishop Wilfred by Eddius Stephanus*. Cambridge.

ed. 1940: *Two Lives of St Cuthbert*. Cambridge.

ed. 1956: *Felix's Life of St Guthlac*. Cambridge.

COLGRAVE, B. and MYNORS, R. A. B. eds 1969: *Bede's Ecclesiastical History of the English People*. Oxford.

COOPER, W. D. 1869: Mayfield. *Sussex Archaeological Collections* XXI, 1–19.

COX, B. 1973: The significance of the distribution of English place-names in -*hām* in the Midlands and East Anglia. *English Place-Name Society Journal* V, 15–73.

1976: The place-names of the earliest English records. *Journal of the English Place-Name Society* VIII, 12–66.

CUNLIFFE, B. 1970: The Saxon culture sequence at Portchester Castle. *Antiquaries Journal* I, 167–85.

DARBY, H. C. 1977: *Domesday England*. Cambridge.

DARBY, H. C. and CAMPBELL, E. M. J. 1962: *The Domesday Geography of South-East England*. Cambridge.

DARBY, H. C. and TERRETT, I. B. 1971: *The Domesday Geography of Midland England*. 2nd edn, Cambridge.

DELMAIRE, R. 1969: Persistance des inhumations avec vases à Saint-Omer au XIVe siècle. *Revue du Nord* LI, 350–52.

DODGSON, J. M. 1966: The significance of the distribution of the English place-name in *-ingas*, *-inga-* in south-east England. *Medieval Archaeology* X, 1–29.

—— 1967a: The *-ing* in English place-names like Birmingham and Altrincham. *Beiträge zur Namenforschung*, N F II, 221–45.

—— 1967b: Various forms of Old English *-ing* in English place-names. *Beiträge zur Namenforschung*, N F II, 325–96.

—— 1968a: The English arrival in Cheshire. *Transactions of the Historic Society of Lancashire and Cheshire for 1967* CXIX, 1–37.

—— 1968b: Various English place-name formations containing Old English *-ing*. *Beiträge zur Namenforschung*, N F III, 141–89.

—— 1973: Place-names from *hām* distinguished from *hamm* names in relation to the settlement of Kent, Surrey and Sussex. *Anglo-Saxon England* II, 1–50.

DOMESDAY BOOK 1783. 2 vols, London, Public Records Commission.

DOUGLAS, D. C. ed. 1944: *The Domesday Monachorum of Christ Church, Canterbury.*

DU BOULAY, F. R. H. 1966: *The Lordship of Canterbury.* London.

DUGDALE, W. 1656: *The Antiquities of Warwickshire.*

DUNNING, G. C. 1967: Late medieval pots with lettering. *Medieval Archaeology* XI, 233–41.

—— 1968: The trade in medieval pottery around the North Sea. *Rotterdam Papers*, ed. J. G. N. Renaud. Rotterdam, 35–58.

—— 1969: Medieval church cruets in pottery. *Medieval Archaeology* XIII, 226–7.

EKWALL, E. 1928: *English River-Names.* Oxford.

—— 1936: *Studies on English Place-Names.* Stockholm.

—— 1960: *The Concise Oxford Dictionary of English Place-Names.* 4th edn, London.

—— 1962: Variation and change in English place-names. *Vetenskaps-Societeten i Lund, Årsbok,* 3–49.

ELLIS, H. E. 1833: *A General Introduction to Domesday Book.* 2 vols.

—— ed. 1838: *The Record of Caernarvon.*

EMANUEL, H. D. ed. 1967: *The Latin Texts of the Welsh Laws.* Cardiff.

EMERY, F. 1974: *The Oxfordshire Landscape.* London.

EVANS, J. G. 1885: Casgliad o Ddiarhebion Cymreig. *Transactions of the Liverpool National Eisteddfod, 1884,* 528–84.

EYRE, S. R. and JONES, G. R. J. eds 1966: *Geography as Human Ecology.* London.

FÄGERSTEN, A. 1933: *The Place-Names of Dorset.* Uppsala.

FÂRRER, W. 1914: *Early Yorkshire Charters* I. Edinburgh.

FELLOWS JENSEN, G. 1972: *Scandinavian Settlement Names in Yorkshire.* Copenhagen.

—— 1975: The Vikings in England: a review. *Anglo-Saxon England* IV, 181–206.

—— 1978a: *Scandinavian Settlement Names in the East Midlands.* Copenhagen.

—— 1978b: Place-names and settlement in the North Riding of Yorkshire. *Northern History* XIV, 19–46.

FINBERG, H. P. R. 1961: *The Early Charters of the West Midlands.* Leicester.

FISHER, R. A. and TAYLOR, G. L. 1940: Scandinavian influence in Scottish ethnology. *Nature* CXLV, 590.

FOARD, G. 1978: Systematic fieldwalking and the investigation of Saxon settlement in Northamptonshire. *World Archaeology* IX, 357–74.

FORD, W. J. 1973: *The Patterns of Settlement in the Central Region of the Warwickshire Avon.* MA thesis, University of Leicester.

FÖRSTER, M. 1942: *Der Flussname Themse und seine Sippe*. Munich.

FOSSIER, R. 1968: *La terre et les hommes en Picardie jusqu'à la fin du XIIIe siècle*. 2 vols, Paris.

FOSTER, C. W. and MAJOR, K. eds 1931–73: *Registrum Antiquissimum of the Cathedral Church of Lincoln*. Lincoln Record Society.

FOWLER, P. J. ed. 1975: *Recent Work in Rural Archaeology*. Bradford-on-Avon.

1966: Two finds of Saxon domestic pottery in Wiltshire. *Wiltshire Archaeological and Natural History Magazine* LXI, 31–7.

GELLING, M. 1953–54: *The Place-Names of Oxfordshire*. Cambridge, EPNS, XXIII–IV.

1960: The element *hamm* in English place-names: a topographical investigation. *Namn och Bygd* XLVIII, 140–62.

1961: Place-names and Anglo-Saxon paganism. *University of Birmingham Historical Journal* VIII (1), 7–25.

1962: Review of Cameron 1961 and of P. H. Reaney, *The Origin of English Place-Names*. *Oxoniensia* XXVI–XXVII, 347–50.

1967: English place-names derived from the compound *wīchām*. *Medieval Archaeology* XI, 87–104.

1967–68: The charter bounds of Æscesbyrig and Ashbury. *Berkshire Archaeological Journal* LXIII, 5–13.

1970, 1971: The place-names of the Isle of Man. *Journal of the Manx Museum* VII (86), 130–39 and (87), 168–75.

1972: The place-name evidence. *Excavations at Shakenoak Farm, near Wilcote, Oxfordshire. Part III, Site F*, ed. A. C. C. Brodribb, A. R. Hands and D. R. Walker. Oxford, 134–40.

1973: Further thoughts on pagan place-names. *Otium et Negotium: Studies in Onomatology and Library Science Presented to Olof von Feilitzen*, ed. F. Sandgren. Stockholm, 109–28.

1973–6: *The Place-Names of Berkshire*. Cambridge, EPNS, XLIX, L, LI.

1974a: Recent work on English place-names. *The Local Historian* XI (1), 3–7.

1974b: The chronology of English place-names. Rowley 1974, 93–101.

1974c: Some notes on Warwickshire place-names. *Transactions of the Birmingham and Warwickshire Archaeological Society* LXXXVI, 59–79.

1976: Introduction to the place-names of Berkshire. *The Place-Names of Berkshire Part III*. Cambridge, EPNS LI, 800–47.

1978: *Signposts to the Past: Place-names and the History of England*. London.

GELLING, M., NICOLAISEN, W. and RICHARDS, M. 1970: *The Names of Towns and Cities in Britain*. London.

GODWIN, H. 1967: Pollen-analytic evidence for the cultivation of *Cannabis* in England. *Review of Palaeobotany and Palynology* IV, 71–80.

GOVER, J. E. B., MAWER, A. and STENTON, F. M. 1940: *The Place-Names of Nottinghamshire*. Cambridge, EPNS, XVII.

GOVER, J. E. B., MAWER, A., STENTON, F. M. and HOUGHTON, F. T. S. 1936: *The Place-Names of Warwickshire*. Cambridge, EPNS, XIII.

GREENWELL, W. ed. 1852: *Bolden Buke*. Durham, Surtees Society, XXV.

GRUNDY, G. B. 1919, 1920: The Saxon land charters of Wiltshire. *Archaeological Journal* XXVI, 143–301; XXVII, 8–126.

HARVEY, M. 1976: *Morphogenetic Analysis of Fields and Settlements in Holderness, Yorkshire*. Ph.D thesis, University of London.

1978: *The Morphogenetic and Tenurial Structure of a Yorkshire Township: Preston in Holderness 1066–1750*. Department of Geography, Queen Mary College, University of London, Occasional Papers XIII.

HARVEY, S. 1971: Domesday Book and its predecessors. *English Historical Review* LXXXVI, 753–73.

HICKS, S. P. 1971: Pollen analytical evidence for the effect of prehistoric agriculture on the vegetation of north Derbyshire. *New Phytologist* LXX, 647–67.

HILTON, R. H. ed. 1952: *The Ministers Accounts of the Warwickshire Estates of the Duke of Clarence, 1479–80.* Oxford, Dugdale Society, XXI.

   ed. 1960: *The Stoneleigh Leger Book.* Oxford, Dugdale Society, XXIV.

HINDE, J. H. ed. 1868: *Historia de Sancto Cuthberto.* Durham, Surtees Society, LI.

HJORTH PEDERSEN, B. 1960: Bebyggelsesnavne på -by sammensat med personnavn. *Ti Afhandlingar.* Copenhagen, 10–46.

HOSKINS, W. G. 1954a: Regional farming in England. *Agricultural History Review* II, 3–11.

   1954b: The medieval period. *The Oxford Region*, ed. A. F. Martin and R. W. Steel. Oxford, 103–20.

   1970: *The Making of the English Landscape.* London.

HOYT, R. S. 1962: A pre-Domesday Kentish assessment list. *Early Medieval Miscellany.* Pipe Roll Society, n s XXXVI, 189–202.

HUGHES, K. 1972: *Early Christian Ireland: Introduction to the Sources.* London.

HURST, J. G. 1957: Saxo-Norman pottery in East Anglia. *Proceedings of the Cambridge Antiquarian Society* L, 29–60.

HVASS, S. 1975: Jernalderlandsbyen i Hodde. *Mark og Montre: Fra sydvestjyske museer* XI, 28–36.

IVERSEN, J. 1949: The influence of prehistoric man on vegetation. *Danmarks geologiske Undersøgelse* IV 1–25.

JACKSON, K. H. 1953: *Language and History in Early Britain.* Edinburgh.

JENKINS, D. ed. 1963: *Llyfr Colân.* Cardiff.

JENNINGS, B. 1970: *A History of Harrogate and Knaresborough.* Huddersfield.

JOLLIFFE, J. E. A. 1926: Northumbrian institutions. *English Historical Review* XLI, 1–42.

   1933: *Pre-Feudal England: the Jutes.* Oxford.

   1934: The era of the folk in English history. *Oxford Essays in Medieval History Presented to H. E. Salter.* Oxford, 1–32.

JONES, G. D. B. and LEWIS, P. R. 1972: *The Roman Gold Mines at Dolaucothi.*

JONES, G. R. J. 1955: The distribution of medieval settlement in Anglesey. *Anglesey Transactions*, 27–96.

   1960: The pattern of settlement on the Welsh border. *Agricultural History Review* VIII, 66–81.

   1961a: The tribal system in Wales: a reassessment in the light of settlement studies. *Welsh History Review* I, 111–32.

   1961b: Settlement patterns in Anglo-Saxon England. *Antiquity* XXXV, 221–32.

   1961c: Basic patterns of settlement distribution in northern England. *Advancement of Science* XVIII, 192–200.

   1961d: Early territorial organization in England and Wales. *Geografiske Annaler* XLIII, 174–81.

   1964: The distribution of bond settlements in north-west Wales. *Welsh History Review* II, 19–36.

   1965: Early territorial organization in northern England and its bearing on the Scandinavian settlement. *The Fourth Viking Congress*, ed. A. Small. Edinburgh, 67–84.

   1966: The cultural landscape of Yorkshire: the origins of our villages. *Yorkshire Philosophical Society Transactions*, 45–57.

   1971: The multiple estate as a model framework for tracing early stages in the evolution of rural settlement. *L'Habitat et les paysages ruraux d'Europe*, ed. F. Dussart. Liège, 251–67.

   1972: Post-Roman Wales. *The Agrarian History of England and Wales* I, ii, AD 43–1042, ed. H. P. R. Finberg. Cambridge, 281–382.

JONES PIERCE, T. 1941: The growth of commutation in Gwynedd during the thirteenth century. *Bulletin of the Board of Celtic Studies* X, 309–32.

JOPE, E. M. 1963: The regional cultures of medieval Britain. *Culture and Environment*, ed. I. Ll. Foster and L. Alcock. London, 327–50.

KEMBLE, J. M. 1839–48: *Codex Diplomaticus Aevi Saxonici*. 6 vols, London.

KING, A. 1978: Gauber high pasture, Ribblehead—an interim report. *Viking Age York and the North*, ed. R. A. Hall, Council for British Archaeology Research Report XXVII, 21–5.

LEEDS, E. T. 1948: A Saxon village at Sutton Courtnay, Berkshire. *Archaeologia* XCII, 79–93.

LENNARD, R. V. 1951: The economic position of the bordars and cottars of Domesday Book. *Economic Journal* LXI, 342–71.

1959: *Rural England 1086–1135*. Oxford.

LE PATOUREL, H. E. J. 1962–64: The pottery. *Pontefract Priory Excavations*, ed. C. V. Bellamy. Thoresby Society, XLIX, 106–22.

1967: The pottery. *Kirkstall Abbey Excavations*. Thoresby Society LI, 36–59.

1968: Documentary evidence and the medieval pottery industry. *Medieval Archaeology* XII, 101–26.

LEWIS, P. R. and JONES, G. D. B. 1969: Dolaucothi gold mines. I, the surface evidence. *Antiquaries Journal* LXIX, 244–72.

LIEBERMANN, F. 1903–16 *Die Gesetze der Angelsachsen*. 3 vols, Halle.

LLOYD, J. E. 1890: Welsh place-names. *Y Cymmrodor* XII, 15–60.

LYNCH, F. 1970: *Prehistoric Anglesey*. Llangefni.

MCPHERSON, A. W. 1946: Warwickshire. *Land Utilization Survey* LXII, ed. L. Dudley Stamp.

MAITLAND, F. W. 1897: *Domesday Book and Beyond*. Cambridge.

MAWER, A. 1920: *The Place-Names of Northumberland and Durham*. Cambridge.

MAWER, A. and STENTON, F. M. 1929–30: *The Place-Names of Sussex*. Cambridge, EPNS, VI–VII.

MAYES, P. and PIRIE, E. J. 1966: A Cistercian ware kiln of the early sixteenth century at Potterton, Yorkshire. *Antiquaries Journal* XLVI, 255–76.

MAYHEW, A. 1973: *Rural Settlement and Farming in Germany*.

MEANEY, A. 1964: *A Gazetteer of Early Anglo-Saxon Burial Sites*. London.

MEITZEN, A. 1895: *Siedelung und Agrarwesen der Westgermanen und Ostgermanen, der Kelten, Römer, Finnen und Slawen*. 3 vols, Berlin.

MINISTRY OF AGRICULTURE, FISHERIES AND FOOD 1968: *Agricultural Land Classification Map of England and Wales: Explanatory Note*. London.

MONEY, J. H. 1941: An interim report on excavations at High Rocks, Tunbridge Wells, 1940. *Sussex Archaeological Collections* LXXXII, 104–9.

MORTIMER, J. R. 1905: *Forty Years' Researches in British and Saxon Burial Mounds of East Yorkshire*. London.

MYRES, J. N. L. 1956: Romano-Saxon pottery. *Dark Age Britain*, ed. D. B. Harden, London, 16–39,

1969: *Anglo-Saxon Pottery and the Settlement of England*. Oxford.

MYRES, J. N. L. and GREEN, B. 1973: *The Anglo-Saxon Cemeteries of Caistor-by-Norwich and Markshall, Norfolk*. London.

NASH-WILLIAMS, V. E. 1950: *The Early Christian Monuments of Wales*. Cardiff.

NICOLAISEN, W. 1957. Die alteuropäischen Gewässernamen der britischen Hauptinsel. *Beiträge zur Namenforschung* VIII, 209–68.

OFTEDAL, M. 1962: Norse place-names in Celtic Scotland. *Proceedings of the International Congress of Celtic Studies, Dublin, 6–10 July 1959*. Dublin.

OWEN, A. ed. 1841: *Ancient Laws and Institutes of Wales*. 2 vols, London.

OWEN, D. 1971: *Church and Society in Medieval Lincolnshire*. Lincoln.

    1978: Bedfordshire chapelries: an essay in rural settlement history. *Worthington George Smith and other studies presented to Joyce Godber*, Bedfordshire Historical Record Society LVII, 9–20.

PARKER, H. 1965: Feddersen Wierde and Vallhagar: a contrast in settlements. *Medieval Archaeology* IX, 1–10.

PETCH, D. F. and THOMPSON, F. H. 1959: Excavations in Commonhall St, Chester, 1954–56. *Chester Archaeological Society Journal* XLVI, 33–60.

PEVSNER, N. 1957: *The Buildings of England: Northumberland*. London.

PHYTHIAN-ADAMS, C. 1978: *Continuity, Fields and Fission: The Making of a Midland Parish*. Leicester University, Department of English Local History, Occasional Papers, 3rd series IV.

PIGGOTT, S. and PIGGOTT, C. M. 1944: Excavations of barrows on Crichel and Launceston Downs, Dorset. *Archaeologia* XC, 47–80.

PLUMMER, C. 1896: *Baedae Opera Historica*. Oxford.

RACKHAM, B. 1972: *Medieval English Pottery*. London.

RAHTZ, P. 1976: Gazetteer of Anglo-Saxon domestic settlement sites. *The Archaeology of Anglo-Saxon England*, ed. D. M. Wilson, London, 405–52.

REDWOOD, B. C. and WILSON, A. E. eds 1958: *Custumals of the Sussex Manors of the Archbishop of Canterbury*. Sussex Record Society, LVII.

REES, W. 1963: Survivals of ancient Celtic custom in medieval England. *Angles and Britons* (O'Donnell Lectures by J. R. R. Tolkien and others). Cardiff, 146–68.

RICHARDS, M. ed. 1954: *The Laws of Hywel Dda (The Book of Blegywryd)*. Liverpool.

RIVET, A. L. F. 1958: *Town and Country in Roman Britain*. London.

ROBERTS, B. K., TURNER, J. and WARD, P. F. 1973: Recent forest history and land use in Weardale, northern England. *Quaternary Plant Ecology*, ed. H. J. B. Birks and R. G. West. Oxford, 207–11.

ROBERTS, E. 1958: *Memoirs of the Soil Survey of Great Britain: The County of Anglesey*.

ROBERTSON, A. J. 1956: *Anglo-Saxon Charters*. Cambridge.

RODWELL, W. 1978: Relict landscapes in Essex. Bowen and Fowler 1978, 89–98.

ROUND, J. H. 1899: The settlement of the south- and east-Saxons. *The Commune of London and Other Studies*. 1–27.

ROWLEY, T. ed. 1974: Anglo-Saxon settlement and landscape. *British Archaeological Reports*, VI.

ROYAL COMMISSION ON HISTORICAL MONUMENTS (ENGLAND) 1970: *An Inventory of Historical Monuments in the County of Dorset* II and III. London.

SALZMAN, L. F. 1931: The rapes of Sussex. *Sussex Archaeological Collections* LXXII, 20–29.

SAWYER, P. H. 1968: *Anglo-Saxon Charters: An Annotated List and Bibliography*. London.

    1974: Anglo-Saxon settlement: the documentary evidence. Rowley 1974, 108–19.

    1978: *From Roman Britain to Norman England*. London.

SCAMMELL, G. V. 1956: *Hugh du Puiset*. Cambridge.

SEEBOHM, F. 1890: *The English Village Community*. London.

SHOESMITH, R. 1968: Hereford city excavations. *Transactions of the Woolhope Naturalists' Field Club* XXXIX, 348–53.

SMALL, A. ed. 1965: *The Fourth Viking Congress*.

SMEDLEY, N. and OWLES, E. J. A sherd of Ipswich ware with face-mask decoration. *Proceedings of the Suffolk Institute of Archaeology* I, 84–7.

SMITH, A. H. 1956: *English Place-Name Elements*. Cambridge, EPNS, XXV–XXVI.

    1961–3: *The Place-Names of the West Riding of Yorkshire*. Cambridge, EPNS, XXX–XXXVII.

    1964–5: *The Place-Names of Gloucestershire*. Cambridge, EPNS, XXXVIII–XLI.

STAMP, L. DUDLEY and HOSKINS, W. G. 1963: *The Common Lands of England and Wales*. London.

STENTON, F. M. 1929: The English element. *Introduction to the Survey of English Place-Names*, part I, ed. A. Mawer and F. M. Stenton, Cambridge, EPNS I pt. i, 36–54.

    1971: *Anglo-Saxon England*. 3rd edn, Oxford.

STOKES, E. ed. 1932: *Warwickshire Feet of Fines 1195–1284*. Oxford, Dugdale Society, XI.

TALLIS, J. H. and SWITSUR, V. R. 1973: Studies on southern Pennine peats. VI, A radiocarbon-dated pollen diagram from Featherbed Moss, Derbyshire. *Journal of Ecology* LXI, 743–51.

TAUBER, H. 1965: Differential pollen dispersion and the interpretation of pollen diagrams. *Danmarks Geologiske Undersøgelse* II, 1–69.

TAYLOR, C. C. 1974: The Anglo-Saxon countryside. Rowley 1974, 5–15.

    1975: Roman settlements in the Nene Valley: the impact of recent archaeology. Fowler 1975, 107–19.

    1977: Polyfocal settlement and the English village. *Medieval Archaeology* XXI, 189–93.

TAYLOR, C. C. and FOWLER, P. J. 1978: Roman fields into medieval furlongs. Bowen and Fowler 1978, 159–62.

THIRSK, J. 1954: Farming in Kesteven 1540–1640. *Lincolnshire Architectural and Archaeological Society Reports and Papers* VI, 37–53.

    1964: The common fields. *Past and Present* XXIX (December), 3–25.

THOMAS, C. 1954: Excavations at Gwithian, Cornwall. *Proceedings of the West Cornwall Field Club*. I (2), 66–72.

THOMPSON, F. H. 1956: Anglo-Saxon sites in Lincolnshire. *Antiquaries Journal* XXXVI, 181–199.

TINSLEY, H. M. 1972: *A Palynological Study of Changing Woodland Limits on the Nidderdale Moors*. PhD thesis, University of Leeds.

TINSLEY, H. M. and SMITH, R. T. 1974: Ecological investigations at a Romano-British earthwork in the Yorkshire Pennines. *Yorkshire Archaeological Journal* XLVI, 23–33.

TURNER, J. 1970: Post-Neolithic disturbance of British vegetation. *Studies in the Vegetational History of the British Isles*, ed. D. Walker and R. G. West. Cambridge, 97–116.

TURNOR, E. 1806. *Collections for the History of the Town and Soke of Grantham*. London.

VAN ES, W. A. 1967: *Wijster: a Native Village beyond the Imperial Frontier, 150–425 A.D.* Palaeohistoria XI. Groningen.

VINOGRADOFF, P. 1908: *English Society in the Eleventh Century*. Oxford.

VINOGRADOFF, P. and MORGAN, F. W. eds 1914: *Survey of the Honour of Denbigh*. London.

VON FEILITZEN, O. 1937: *The Pre-Conquest Personal Names of Domesday Book*. Uppsala.

WADE-EVANS, A. W. ed. 1909: *Welsh Medieval Law*. Oxford.

WAINWRIGHT, F. T. 1945: Field-names of Amounderness Hundred. *Transactions of the Historic Society of Lancashire and Cheshire* XCVII, 181–222.

    1945–46: The Scandinavians in Lancashire. *Transactions of the Lancashire and Cheshire Antiquarian Society* LVIII, 71–116.

WAINWRIGHT, F. T. 1962: *Archaeology, Place-Names and History*. London.

WALMSLEY, J. F. R. 1968: The *Censarii* of Burton Abbey and the Domesday population. *North Staffordshire Journal of Field Studies* VIII, 73–80.

WARD, G. 1936: The Haeselersc Charter of 1018. *Sussex Archaelogical Collections* LXXVII, 119–29.

WATTS, V. E. 1970: Place-names. *Durham County and City with Teeside,* ed. J. C. Dewdney. Durham, 251–65.

WEBSTER, G. and HOBLEY, B. 1964: Aerial reconnaissance over the Warwickshire Avon. *Archaeological Journal* CXXI, 1–22.

WELCH, M. G. 1971: Late Romans and Saxons in Sussex. *Britannia* II, 232–7.

WEST, S. E. 1963: Excavations at Cox Lane and at the town defences, Shire Hall Yard, Ipswich. *Proceedings of the Suffolk Institute of Archaeology* XXIX, 233–303.

1969a: The Anglo-Saxon village of West Stow. *Medieval Archaeology* XIII, 1–20.

1969b: Pagan Saxon pottery from West Stow, Suffolk. *Berichten van de Rijksdienst voor Oudheidkundig Bodemondeerzook* XIX, 175-81.

WHITE, R. B. 1974: *Excavations at Aberffraw, 1973.* BA thesis, University College of North Wales.

WHITELOCK, D. 1930: *Anglo-Saxon Wills.* Cambridge.

1951: *The Audience of Beowulf.* Oxford.

1952: *The Beginnings of English Society.* London

1955: *English Historical Documents* I c. 500–1042. London.

WILIAM, A. R. ed. 1960: *Llyfr Iowerth.* Cardiff.

WILLIAMS, H. ed. 1899: *Gildas, De Excidio Britanniae.* Cymmrodorion Record Series, III.

WILLIAMS, S. J. and POWELL, J. E. eds 1961: *Llyfr Blegywryd.* Cardiff.

WILLIAMSON, D. M. 1955–58: Kesteven villages in the Middle Ages. *Lincolnshire Historian* II, 10–17.

WILSON, A. E. 1959: Farming in Sussex in the Middle Ages. *Sussex Archaeological Collections* XCIV, 98–118.

WILSON, H. E. 1939: Excavations at the Caburn, 1938. *Sussex Archaeological Collections* XC, 193–213.

WINBOLT, S. E. 1930: Excavations at Saxonbury camp. *Sussex Archaeological Collections* LXXI, 223–36.

Index

Figures and plates are indexed by reference to the pages on which they occur. The following abbreviations are used: